FAMILY FORMATION PATTERNS AND HEALTH

FAMILY FORMATION PATTERNS AND HEALTH

An international collaborative study
in
India, Iran, Lebanon, Philippines, and Turkey

STUDY COORDINATORS AND EDITORS

A. R. OMRAN
Chapel Hill
USA

C. C. STANDLEY
WHO
Geneva

PRINCIPAL INVESTIGATORS

J. E. AZAR
Beirut
Lebanon

M. BERTAN
Ankara
Turkey

V. GUZMAN
Manila
Philippines

V. NAHAPETIAN
Teheran
Iran

K. A. PISHAROTI
Gandhigram
India

WORLD HEALTH ORGANIZATION

GENEVA

1976

ISBN 92 4 156053 3

PRINTED IN SWITZERLAND

CONTENTS

Chapter 4 : Family formation and childhood mortality

Chapter 5 : Family formation and child development

I. Child growth and health

II. Intelligence quotient

Chapter 6 : Family formation and maternal health

Chapter 7 : Child loss and family formation

PART III : AN OVERVIEW OF THE STUDY

COLLABORATING CENTRES

GANDHIGRAM INSTITUTE OF RURAL HEALTH AND FAMILY PLANNING, INDIA

PRINCIPAL INVESTIGATORS

P. R. Dult, Advisor to the Director
S. Gunasekaran, Statistician
S. Kalyanasundaram, Medical Officer
R. S. Kurup, Head of the Department of Population Studies
K. A. Pisharoti, Director

OTHER STAFF INVOLVED IN THE STUDY

M. Lakshmi, Health Educator
R. Lalithambal, Research Officer
P. Padmavethiamma, Health Educator
N. Palanisami, Health Educator
N. Radhakrishnan, Medical Officer
S. Rajamanickam, Research Assistant
P. Rajasekharan, Microbiologist, Sanitation Faculty
S. Sethu, Programme Development Officer
S. Vijayabharathi, Medical Officer

ACKNOWLEDGEMENTS

The investigators wish to express their gratitude for the leadership and guidance given by Dr K. V. Ranganathan, who was the coordinator for the study at the initial stages of designing and planning. They also acknowledge the contribution of the following persons in the initial planning of the study and preparation of the study instruments :

M. Kachirayan, Senior Statistician
S. Krishnamoorthy, Statistician
K. Mahadevan Pillai, Senior Social Scientist
A. Muthiah, Research Officer
P. S. Nair, Demographer
K. E. Vaidyanathan (former Head of the Department of Population Studies at the Gandhigram Institute of Rural Health and Family Planning), Demographic Expert, Demographic Centre, Cairo

The investigators also thank the Research Assistants, Medical Officers, Interviewers, Laboratory Technicians and Machine Operators of the Data Processing Unit of the Institute, without whose hard work the study could not have been successfully completed. The help of the village leaders, officials of the Primary Health Centres and Panchayat Unions in Palani, Thoppampatti, Madathukkulam and Dharapuram blocks, Tamil Nadu, is greatly appreciated. The cooperation of the respondents in the study is also gratefully acknowledged.

Finally, the investigators wish to record their gratitude to the Government of India which permitted this collaboration with the World Health Organization.

SCHOOL OF PUBLIC HEALTH, TEHERAN UNIVERSITY, IRAN

PRINCIPAL INVESTIGATORS

> Simin Azari, Assistant Professor, Department of Human Ecology
> Gholam Hossein Jalali, Professor and Chairman, Department of Human Ecology
> Aliyeh Majd, Assistant Professor, Department of Human Ecology
> Vardges Nahapetian, Professor and Chairman, Department of Epidemiology and Biostatistics
> Behin Dokht Navidi-Kasmaii, Associate Professor of Maternal and Child Health

OTHER STAFF INVOLVED IN THE STUDY

> Seda Bagratouni, Interviewer
> Manijeh Bavar, Social Worker
> Aazam Farrokhi, Nurse
> Ghassem Ghazi, Field Supervisor
> Nassrin Hendi, Psychologist
> Lili Koutikian, Interviewer
> Farah Manavi, Interviewer
> Simin Manavi, Interviewer
> Mehrnoush Mohtadi, Nurse
> Reza Molaii, Laboratory Technician
> Khadijeh Nazari, Laboratory Technician
> Mahin Rakhsha, Interviewer
> Gloria Rouhani, Laboratory Technologist
> Dora Sabonjian, Interviewer
> Nourollah Tabibian, Secretary
> Seza Temrazian, Statistician
> Parvin Vaseghi, Nurse
> Marian Yazdan Parast, Psychologist

ACKNOWLEDGEMENTS

The investigators wish to thank Dr Abolhassan Nadim, Dean of the School of Public Health, Teheran University, and Dr Chamseddin Mofidi and Dr Mohammad Ali Faghih, former Deans of the School, for their valuable advice, encouragement and assistance during this research project.

SCHOOL OF PUBLIC HEALTH, AMERICAN UNIVERSITY OF BEIRUT, LEBANON

PRINCIPAL INVESTIGATORS

Joseph A. Azar, Professor of Infectious Diseases and Epidemiology, Chairman, Department of Epidemiology and Biostatistics

Charles W. Churchill, Professor of Public Health Statistics, Department of Epidemiology and Biostatistics

Irini A. Lorfing, Instructor in Public Health Statistics, Department of Epidemiology and Biostatistics

Huda C. Zurayk, Assistant Professor of Public Health Statistics, Department of Epidemiology and Biostatistics

OTHER STAFF INVOLVED IN THE STUDY

I. Samara, IQ Testing

H. Shedid, Interviewer/Field Studies

ACKNOWLEDGEMENTS

The investigators wish to express their gratitude for the guidance and assistance they received from the following persons : Dr C. Lichtenwalner, Dean, Faculties of Medical Sciences, American University of Beirut (AUB) ; Dr L. Verhoestraete, Former Director, School of Public Health (AUB) ; Dr J. Harfouche, Professor of Maternal and Child Health, Chairman, Department of Community Health Practice, School of Public Health (AUB), and Coordinator, Mreyjeh Health Center Project ; Dr K. Abou-Daoud, Associate Professor of Epidemiology, Department of Epidemiology and Biostatistics, School of Public Health (AUB) ; Dr L. Melikian, Professor of Psychology (AUB) ; Dr N. Naaman, Obstetrician/Gynaecologist ; Drs H. Alami and N. Fakhoury, Pediatricians ; Dr S. Alami, Chairman, Department of Clinical Pathology (AUB) ; Dr J. Tomb, Assistant Professor of Pathology, Department of Pathology (AUB) ; and Miss S. Nasser, Research Assistant.

INSTITUTE OF PUBLIC HEALTH, UNIVERSITY OF THE PHILIPPINES, MANILA

PRINCIPAL INVESTIGATORS

Virginia B. Guzman, Professor of Maternal and Child Health, Chairman, Department of Community Health

Susie Ignacio-Morelos (formerly Head of Data Processing Unit, Institute of Public Health, University of the Philippines), Junior Scientist, Epidemiology and Biostatistics Section, Division of Research, Philippine Heart Center for Asia

Generoso B. Roman, Associate Professor of Epidemiology and Biostatistics

Lina C. Somera, Assistant Professor of Environmental and Occupational Health

Victor O. Tantengco, Professor of Nutrition

Amanda H. Tayag, Directress, Child Study Center, Philippines Normal College

OTHER STAFF INVOLVED IN THE STUDY

Alonso Alunan, Statistics
Honorata Apolonio, Cattell IQ Test
Eva Balediata, Statistics
Teresita Bobis, Statistics
Gloria Carandang, Dietary Survey
Nora Cruz, Statistics
Ana Marie O. Eustaquio, Cattell IQ Test
Elsie Lazaro, Statistics
Telly Q. Lim-de Mesa, Obstetrician
Lolita N. Llamado, Gesell IQ Test
Myrna I. Lomotan, Cattell IQ Test
Julieta M. Lopez, Dietary Survey
Virginia S. Luis, Dietary Survey
Leilani Mamaril, Anthropometry
Estelita Mariano-Fullantes, Pediatrician
Aurora V. Nicolas, Gesell IQ Test
Marita Paragas, Laboratory Tests
Purita Planta, Laboratory Tests
Lucila B. Rabuco, Laboratory Tests
Josefina Regio, Statistics
Imelda Sahagun, Cattell IQ Test
Bella A. San Juan, Secretary
Violeta Z. Trovela, Anthropometry
Clarissa Villamor, Laboratory Tests

ACKNOWLEDGEMENTS

The investigators acknowledge with deep appreciation and gratitude the help and guidance given by the late Dr Ida Van Dijk, WHO Regional Adviser on Maternal and Child Health, and Dr V. K. Bailey, Regional Adviser on Nutrition, WHO Regional Office for the Western Pacific, Manila.

Their thanks go to the staff of the Rizal Provincial Health Office and Pasay City Health Department, particularly the personnel of Dona Marta Maternity and Lying-In Hospital, for giving access to their facilities.

The investigators are indebted to the Nestlé Company for their donation of several boxes of coffee which served as incentives for mothers to join the study, and to the United Drug Company for the generous donation of drugs used for treating the sick children and mothers encountered in the study.

Last, but not least, it is with sincerest thanks that the investigators acknowledge the permission given by Dean Benjamin D. Cabrera to do the research in spite of their teaching and administrative duties.

INSTITUTE OF COMMUNITY MEDICINE, HACETTEPE UNIVERSITY, TURKEY

SCIENTISTS INVOLVED IN THE STUDY

D. Benli, Director of Etimesgut Rural Health District, Institute of Community Medicine, School of Medicine, Hacettepe University
M. Bertan, Professor of Community Medicine and Social Pediatrics
A. Egemen, Instructor
N. H. Fişek, Director and Professor of the Institute of Community Medicine
K. Sümbüloglu, Lecturer in Health Statistics
S. Tezcan, Instructor

OTHER STAFF INVOLVED IN THE STUDY

D. Arici, Psychological Tests
M. Ulusoy, Programmer

ACKNOWLEDGEMENTS

The investigators wish to thank the collaborating doctors, nurses and midwives of the Etimesgut Health District, and the staff of the Computer Center of the Hacettepe University.

WHO INTERNATIONAL REFERENCE CENTRE FOR EPIDEMIOLOGICAL STUDIES OF HUMAN REPRODUCTION

M. N. El-Khorazaty, Research Associate (Statistician)

A. R. Omran, Professor of Epidemiology, School of Public Health and Director of the IRC, University of North Carolina, Chapel Hill, USA

OTHER STAFF INVOLVED IN THE STUDY

J. Dunigan, Research Assistant

M. Eldredge, Research Assistant

D. Horne, Research Assistant

A. Leung, Computer Programmer

L. Southerland, Research Assistant

ACKNOWLEDGEMENTS

The Director and staff of IRC recognize with appreciation the continued support of Dr John Cassel (former Chairman, Epidemiology Department), Dr Michel Ibrahim (Chairman, Epidemiology Department), Dr Moye Freymann (former Director, Carolina Population Center), Dr Thomas Hall (Director, Carolina Population Center), and Dr Bernard Greenberg (Dean of School of Public Health, University of North Carolina).

WORLD HEALTH ORGANIZATION

P.-C. Kaufmann, Statistician, Health Statistical Methodology

A. Kessler, Chief, Human Reproduction

C. C. Standley, Scientist, Human Reproduction

H. Woodward, Secretary, Human Reproduction

CONSULTANTS

M. R. Bone, Office of Population Censuses and Surveys, London, England

A. M. Woolman, Consultant Editor, Eastbourne, Sussex, England

J. R. Wray, Harvard School of Public Health, Boston, USA

These studies were in part supported by the United Nations Fund for Population Activities and the Swedish International Development Agency.

PART I. BACKGROUND TO THE STUDY

Chapter One

REVIEW OF THE EVIDENCE

A. R. Omran

The collaborative studies described in this volume were begun in 1970 with the aim of elucidating the relationship between family health and factors affecting fertility formation. As a preliminary step, a review of the literature was undertaken to determine whether some of the specific research questions had already been answered by others ; to refine or even generate research hypotheses for the studies ; to improve the research design on the basis of the experience of other investigators ; and to facilitate the interpretation of the results of the studies and their comparison with those of previous ones.

This review does not claim to be exhaustive. The findings are summarized in the present chapter, which is divided into several sections, each dealing with a major topic. Each section opens with a summary statement, followed by more detailed consideration and selected studies. It must be emphasized that the relationships among the three main sets of variables —family formation, family health, and socioeconomic conditions—are extremely complex and that there is a close correlation among the variables within each of the three sets. For example, high parity at young ages, involving short pregnancy intervals, is commonly associated with poverty, poor housing, poor nutrition, and lack of medical care, each of which may have an adverse effect on the health of the mother and child. With such constraints in mind, the review attempts to isolate the relatively independent effect of variations in the family formation. More detailed discussions of these topics have been published elsewhere (Omran, 1971 ; Wray, 1971).

HEALTH RISKS RELATED TO FAMILY FORMATION

Fetal, Perinatal, Infant, and Childhood Mortality in Relation to Birth Order

Summary The general pattern that emerges from various studies, mostly undertaken in industrialized countries, indicates that the risk of late fetal death (stillbirth) is relatively high for first births, decreases for second and third births, increases slightly for fourth births, and increases much more sharply for later order births. Such a pattern is frequently described as a J-shaped curve. When risks for first births are very high, the curve becomes U-shaped.

The relationship between neonatal mortality rates and birth order shows a similar U-shaped or J-shaped curve. Both postneonatal and total infant mortality rates increase steadily with increasing birth order, as do the mortality rates for early childhood (1–4 years). If allowance is made for maternal age, infant mortality rates may continue to show a linear increase with parity or they may take the form of a U-shaped curve, especially for older mothers. Some of the more detailed studies indicate that, although a strong inverse relationship exists between mortality and social class, the variations in mortality with birth order are maintained within each social class.

Evidence from developed countries

In an early study of stillbirths, Yerushalmy (1945) analysed records of all births and stillbirths in the USA during the period 1937–41. He found that stillbirth rates were lowest for second order births and increased thereafter with birth order, this increase being more dramatic for younger than for older women. Even when the effect of maternal age was eliminated to produce a theoretical curve of the association between stillbirths and birth order, stillbirths continued to increase with birth order, especially at birth orders of ten and above.

In another study by Yerushalmy (1938), using 1936 data from New York State exclusive of New York City, a similar J-shaped curve was demonstrated for the relationship of both stillbirths and neonatal mortality to birth order.

An indication that similar patterns may exist even for women under relatively good medical care comes from a study by Shapiro et al. (1970) of approximately 12 000 women belonging to the Health Insurance Plan (HIP) of Greater New York. Throughout their pregnancies, these women were under medical care. Fetal death within the first 20 weeks of gestation increased progressively with pregnancy order, while the rates for late fetal loss (20 weeks or more of gestation) followed the typical J-shaped curve with pregnancy order.

The J-shaped pattern for the relationship of late fetal death rates to birth order was also found in national data from several developed countries (Czechoslovakia, Hungary, Italy, Japan, Portugal, Scotland, and

18

the USA) and one less developed country (Chile). The data, which covered the periods 1955–57 and 1965–67, showed that, despite the demonstrable decline in mortality over time, the pattern persisted (World Health Organization, 1971).

Several comprehensive British and North American studies have been carried out to examine the effect on childhood mortality of birth order, maternal age, and social class. In the United Kingdom, the Medical Research Council's Social Medicine Research Unit matched the birth and death registrations for the 80 000 stillbirths and infant deaths that occurred among the 1.5 million births in England and Wales in 1949 and 1950 (Morris & Heady, 1955).[1] In a later report (Heady & Morris, 1959), the second year mortality was examined as well. The study demonstrated an inverse association between mortality and social class. Within each social class, the mortality rates varied with maternal age and parity. Because these two variables may exert independent influences on mortality, the following statements refer to instances where one is varied while the other is kept constant. Stillbirth rates increased directly with maternal age and showed a reversed J-shaped relationship with parity. The pattern of neonatal mortality rates followed a reversed J-shape curve in relation to both maternal age and parity. Post-neonatal and second-year mortality rates varied in a reversed J-shaped pattern with maternal age, but increased directly with parity.

These findings were confirmed by a later study in Great Britain by Spicer & Lipworth (1966), which was modelled on the Morris & Heady studies and based on data collected for 1963–64. Despite the decline in mortality risks, the patterns persisted. A detailed comparison of the two sets of studies (1949–50 and 1963–64) was made by Omran (1971) for stillbirths and for neonatal and post-neonatal mortality.

Additional support is available from other British studies, especially the British Perinatal Mortality Survey based on 7117 deaths among single, legitimate births in Great Britain in the three months from March through May 1958 (Butler & Bonham, 1963 ; Butler & Alberman, 1969).

In the USA, several comprehensive studies have been carried out. Yerushalmy et al. (1956) gathered retrospective data on pregnancy outcome on the Island of Kauai, Hawaii, which showed that neither fetal death rates under 20 weeks of gestation nor death rates in the post-neonatal period bore any clear relationship to parity. On the other hand, late fetal and neonatal mortality rates both showed a U-shaped relationship to parity, while mortality rates in childhood (1–4 years) increased steadily with parity.

Chase (1961, 1962) studied nearly half a million births in New York State, exclusive of New York City, between 1950 and 1952. She found

---

[1] Several articles by Morris & Heady and others from the Social Medicine Research Unit were published under the general title : " Social and biological factors in infant mortality " in *Lancet* in 1955. A useful summary of their work appears in *Uses of epidemiology*, 2nd ed., Baltimore, Williams & Wilkins, pp. 156–157, which includes sources of the original articles.

that post-neonatal and early childhood mortality rates rose steadily with parity and that fetal and neonatal death rates had a J-shaped relationship with birth order. The Institute of Medicine of the US National Academy of Sciences, in a study reported by Kessner et al. (1973) investigated infant mortality among the 142 017 total live births registered in 1968 in the New York City Health Department. Mortality rates were lowest among first-born infants (18.0 per 1000 live births), while the rate was almost double (33.1 per 1000) for infants of sixth or higher birth order. This linear increase with birth order was maintained within specific maternal age groups until age 30, after which age the rates followed a reversed J-shaped or U-shaped curve, owing to increased risks to the first child born to older women.

In an analysis of matched birth and neonatal/post-neonatal death records for Baltimore City between 1960 and 1964, Shah & Abbey (1971) demonstrated that birth weight was " the single most important factor in neonatal mortality " and that it was among the important factors in the post-neonatal period as well. The authors pointed out that race, socio-economic status, and maternal age were important because they were all related to birth weight. In addition, it was found that mortality generally increased with birth order.

A national infant mortality study covered all births in the USA (except Massachusetts) between 1 January and 31 March, 1950, where the child had died during the first year of life. Neonatal mortality rates followed the typical J-shaped or U-shaped curve with both maternal age and total birth order (children ever born, including stillbirths). When both factors were considered, the highest risks were found for the later birth orders of young mothers, probably because of short birth interval. For all maternal ages and birth orders, nonwhites had higher neonatal mortality rates than whites (Loeb, 1965).

More recently the US National Center for Health Statistics (1973) reported on a 100% sample (107 038) of those members of the birth cohort registered in 1960 who died when they were under one year of age (if both events occurred in the USA). Infant mortality rates were consistently higher for nonwhites than for whites ; they were also consistently higher for illegitimate than for legitimate births, and for males than for females. Infant mortality showed a U-shaped relationship to maternal age and a linear relationship to total birth order, in all groups. Considering both maternal age and birth order simultaneously, rates for first order births maintained a J-shaped relationship to maternal age, while those for second and higher birth orders showed a reversed J-shaped relationship to maternal age. The highest mortality risks were registered for high birth order infants of young mothers (especially teenagers) and for infants of older mothers at extreme birth orders. The best survival chances were those for first infants born to mothers between 20 and 34 years of age, first and second infants born to those aged 25 to 29 years ; and third infants born to mothers aged 30 to 34 years.

Similar results for birth order and maternal age were reported in Canada by Newcombe (1965), who examined published birth and infant death records for British Columbia (1952–60). Examining a subsample of those born between 1953 and 1958 and excluding the effect of maternal age, he found a J-shaped relationship between stillbirth rates and birth order and a steady rise of infant death rates with birth order.

Evidence from developing countries

Many of the studies published from developing countries, especially those based on hospital deliveries, should be examined with considerable caution. With only a small fraction of deliveries in such countries occurring in hospitals, such samples are highly selective and include mainly emergency or complicated deliveries from surrounding areas. Differences in admission policies between areas make comparisons difficult. The samples included in such studies were : (*a*) 1000 consecutive births in a Lucknow hospital, India (Bajpai et al., 1966) ; (*b*) 13 634 consecutive deliveries in Hyderabad hospitals, India (Mehdi et al., 1961) ; (*c*) 569 patients at Tema General Hospital, Ghana, over a ten-month period (Radovič, 1966) ; and (*d*) records of 1624 births over the period 1952–57 for the Hangaza, a Bantu-speaking people in Tanganyika (Roberts & Tanner, 1963). These studies found the usual patterns of risks with parity and maternal age. Four other studies from developing countries are considered in rather more detail.

The Khana Longitudinal Study, conducted in 11 Punjab villages and reported by Wyon & Gordon (1962) and Gordon (1969), covered 1479 births during 1955–58. Although relatively higher mortality rates were evident for first births and for higher than seventh order births, the intermediate rates fluctuated so much (probably because of small absolute numbers of deaths) that no consistent pattern could be discerned.

In Bangladesh, birth and death reports were collected in 132 villages (total population 117 000) of Matlab Thana between May 1967 and April 1969 through repeated household visits by local female residents. Neonatal mortality rates clearly described a reversed J-shaped relationship, both with maternal age and with birth order. The post-neonatal mortality rate was high for young mothers (under 20 years of age) and highest for mothers aged 35–39 years, with fluctuations for other maternal age groups. In relation to birth order, post-neonatal mortality rates generally followed a J-shaped curve, the highest risks being observed for birth orders of 8 and above. A striking finding was the comparatively low infant mortality rates among children born to mothers who had large families and had had either no previous child losses or lost only one child (Stoeckel & Chowdhury, 1972).

In Taiwan, the Vital Demographic and Registration Survey collected data on births and infant deaths from a stratified sample of 57 townships out of 361 administrative districts for the period May 1966 to February

1969 through household visits (with 5-month intervals). Over 200 000 persons were covered. Neonatal mortality rates followed a U-shape in relation to birth order and post-neonatal mortality rates bore a linear relationship to maternal age, but a steady rise in both was observed as birth order increased. Higher rates were found in rural than in urban areas, although under-reporting—especially of neonatal deaths—may have affected the results in rural areas. Higher mortality rates were associated with lower education and were attributed partly to less adequate medical care (Sullivan, 1972).

Finally, an inter-American investigation of mortality in childhood, reported by the Pan American Health Organization (1971), showed a steady rise in both neonatal and post-neonatal infant mortality rates with birth order.

Physical and Intellectual Development of the Child
in Relation to Birth Order and Family Size

Summary Several studies, again mainly from developed countries, describe a detrimental effect of large family (or sibship) size and high birth order on physical and intellectual development. However, in view of the many competing variables (genetic and environmental) and the difficulties of assessing intellectual attainment in developing societies, these data must be interpreted cautiously.

Birth weight and prematurity provide measures of infant physical development. However, controversy exists about the relationship of birth weight and prematurity to birth order. Mean birth weight seems to increase with birth order (although not consistently), while the rates for prematurity (defined as birth weights below 2501g) have either a linear or a J-shaped relationship to birth order.

As measured by weight, height, and sexual maturity, the physical growth of children from large families compares unfavourably with that of children from small families. The difference is, however, small and is evident mainly in large studies.

In regard to intellectual development, increasing evidence shows that children from large families obtain lower intelligence scores than those from small families. Mental retardation is also positively associated with family size. This area, however, will require further research, especially in the developing world.

Physical growth and development during infancy

While many studies show no clear-cut relationship between birth weight (or prematurity) and parity, the pattern emerging from several other investigations indicates that prematurity rates and mean birth weights differ in their relationship to parity.

Two early studies used similar methodology to examine the relationship of birth weight to parity. In Great Britain, Karn & Penrose (1951) considered 13 780 hospital births between 1935 and 1946, and in Italy,

Fraccaro (1956) studied 5486 births at an obstetric clinic between 1942 and 1951. In both studies the same pattern was found. Non-survivors (stillbirths and infants who died within 28 days) were significantly lighter in weight than survivors and were born of " somewhat older " mothers, while the birth weight of survivors increased with birth order. This pattern of an increase in mean birth weight by parity was found in many other studies, including those of Roberts & Tanner (1963) in Tanganyika, Simpkiss (1968) in Uganda, Millis & Seng (1954) in Singapore, Namboodiri & Balakrishnan (1959) in India, and Crump et al. (1957) in 3 Negro samples in the USA.

A number of studies describe a U-shaped or J-shaped relationship of prematurity rates to both parity and maternal age. Examples include a study of 100 277 live births in Baltimore City by Wiener & Milton (1970) and a special tabulation, requested by the Population Council, of 1 per 1000 of all births in the 1964–65 National Fertility Survey in the USA (Nortman, 1974).

A study reported by Loeb (1965) of a national sample of births in the USA during the first quarter of 1950 and another study in New York City by Selvin & Garfinkel (1972) of over 1.5 million birth certificates showed both an increase in median birth weight with parity (and maternal age) and a J-shaped relationship between immature birth rates and birth order (as well as with maternal age).

Studies that found little or no relationship between prematurity and parity include a North Carolina study by Donnelly et al. (1964) and the study by Crump et al. (1957) cited above.

Physical growth and development beyond infancy

In all the studies reviewed, it was found that family size and/or birth order may influence the physical growth of children, as measured by height, weight, and sexual maturity.

Scott (1962) in a study of elementary school children in London, found that the mean heights and weights of both boys and girls declined progressively as the number of children per family increased from 1 to 5 and over.

Grant (1964), who followed the development of 1310 children on a housing estate in London, measuring height and weight at or about the sixth, tenth, twelfth, and fourteenth birthdays, was able to compare consecutive siblings in some families. She concluded that " The smaller size of children in large families is common to all of them and ... the first-born does not achieve the height and weight attained by first-borns who remain only children." Even though the higher parity children in large families may retain some weight advantage over their older siblings, they apparently do not achieve the growth norms of children of the same age from small families.

Similar effects of family size on weight and height were reported by Douglas & Simpson (1964) in a British national sample of about 3000 schoolchildren (1456 girls and 1577 boys). The influence of family size was not apparent in the upper middle class, but increased as the social class became lower. The authors also investigated sexual maturity of boys (determined by a physician) and age at menarche in girls. The percentage of sexually mature boys at age 15 and the percentage of girls with early onset of menses (by age 12) varied inversely with family size. The authors suggested that some of the social class effects—such as poor diet, frequent infection, and inadequate care—common to large families may partially explain the association between family size and slow physical development.

A similar effect of sibship size on age at menarche in the index girl has also been found in Czechoslovakia and England, as cited by Tanner (1968), who suggests that a possible explanation of the delay of menarche may lie in the relative malnutrition and high frequency of disease in large families.

Intelligence

Studies have been conducted in many countries during the last 30 or 40 years. A large study in France in 1943–44 included approximately 2% of the schoolchildren between the ages of 6 and 12 ; the total number in the sample was 95 237 and the sample was representative of 20 regions of the country. The mean test scores on René Gille's intelligence test dropped consistently as size of sibship increased. The mental age of children with no siblings was one or two years higher than that of children with seven or more siblings. The association was more apparent among the children of farmers, manual workers, and clerical workers, and was barely discernible among the children of professionals (Heuyer et al., 1950 ; Gille et al., 1954).

The Scottish Council for Research in Education (1949) reported similar results in two large surveys in Scotland, one in 1932 among 87 498 schoolchildren and one in 1947 among 70 805 schoolchildren. Additional evidence was reviewed by Anastasi (1956), who cites similar findings in England, the Federal Republic of Germany, Greece, and the USA.

More recent studies confirm this relationship and consider additional interactions. Reed & Reed (1965), with a sample of 1016 families in Minnesota, found that the mean IQ scores for children with family sizes of 1–5 were similar, but that the mean dropped significantly for those from larger families. IQ scores of parents (obtained from their school records) showed a similar pattern. One interpretation was that parents with higher IQ scores chose to have smaller families, suggesting that the association of children's intelligence with family size could be secondary. Further analysis, taking into account the parents and their childless siblings (who happened to be lower in IQ scores), showed that " the lowest IQ group produces the fewest children and the highest IQ group produces the most".

In England, Record et al. (1969) investigated 50 172 Birmingham children and found a decrease in verbal reasoning test scores with increase in family size. When the social class effect was considered, it was apparent that higher social class children had higher scores than lower social class children; however, within each social class a parity effect was evident—that is, the higher birth order children in all social classes consistently scored lower on the verbal reasoning test. A refinement over previous studies was the matching of 5083 sibling pairs; comparison of the scores of adjacent siblings from the same family showed only small decreases in scores from early to late birth positions (with the greatest average difference apparent between the first and second children). From this evidence, the authors concluded that the association between intelligence and sibship size was due more to differences between families than within families. Record et al. (1969) also matched verbal reasoning scores with maternal age and found a rise in scores with increasing maternal age at the birth of child. The increase in mean IQ of children with increasing maternal age was confirmed in a Johns Hopkins study by Lobl et al. (1971).

In the Netherlands, 5 tests measuring various kinds of faculties were administered to 386 114 nineteen-year-old military recruits. Family size and birth order in this population had independent linear negative effects on intellectual performance. The birth order effects were consistent in each social class (Belmont & Marolla, 1973).

The US National Center for Health Statistics (1974) reported the results of intelligence studies in a national sample of 7119. A battery of intelligence tests was used, including the vocabulary and block design subtests of the Wechsler Intelligence Scale for Children (WISC) and the Goodenough-Harris Drawing Test (HFD). The intelligence of children (or the measurement of both intellectual development (WISC) and intellectual maturity (HFD)) was found to decrease consistently as the number of other children in the household increased. The pattern persisted after correcting for parents' education. The negative relationship was stronger for boys than for girls. This study also found that (a) intelligence of children increased with both maternal and paternal age up to a certain point (25–39 years for mothers and 25–44 years for fathers); (b) children weighing 5–10 lb (2.3–4.5 kg) at birth rated better than those weighing either less or more; (c) children who had a history of not walking or speaking until after 18 months of age and children who were rated by their mothers as being slow in learning how to do things like feeding and dressing themselves when they were young scored lower; (d) other things being equal, girls scored better than boys.

Some comments on the intelligence studies

Three remarks on this review are in order:

1. A number of other studies failed to produce such negative correlations between family size and intelligence and birth order and intelligence, or between the intelligence of parents and the size of the families they produce, particularly those studies in which the sample populations were

highly selected. Collectively, however, the evidence from the literature supports the negative correlation between family size and/or birth order and intelligence levels of children.

2. One explanation of these findings relating family size and intelligence is that the parents of small families are better able to foster the physical and mental development of their children by giving them more individual attention whereas in large families, no matter how great the parents' concern for their children's wellbeing, there is simply less opportunity for individual parent–child contact. This smaller degree of contact in large families may be reflected in the poorer—or at least slower— development of verbal ability in these children, a factor that may affect their performance in intelligence tests. Neligan & Prudham (1969), in their investigations aimed at determining normal milestones in childhood development, found evidence of this phenomenon very early in life. They found that the age at which children begin to talk increased with birth order. Extensive studies done by Nisbet (1953) and by Nisbet & Entwistle (1967) tested and confirmed the hypothesis that at least part of the inverse relationship between family size and intelligence could be traced to poorer verbal ability in large families as compared to small families ; this led Nisbet to conclude that part of the negative correlation between family size and intelligence may be attributed to " an environmental influence of the size of family on verbal development and through it on general mental development " (Nisbet, 1953).

3. Culture-specific, or at least culture-fair, intelligence tests, which unfortunately are yet to be developed and/or refined, are greatly needed in order to test this relationship in the developing world.

Child Health and Family Formation

Summary A number of child health conditions have been linked to family size and birth order (as well as to maternal age). Included are congenital malformation, physical handicaps, malnutrition, dental problems, infectious diseases, emotional problems, and mental illness. Some conditions—like malnutrition—are probably directly related to increased strain on family and maternal resources with each additional child ; in the case of common infections, larger family size may simply lead to more frequent exposure to infectious agents through other family members.

Congenital malformations and handicapping conditions

Among the methodological difficulties in studying congenital malformations is the fact that most studies use the birth certificate as the source of information. Since not all congenital malformations are recognizable at birth, this method of data collection introduces a considerable element

26

of bias. An attempt to reduce this bias has been made by considering also the death certificate for those who die in infancy. A comparative study in New York City (Erhardt & Nelson, 1964) discovered that 28% of the congenital malformations listed as causes of infant death on the death certificate were missed on the birth certificate, and this study identifies only conditions that were severe enough to be fatal. Furthermore, children with malformation may die of competing causes, and malformation may not be listed as a leading or contributing cause of death. Great caution should be exercised, therefore, in considering the evidence from studies of congenital malformation.

Of the family formation variables, maternal age (and sometimes paternal age as well) is strongly correlated with congenital malformations and handicapping conditions among children. This relationship has been documented in the literature for many conditions, especially for Down's syndrome (mongolism). (See, for example, Penrose, 1933, 1962, 1967; Smith & Record, 1955; Stevenson et al., 1966; and Spiers, 1972.)

When birth order is considered, the evidence is controversial. The careful studies of the Social Medicine Research Unit of the Medical Research Council (Morris & Heady, 1955), which considered births, stillbirths, and infant deaths in England in 1949–50, found no association between congenital malformation and birth order. Some other studies showed that if an association exists, it disappears once a correction is made for maternal age. Hay & Barbano (1972) calculated incidence rates for selected categories of congenital malformation reported on birth certificates from a population of more than eight million registered, white, single, live births from 29 states and two large cities in the USA from 1961 through 1966. Most of these categories of malformation exhibited increasing incidence as maternal age increased. With maternal age held constant, none of the conditions showed a consistent increase with increasing birth order. Hypospadias, oesophageal defects, omphalocele, and Down's syndrome decreased somewhat with increasing birth order. Especially high rates of several malformations were observed among first births to women over 40 years of age.

A few studies have shown a small but independent effect of birth order on congenital malformation. A study of 586 neural tube defects among 328 053 Hungarian newborns (Czeizel & Révész, 1970) demonstrated small increases with maternal age and a U-shaped relationship to birth order. When allowance was made for maternal age, the U-shaped relationship to birth order persisted for two maternal age groups, 20–24 and over 40 years.

Extensive studies by Newcombe (1964) and Newcombe & Travendale (1964) demonstrated a high risk of handicapping conditions for infants of " young " mothers (under 20 years) and " old " mothers (over 35 years) and for those of first order or high order births. The risks were accentuated by " unusual " combinations, such as high order births to young mothers and first order births to old mothers. The authors suggested that the association, especially of mental and related disorders, including Down's disease, with older maternal age may result from a high rate of degenerative change in the ova of older mothers. It was also suggested that the risks associated primarily with birth order, particularly handicaps of infective origin, might be environmental rather than congenital in origin.

In a large study of congenital malformations sponsored by the World Health Organization among consecutive births in 24 medical centres in 16 countries, the maternal age effect was demonstrated. Unfortunately, tabulations of malformation by birth order were not provided in the voluminous report (Stevenson et al., 1966).

Malnutrition

The family's nutrition can be decisive in determining each member's health and affecting children's growth and development, dental health, and resistance to infection. In a study which sought to examine demographic and social factors contributing to malnutrition, Wray & Aguirre (1969) surveyed protein-calorie malnutrition among the preschool children of Candelaria, Colombia. They collected complete socioeconomic data as well as measurements of malnutrition in a house-to-house survey of the town. A total of 1094 children under 6 years of age were included in the survey.

The results showed that the difference between the prevalence of malnutrition in children from families with 4 living children or fewer (38% malnourished among 642 children) and that in children from families with 5 or more (44% malnourished among 462 children) was statistically significant. It was also found that the number of pesos per person per week spent on food decreased steadily with increasing family size.

Poor nutrition seems to be associated with large family size, both in developed and in less developed nations. Hubble (1966) found that the incidence of iron-deficiency anaemia in Great Britain showed " a positive correlation with the size of the family ". He also reported that the British National Food Survey of 1962 showed that, regardless of social class, " families with four or more children had diets which on the average contained less calcium (too little milk), less protein (too little meat and fish) and less energy value (inadequate total calorie intake) than the standards recommended by the British Medical Association ".

A study by Robertson & Kemp (1963) among a " coloured " group in Cape Town, South Africa, resulted in the conclusion that large family size *per se* did not put families at risk of malnutrition, but that poverty and poor parental care did. This study also confirmed the belief that poorly nourished children die of diseases of malnutrition and of gastroenteritis and bronchopneumonia more frequently than well-nourished, well-developed children. Finally, the study found that generally whole families were at risk of suffering malnutrition (not just later-born children) and that this was the case " whether there are three children or ten ". However, as pointed out by Wray (1971), the methodology used in data collection in

28

this study is open to criticism. The study compares the distribution of differing numbers of children per family in 3 groups of families, each selected quite differently. The first group was chosen because there was a malnourished preschool child in the family, the second because a child died of a specific cause, and the third because the mother delivered a newborn infant during a defined period of time. A valid statement concerning the presence or absence of increased risk of malnutrition associated with family size can be made only after selecting a substantial population of children grouped according to family size.

Infection

In a longitudinal study of Cleveland families, Dingle et al. (1964) found an increasing incidence per person-year of common respiratory diseases and infectious gastroenteritis with increasing family size. This increase seemed to be attributable to the greater likelihood of direct exposure of family members to infections. Similar findings were reported by two extensive British studies, one by Spence et al. (1954) and one by Douglas & Blomfield (1958).

Family health

Hare & Shaw (1965) collected information on several indices of health for 499 urban British families. The indices include the number of times the subject consulted his physician (from physician's records), the subject's evaluation of his own general health (in an interview), and the extent to which his activities had been restricted by health problems. With parents, particularly mothers, they found an association between poor health and large family size. The health of children in large families appeared to be better than that of children in small families. However, the authors suggested that illness among children in large families might receive less attention and that, consequently, fewer visits to the doctor would be recorded for them.

Maternal health and parity

Summary Several studies, both early and recent, have found that multiparity, especially grand multiparity, carries increased risks of maternal mortality and obstetric complications such as placenta previa, abruptio placentae, malpresentation of fetus, postpartum haemorrhage, anaemia, toxaemia, and rupture of the uterus. Some evidence also links parity with other maternal health problems, such as prolapse, cancer of the cervix, and diabetes. The evidence for hypertension in relation to parity is equivocal, while cancer of the breast may decrease with parity.

Maternal mortality

Increased risks of maternal mortality with high parity, especially grand multiparity—defined in some studies as parities of 6 or over and in others as those of 8 and over—were recognized by early gynaecologists.

Many studies in modern, well-equipped hospitals show a reduction in maternal mortality among grand multiparas in recent years. Oxorn (1955), for example, reported on 1056 cases of grand multiparity that occurred among 63 140 confinements at a Montreal hospital between 1926 and 1952 ; he found that maternal mortality for the whole series increased with parity, but that *all* the deaths for grand multiparas occurred in the period 1926–42.

Despite the apparent decline in the absolute risk of mortality among multiparas, it is still possible to demonstrate the relatively high risk of grand multiparity, but only in large samples.

Jaffe & Polgar (1964), for example, showed that for 348 393 live births in the USA between 1951 and 1961, maternal mortality generally increased with both age and parity. Furthermore, a comparison of maternal mortality for second to fourth births with that for fifth and later births *within* each of 4 maternal age groups (under 20, 20–29, 30–39, and over 40 years) revealed higher maternal mortality for the women of higher parities, in some cases more than twice as high as the mortality for those of low parity.

Obstetric and gynaecological morbidity

Morbidity among multiparas does not appear to have been as much reduced by recent improvements in medical care as has mortality. Most authors still report a markedly higher incidence of obstetric complications in grand multiparas than in low-parity patients. Oxorn's report gives higher rates of toxaemia, placental disorders, malpresentations, and haemorrhage among grand multiparas. In order to try to separate the effects of age and parity, Oxorn divided his grand multipara group into those under 35 years of age, those aged 35 to 40, and those over 40 years. He also compared grand multiparas over 40 to women over 40 with 2 or 3 children. He found that among the older grand multiparas there were relatively high risks of toxaemia, occiput posterior and transverse positions, caesarean section, and mid-forceps deliveries. However, comparing the grand multiparas over 40 to the women of low parity over 40, he concluded that high parity rather than age was of greatest importance as a cause of complications of pregnancy. His analysis suggested that parity alone seemed to affect fetal and maternal mortality, but that for many other complications, " age and parity working together have a greater effect than parity alone ".

Israel & Blazar (1965) in a collaborative obstetrical statistical survey in 13 United States hospitals between 1958 and 1960 reported higher rates of anaemia, pre-eclampsia, chronic hypertension, placental disorders, uterine rupture, and postpartum haemorrhage among women of parity 7 and higher. Vehaskari et al. (1968), reporting on 1567 grand multiparas and 16 432 lower-parity women delivered in a Finnish hospital between 1951 and 1960, show statistically significant higher rates among the grand multiparas for hypertensive disease, abruptio placentae, placenta previa, retained placenta, and breech presentation. Similar results have been reported by Nelson & Sandmeyer (1958) for patients at a Washington, DC, hospital, by Petry & Pearson (1955) for a southeastern Kentucky hospital, and by Ziel (1962), who also worked in southeastern Kentucky.

Prolapse. Prolapse is a gynaecological condition related to childbirth. It may take the form of a cystocele (protrusion of the bladder into the anterior vaginal wall), a rectocele (protrusion of the rectum into the posterior vaginal wall), prolapse of the uterus, or combinations thereof. (See, for example, Shirodkar, 1967 ; Novak et al., 1970.)

Prolapse arises from one or more of the following : (*a*) injury or over-stretching of the pelvic floor, (*b*) devitalization or damage of tissues during prolonged labour and/or obstetric operations, or failure of the uterosacral ligament to involute after labour, and (*c*) laxity of the cardinal ligaments.

These mechanisms are accentuated by repeated pregnancies and labour and/or by poor obstetric management resulting, under the stress and strain of active life, in protrusion of the bladder, the rectum, and/or the uterus into the vagina or outside the body. The damage produced by pregnancy and labour may not show in the form of prolapse until later in life. Prolapse may sometimes occur in nulliparas with congenital weakness of the concerned ligaments and other supporting structures.

Despite the significance of prolapse in gynaecological practice, its epidemiology has not been given due attention. Even its incidence is not well documented. It has been suggested that the incidence of prolapse is higher in India (1 : 547 deliveries) than in the USA (1 : 7500 deliveries). It is also claimed that the incidence of spontaneous abortion in the presence of prolapse is increased to 20 per 100 pregnancies.

Almost all the studies relating prolapse to parity, age, obstetric operations, etc., are based on numerator data or case reports. Limited as this approach may be, two are quoted with this caution in mind.

Tyrone (1957) described 166 cases of procidentia or complete uterine prolapse and found that obstetric trauma was the chief cause. Of the 166 patients in the series, 159 had borne children. The fact that there were 7 nulliparas with prolapse was explained by the possibility that congenital laxity of ligaments and supporting structures could have been involved. The age of the group ranged from 27 to 87 years, with a high number in the fifth decade or after.

Kinzel (1961) reported a study of 265 cases ranging in age from 26 to 78 years, with the greatest number between 50 and 70 years of age. In regard to parity, 6% of the group had never borne a child. The greatest number had 2 or more children.

Cancer of the cervix. Several reports suggest an association between parity and cancer of the cervix (Maliphant, 1949 ; Wynder et al., 1954 ; Wahi et al., 1969).

Although Logan (1953) reported a similar association between cervical cancer and marital and childbearing experience, he pointed out that no causal relationship had been established. Some of these articles and others on environmental factors associated with cervical cancer, of which parity is only one, are reviewed by Lundin et al. (1964). In their own study of Memphis women, Lundin and his associates found that age at first pregnancy was highly correlated with cancer of the cervix. They also found a small positive association between high parity and intraepithelial carcinoma of the cervix in white women, but not in Negro women, and they found no consistent association for squamous cell carcinoma of the cervix.

Breast cancer. An international collaborative study of breast cancer and reproductive experience was undertaken by MacMahon et al. (1970) in hospitals in Brazil, Greece, Japan, Taiwan, the USA, Wales, and Yugoslavia. In all, more than 400 women who were hospitalized for a first diagnosis of breast cancer and nearly 13 000 controls (patients in the same hospitals for conditions other than breast cancer) were interviewed. Although the trends are not regular, estimated risks of breast cancer for women of parity 5 or more are between 40% and 60% of the risk for the nulliparous. Furthermore, in all 7 centres, breast cancer increased with increase in the age at which a woman bore her first child, with births after the first having substantially less additional protective influence than that of a first birth at the same age.

Other selected health problems

Diabetes. Pyke (1956) in England concluded that " A woman who has had five children appears to have about three times as great a chance of developing diabetes as a woman who has had none … ". Middleton & Caird (1968) sought to overcome some of the methodological shortcomings of earlier studies by examining the records of 543 women and 413 men between the ages of 40 and 80 years who represented virtually all newly diagnosed diabetics in a population whose age and sex structure were known. For diabetic women they found an " excess " of those with 4 or more children. They also found that while the likelihood of diabetes increased with age, within each age group the rates also increased " with fair regularity with increasing parity ". The results of this study were in close agreement with others and showed that in the post-menopausal years (between the ages of 50 and 80 years) " the excess risk, above that of a nullipara, is 20% for one child, 45% for two, 100% for three, 200% for four or five, and 400% for six or more children ". For men, the risk of diabetes was approximately the same as that of women who had borne 2 children.

An interesting point about these studies is that they were looking at the onset or at least the existence of diabetes in menopausal or post-menopausal women. Their evidence suggests that there may be certain conditions, such as diabetes, that are associated with multigravidity but do not appear until later in life. It is therefore possible that excessive childbearing may alter women permanently. The same may also be true of other conditions, like prolapse and malignancy.

The United States National Health Examination Survey (O'Sullivan & Gordon, 1966) examined mean blood glucose levels by parity for specific age groups. The results indicate that these levels did not rise with increasing parity and that the correlation of parity with blood glucose levels was very low when all parties were considered together. The high parity groups, however, had significantly higher blood glucose levels. Because of the small numbers and a negative finding in a study in Massachusetts, the reporters pointed out that a causal relationship could not be established.

Hypertension. Studies of parity and hypertension are of uneven methodological quality, and conclusions vary from finding a positive or negative association to no association at all.

Miall has almost consistently found a negative association between parity and hypertension. In a 1954 cross-sectional study (Miall & Oldham, 1958) among a sample of 623 persons in two communities in South Wales, age-adjusted scores of blood pressure decreased with parity for all women. The samples were small, however, especially for those with high parity. Interestingly, Miall (1959) in a follow-up study in a Welsh mining community (including 223 propositi from the 1954 sample and 891 relatives), found that those persons who had had a child in the interval between 1954 and 1958 had less increase in mean blood pressure than those who did not. Miall et al. (1962) in a larger study in Jamaica (a sample of 1666 females), found higher means of blood pressure for nulliparous than for parous women. Within the parous groups, mean blood pressure decreased from parity one to parities 2–5 and then increased for higher parities. A negative association between parity and hypertension was also found by Humerfelt & Wedervang (1957) among 1350 women aged 40–42 years who were residents of Bergen, Sweden, in 1950.

In other studies, an increase of blood pressure with parity has been found. Nelson & Sandmeyer (1958) reported such a relationship among 812 multiparas delivered in a Washington hospital, compared to 19 214 patients in the general clinic. Using similar methods of selection, Ziel (1962) confirmed these results among multiparas and controls in another American hospital. In a study of a rural and an urban Zulu community, it was found that, in the urban area, women with 5 or more children had higher rates of hypertension than women with 4 or less. The difference in the rural sample was not significant. In Jamaica, Roopnariensingh et al. (1971) also found a positive association between hypertension and high parity among women delivered at the university hospital.

On the other hand, two recent studies, one by Gordon et al. (1970) in Cape Town and the other by the National Center for Health Statistics in the USA (1972), found no significant association between parity and hypertension. The latter study included a national sample of 3435 women from whom standardized blood pressure measurements were obtained.

The study concluded that " in comparable age groups there was no evidence to suggest that either parity or gravidity played a part in the etiology of cardiovascular hypertension ".

Maternal Age at Pregnancy and Family Health

Summary The effect of maternal age is discussed here as a separate entity in order to emphasize the significance of timing in family formation. Several studies have revealed a consistent association between maternal age and mortality and morbidity in mothers and children. These studies uniformly suggest that there is an age-band in the fertility span of a woman during which the reproductive risks are at a minimum ; on either side of this relatively safe age-band, the risks progressively increase, describing J-shaped, U-shaped or reversed J-shaped curves. These patterns are particularly typical of late fetal deaths, perinatal mortality, infant mortality, prematurity, and maternal mortality. Congenital malformations, especially Down's syndrome, increase steadily with age.

Some of the evidence concerning the relationship of maternal and child health to maternal age has already been presented. In this section, some reference to these studies will be made with additional evidence from other studies.

Fetal and child health

Two of the early pieces of evidence for a U-shaped or J-shaped relationship between stillbirth and maternal age were given by Yerushalmy (1938) in a study of neonatal mortality using 1936 data from New York State, exclusive of New York City, and in another study of stillbirths published by Yerushalmy in 1939 and based on data from the United States Registration Area for the period 1931–35.

In a still later report, Yerushalmy (1945) tried to determine quantitatively the degree to which the stillbirth rate for the period 1937–41 in the USA was affected by parity, rather than by maternal age. He found that the risk of stillbirth was high for young mothers (under 20 years), declined for mothers aged 20 to 29, and rose thereafter with maternal age. When the effect of birth order was eliminated, the relative stillbirth ratios became higher for the young mother, and the rise with age after 30 became less significant. Data on late fetal death reported to the World Health Organization by 8 countries confirm the U-shaped or J-shaped relationship with maternal age (World Health Organization, 1971).

Donnelly et al. (1964), reporting on 2521 premature infants among 29 561 deliveries in 3 North Carolina hospitals between 1954 and 1961, and Douglas (1950), reporting on 13 686 mothers who delivered during the week of March 3–9, 1946, in England, Scotland, and Wales, both concluded that prematurity rates were greatest for young mothers of 20 years or less from low socioeconomic backgrounds. Douglas suggested that the high rates among poor women could be accounted for, to some extent, by poor parental and obstetric care.

The Social Medicine Research Unit of the Medical Research Council (Morris & Heady, 1955, and others), reporting on data for 1949–50 for England, and Spicer & Lipworth (1966), reporting on data for 1963–64, also for England, noted particularly marked increases in stillbirths per 1000 births with maternal age. For neonatal mortality, the highest rates were for fourth or later births to mothers under 25 years and first births to mothers aged 30 and over. Neonatal mortality was generally lowest for infants of mothers between 25 and 29 years. Postneonatal mortality rates were generally highest for mothers under 25, especially those who had had more than 3 children. Likewise, the British Perinatal Mortality Survey (Butler & Bonham, 1963) reported that, in general, the risk of perinatal mortality was greatest among infants born to mothers over 35 years of age and next greatest for those of mothers under 25 (particularly those under 20).

A survey of all births in the USA (except Massachusetts) for the first quarter of 1950 found that while the median birth weight increased with maternal age, immature births were comparatively frequent among very young mothers, amounting to 9% of births at maternal ages of 15 to 19 years, dropping to a minimum of 6.7% at maternal ages of 25 to 29 years, and increasing again thereafter. For first pregnancies, the likelihood of immaturity rose steadily with maternal age, 7.1% of births being premature at ages 25 to 29 and 13.7% at 40 to 44 years. Similarly, neonatal mortality was lowest at maternal ages of 25 to 29 years and was higher among infants born to mothers of less than 25 or more than 29 years of age (Loeb, 1965).

A more recent report of the National Center for Health Statistics (1973) on a 1960 birth cohort describes a similar pattern for infant mortality. Interesting details have already been discussed in this review in the section concerning childhood mortality in the developed countries (p. 20).

In that section, reference was also made to the New York City Study (Kessner et al., 1973). Infant mortality risks were highest for infants born to mothers under 15 years of age and to those aged 45 and over, with rates of 43.5 and 47.9 per 1000 live births, respectively. High relative risks were also found for infants of mothers aged 15–19 and 35–44 years, with the lowest risks recorded for infants of mothers in the intermediate age groups (20–34 years). This trend was maintained, with some variation, when birth order was considered simultaneously with maternal age. The highest risks were registered for the young mothers (15–19 years) having their fourth child, and lowest among offspring of women aged 25–34 years having their second child.

The relationship between maternal age and increasing incidence of congenital malformations, especially Down's syndrome, has also been discussed earlier.[1]

---

[1] See, for example, the studies of Newcombe (1964) in British Columbia and WHO's congenital malformation studies in 16 countries (Stevenson et al., 1966).

Additionally, Israel & Deutschberger (1964), who examined the age factor in pregnancy outcome among a sample of 22 201 unselected women from institutions in the Collaborative Project on Cerebral Palsy, arrived at conclusions similar to those outlined above on stillbirth and neonatal mortality. They also reported a steady increase in congenital anomalies with increasing maternal age and an increase in neurological abnormalities among infants of the youngest and oldest mothers in their samples.

As has already been discussed, another area of development, the intellectual attainment of the child, appears to improve with rising maternal age.

Maternal mortality

An early study by Yerushalmy et al. (1940), based on data for New York State exclusive of New York City, demonstrated a steady increase in maternal mortality with age (independently of parity).

An examination of national data from 48 countries for several years (mostly 1961–66) revealed either a progressive increase in mortality with increasing age or a J-shaped pattern (World Health Organization, 1969).

Birth Interval and Family Health

Summary Many studies from developed countries and some from the less developed countries have shown an association between short birth intervals and higher relative risks to child health. Research concerning the influence of birth interval on family health is scanty and fraught with methodological problems. This is an area for further investigation, especially in developing countries where the factors of lactation and nutrition play an important part in these interactions.

Child health and birth interval

It is important to note that the term " interval " is often in published literature used without clear definition of what it specifically measures in a particular study. There are several types of intervals, including:

1. " Interbirth interval " : the interval between two successive births including live and/or stillbirths. This interval will miss an intervening pregnancy ending in abortion or fetal loss ; if the second child is born prematurely the interval is automatically shortened by a number of weeks.

2. " Inter-live-birth interval " : the interval between two successive live births. It has the advantage over the " interbirth interval " that it includes only live births, which are usually less under-reported than stillbirths in surveys. It still disregards an intervening pregnancy that did not end in a live birth, and is also shortened if the second child is born prematurely.

3. " Interpregnancy interval " or " interconception interval " is the interval between the onset of one pregnancy and the onset of a successive one. It has the disadvantage that the exact onset of pregnancy cannot

36

usually be accurately identified in interview surveys. If one or both pregnancies end in abortion, fetal loss, or premature birth, the interval is automatically shortened.

4. " Birth-to-conception interval " : the interval between a birth (can be specified as live or stillbirth) and the onset of a succeeding pregnancy. This is the most commonly used interval. While it does not miss an intervening pregnancy, there is still the problem of defining the onset of the succeeding pregnancy.

Another problem in published reports is the paucity of studies that distinguish between the effect of the preceding interval and that of the succeeding interval. Most of the studies reviewed emphasize the effect of the preceding interval on an index child, although its health may also be influenced by the succeeding interval.

Early studies by the Children's Bureau in the USA demonstrated the association between high infant mortality and short birth intervals. These studies are of special interest because they were carried out at a time when infant mortality in the USA was still high. In one study in Gary, Indiana, in 1916 (Hughes, 1923), the infant mortality rate was 169.1 deaths per 1000 live births when the preceding birth interval was less than 15 months, compared to 102.8 for intervals of 24 months or more. In Baltimore in 1915 (Woodbury, 1925), the infant mortality rate was highest (146.7 deaths per 1000 live births) when the preceding birth interval was less than 2 years ; the rate dropped steadily for longer birth intervals. Eastman (1944) noted in his studies that prematurity rates (among the " coloured " population) and rates for hypertensive toxaemia were higher for short birth intervals, but his sample was highly selective. Yerushalmy (1945) analysed records of all births and stillbirths in the USA during the period 1937–41. Using an indirect method of assessing the influence of the birth interval, Yerushalmy demonstrated that relatively short and relatively long intervals were associated with higher stillbirth rates. He acknowledged, however, the urgent need for studies based on exact knowledge of birth intervals rather than on mathematical estimations of the intervals. He and his associates attempted to meet this need in a study in Kauai, Hawaii, in 1953 (Yerushalmy et al., 1956). The study was based on reproductive histories and demonstrated that very short intervals of 4 months (from the end of one pregnancy to the beginning of another) were associated with high fetal and childhood mortality.

Similarly, Bishop (1964), in a study of 16 000 consecutive deliveries in Philadelphia, found an increased incidence of premature births with pregnancy intervals of less than 1 year. This finding was supported by Douglas (1950), who studied a nationwide sample of 13 000 births in England during 1 week in 1946. The study found that the highest risks were associated with intervals of 1 year or less and the least risks with intervals of 2–4 years. A second increase in risk was also noted for very long intervals (6 years or more), probably because of aging of the mother.

In an ongoing longitudinal study by the Perinatal Research Branch of the National Institute of Neurological Diseases and Stroke (USA) in collaboration with 14 American medical centres, it was found that " the children with an intersib interval of less than one year had lower birth weight, lower Bayley developmental scores at eight months of age, lower Binet IQ scores at four years of age, and a greater incidence of neurologically suspicious or abnormal outcome at one year of age " (Holley et al., 1969).

Among studies in the less developed countries, the Khana study (Wyon & Gordon, 1962) showed that preceding intervals of less than 2 years were associated with higher neonatal and infant mortality in 11 Punjab villages. Second-year mortality was highest for intervals of less than 12 months, fluctuating thereafter, probably because of the small absolute numbers of deaths. Wray & Aguirre (1969), in their Colombian study, considered the relationship of the succeeding birth interval and malnutrition of index children. This study included 489 children under 6 years of age, for whom interval data were available. They found that the rate of malnutrition was about 40% in various 6-month sibling intervals up to 2 years, but rose appreciably to 51% and 57%, respectively, for an interval of 25–30 and 31–36 months. Only when the interval between a given child and the succeeding sibling was more than 3 years was there a marked decline in malnutrition (to 26%). Although the differences (between those with an interval of less than 3 years and those with longer intervals) were of border-line significance, the authors felt that the percentages clearly suggest that an interval of at least 3 years between children in that community " protects " the older child, to some extent, from malnutrition. As the authors mention, Cicely Williams has explained that " kwashiorkor " meant, in the African tribal language in which the term originated, " the disease of the deposed baby when the next one is born ". More recently, a study in Guayaquil, Ecuador (Wolfers & Scrimshaw, 1974), based on reproductive histories of 1934 mothers, found higher risks of miscarriage and stillbirth for very short and very long interpregnancy intervals (both preceding and succeeding). A minimal risk for post-neonatal mortality was found for intervals of about 3 years.

THE IMPACT OF CHILD LOSS ON FAMILY FORMATION

Introduction

Family formation patterns and objectives (including actual and ideal family size, desired number of male and female children, and regulation of fertility) may be influenced by the child loss experience of individual couples and/or by the fear of child loss based on community experience. According to this view, as long as childhood mortality remains high, there is a major psychological barrier to fertility limitation (Taylor, 1965 ; Frederiksen, 1969 ; Omran, 1971). Theoretically, there are 4 possible mechanisms through which child loss may affect fertility behaviour :

(a) involuntary or biological mechanisms, whereby the birth interval following child loss is shorter than that following the birth of a child who survives ; among factors to be considered are length of lactation and lactation amenorrhoea, as well as social customs that make for the shunning of a new pregnancy while another child is being nursed ;

(b) volitional response to own child loss (replacement motivation) ;

(c) volitional response to anticipation of loss, i.e., fear of child loss (insurance motivation) ; and

(d) societal response whereby social organizations responding to reduction in child loss may endorse and/or subscribe to fertility regulation.

Appealing as these hypotheses may seem to be, relatively little unequivocal empirical evidence for them exists. The evidence presented below has become available only in the last few years, and there is still a need for additional epidemiological studies of the relationship between child loss and fertility in different geopolitical settings. For descriptive purposes the evidence will be classified under separate headings, depending on the basic nature of the study reviewed.

Studies of Pre-Industrial Europe

In these studies family reconstruction has been attempted by linking together the entries of births, marriages, and deaths from parish records or some similar sources into family histories of vital events.

The evidence from these studies is either weak or controversial in regard to child loss and fertility. Knodel (1975), for example, found that in villages where breast feeding was common the birth interval was from 2 to 13 months shorter following a child death, compared to those following a surviving child (the biological mechanisms). Matthiessen (1975), on the other hand, could not find any conclusive relationship between child loss and fertility in many European communities during the demographic transition. These parish studies, however, have to be taken with great caution for many reasons :

(a) the parish records are by no means representative of the events in their communities ; remote areas, in particular, were less represented ;

(b) under-reporting was probably significant, especially of abortion, which was prohibited by the church and, hence, the birth intervals may not be accurate ; and

(c) wrong linkage could have happened in cases of twins, cousins with the same name, prevalence of similar names, etc.

Studies of National Demographic Trends

Demographic trends from many European countries indicate that the falling infant mortality rate has preceded the fall in the fertility rate by one or more decades (see, for example, Swedish data reported by Omran,

1971). This phenomenon is also evident in several developing countries since the Second World War. A prominent example is Sri Lanka, where infant mortality rates dropped below 100 deaths per 1000 live births for the first time in 1948 and continued to decline thereafter. Fertility began to fall 10 to 15 years after infant mortality fell (Lapham et al., 1975).

Data from demographic yearbooks for 53 developing countries were used in a recent WHO report to calculate the interval from the onset of decline in the infant mortality rate to the onset of decline in the crude birth rate since 1945–49. With the exception of one country (Dominican Republic), it was found that the greater the mean postwar rate of fall of infant mortality, the shorter has been the interval between infant mortality decline and the onset of fertility decline (World Health Organization, 1974).

Simulation and Econometric Models

Simulation models, including those incorporating assumptions about son survivorship, attempt to evaluate the influence of child loss upon fertility behaviour (Heer, 1966a ; Heer & Smith, 1968 ; May & Heer, 1968 ; Immerwahr, 1967 ; O'Hara, 1972). In general terms, these models consider the fertility rates required to offset varying child mortality rates with a given degree of certainty. In a provocative conclusion in one of the papers (Heer 1966a), the author showed, by a rough calculation based on a simulation model, that " If birth control was perfect and if parents wanted to be highly certain of at least one surviving son, one might expect rates of population growth to be greater when mortality is of intermediate magnitude than when mortality is either quite high or quite low ". If this model is a reasonable predictor, and since mortality rates in most developing countries are at intermediate levels, the likelihood of " overshooting " is substantial in several countries.

Econometric models (Schultz, 1973 ; Retherford, 1975) postulate that reproductive behaviour is economically-oriented in the sense that it is part of an attempt to maximize utility for a given fund of resources ; that is to say that additional children are one of a large variety of goods (material and otherwise) on which couples may choose to spend their money, time, attention, and so on. A model developed by Retherford examined the relationship between child mortality and fertility in this microeconomic framework. It differentiated between demand effect (the change in family fertility due to a change in the demanded number of surviving children) and the replacement effect (the desire to replace a lost child).

This area of modelling needs extensive revision, expansion, and refinement.

Cross-Sectional Correlation and Regression Analysis

A strong positive correlation between infant mortality and fertility was found by various authors using national data from various countries. Where regression analysis was done, infant mortality was shown to be an important predictor of fertility level (see, for example, Adelman, 1963 ; Heer, 1966b). These analyses have unfortunately lumped together data of varying quality and from countries passing through different stages of their demographic transition.

Specific Family Surveys

Several studies based on pregnancy history analysis have been undertaken in recent years. These studies tend to support the view that child loss has some impact on fertility. As the quality of the data on which these studies were based varied, they are discussed in some detail.

Hassan (1966), in Cairo, studied the pregnancy histories of 2695 women, who had been married for at least 5 years, had at least 1 child, and were aged 20–49 years at the time of survey (1963). He found that child loss experience had an inflationary effect on both actual and desired family size within each educational and occupational category. Among illiterate mothers aged 45–49 years, for example, those with no child loss had, on the average, only one child in excess of the average desired number of 3.8 ; in contrast, those with child loss averaged 4.8 children more than the number desired. These figures may be suspect, however, because the birth order of the last child was not controlled.

Adlakha (1970), using data from a sample survey of 803 women in Ankara who had 2692 live births, found that (a) the average birth interval was shorter in the case of an infant death than when a child had survived to the age of 1 year ; (b) this was true after adjusting for status and age ; (c) infant death was also associated with a low level of contraceptive practice ; (d) for women who had suffered child loss there was an increase in the number of live births (amounting to 2.6 for women aged 45), compared with women who had not lost a child ; (e) there was also an increase in the expected number of births with child loss. Unfortunately, the intervals used in this study were not corrected for fetal loss. The sample was also rather small.

Harrington (1971) reanalysed data from 3 surveys in West Africa (including women over 30 numbering 5536 in Ghana, 1834 in Upper Volta, and 2988 in Niger). The evidence was largely indirect and was based on the observations that (a) in both Ghana and Upper Volta [1] the proportion of children dying in large families was higher than might be expected on the basis of the higher risks of death associated with high parity births alone ; (b) in larger families the proportion of early birth order children dying was considerably higher than for children of the same birth orders in small families. Unfortunately, it was difficult to separate precisely the effect of mortality on fertility from that of fertility on mortality.

---

[1] Harrington felt the Niger data were not comparable.

Rutstein (1975) used data from a sample survey of Taiwanese women aged 20–44 years and of their husbands who were interviewed 20 months later. A total of 2277 couples were included. Couples with no child loss had lower parity progression ratios than those with child loss at each parity level until the sixth. There was also some increase in parity progression ratio attributable to fear from loss. The observed effect was reduced but not eliminated by adjusting for social and other variables.

Heer & Wu (1975) analysed interview data from 2 towns in Taiwan and 9 cities in Morocco. In the 2 Taiwanese townships, all households with an ever-married woman were included and 6814 women and 1364 men therein were scheduled for interview. After adjusting the data for the effect of other variables, it was found that the respondents with 1 death among their first 3 live births went on to have 0.285 more children than those with no loss (i.e., they had made up 28.5% of their loss by the time of interview). The corresponding figure for Moroccan towns was 0.360 children more for those with child loss. The authors concluded that " it can be definitely confirmed that both in Taiwan and in Morocco the occurrence of child death among the first three births serves to increase later fertility ".

Lery & Vallin (1975) used data from a 1962 French interview survey of family structure covering 92 000 ever-married women between the ages of 46 and 70 years. It was found that only 61% of the index children still alive at the date of survey were followed by another live birth, whereas 74% of the children who died before or after their first birthday were followed by another live birth. " Overfertility " consecutive to death was calculated to be $\frac{74-61}{61} = 0.22$ or 22%, a rough estimate of "wish for replacement". The analysis did not demonstrate any influence of the sex of the lost child on wish for replacement. It also indicated that in the case of infant mortality, the diminution of the average interval between births was generally 20% or 25%.

An analysis has been carried out of data from the KAP-type fertility survey (around 1970) in rural and semi-urban areas in Colombia, Costa Rica, Mexico, and Peru, with samples of 1400 to 2100 women (who had had at least one birth) in each country. The proportion ever using contraception has been lowered by child loss in all 4 countries. In Peru and Costa Rica, a small increase in fertility due to child loss was observed, but there was no similar effect in Colombia or Mexico.

Chowdhury et al. (1975) used data from two sources : (a) retrospective pregnancy histories of 2910 currently married women interviewed in the Pakistan National Impact Survey (1968–69), and (b) longitudinal vital registration data (1966–70) of 5236 women residing in a rural area of Bangladesh collected by the Cholera Research Laboratory. The report concentrates on the influence of child loss on the live-to-live birth intervals. In the retrospective data, no consistent difference was observed between women with and women without previous child loss. In the Bangladesh prospective study the median birth interval for women with a surviving infant was 37.2 months. This was shortened to 24.1 months by an infant death. Most of the effect, the authors explained, was biological rather than behavioural. Unfortunately no consideration was given to fetal loss or abortion between two live births. The interval data are therefore suspect.

REFERENCES

ADELMAN, I. (1963) An econometric analysis of population growth. *American economic review*, 53 : 314–339.

ADLAKHA, A. L. (1970) A study of infant mortality in Turkey. Thesis, University of Michigan.

ANASTASI, A. (1956) Intelligence and family size. *Psychological bulletin*, 53 : 187–209.

BAJPAI, P. C. et al. (1966) Observations on perinatal mortality. *Indian pediatrics*, 3 : 83–98.

BELMONT, L. & MAROLLA, F. A. (1973) Birth order, family size, and intelligence. *Science*, 182 : 1096–1101.

BISHOP, E. H. (1964) Prematurity : Etiology and management. *Postgraduate medicine*, 35 : 185–188.

BUTLER, N. R. & ALBERMAN, E. D., ed. (1969) *Perinatal problems : The second report of the 1958 perinatal mortality survey*, Edinburgh, Livingstone.

BUTLER, N. R. & BONHAM, D. G. (1963) *Perinatal mortality : The first report of the 1958 British perinatal mortality survey*, Edinburgh, Livingstone.

CHASE, H. C. (1961) *The relationship of certain biologic and socio-economic factors to fetal, infant and early childhood mortality—I. Father's occupation, parental age, and infant's birth rank*, Albany, New York State Department of Health (mimeographed document).

CHASE, H. C. (1962) *The relationship of certain biologic and socio-economic factors to fetal, infant and early childhood mortality—II. Father's occupation, infant's birth weight and mother's age*, Albany, New York State Department of Health (mimeographed document).

CHOWDHURY, A. K. A., KHAN, A. R. & CHEN, L. C. (1975) *The effect of child mortality experience on subsequent fertility : An empirical analysis of Pakistan and Bangladesh data*. Paper presented at a Seminar on Infant Mortality in Relation to the Level of Fertility, Bangkok, Thailand, 6–12 May 1975.

CRUMP, E. P. et al. (1957) Growth and development—I. Relation of birth weight in Negro infants to sex, maternal age, parity, prenatal care, and socioeconomic status. *Journal of pediatrics*, 51 : 678–697.

CZEIZEL, A. & RÉVÉSZ, C. (1970) Major malformations of the central nervous system in Hungary. *British journal of preventive and social medicine*, 24 : 205–222.

DINGLE, J. H., BADGER, G. F. & JORDAN, W. S. (1964) *Illness in the home : A study of 25,000 illnesses in a group of Cleveland families*, Cleveland, Press of Western Reserve University.

DONNELLY, J. F. et al. (1964) Maternal, fetal and environmental factors in prematurity. *American journal of obstetrics and gynecology*, 88 : 918–931.

DOUGLAS, J. W. B. (1950) Some factors associated with prematurity : The results of a national survey. *Journal of obstetrics and gynaecology of the British Empire*, 57 : 143–170.

DOUGLAS, J. W. B. & BLOMFIELD, J. M. (1958) *Children under five : The results of a national survey*, London, Allen & Unwin.

DOUGLAS, J. W. B. & SIMPSON, H. R. (1964) Height in relation to puberty, family size and social class : A longitudinal study. *Milbank Memorial Fund quarterly*, **42** : 20–35.

EASTMAN, N. J. (1944) The effect of the interval between births on maternal and fetal outlook. *American journal of obstetrics and gynecology*, **47** : 445–466.

ERHARDT, C. L. & NELSON, F. G. (1964) Reported congenital malformations in New York City, 1958–1959. *American journal of public health*, **54** : 1489–1506.

FRACCARO, M. (1956) A contribution to the study of birth weight based on an Italian sample. *Annals of human genetics*, **20** : 282–298.

FREDERIKSEN, H. (1969) Feedbacks in economic and demographic transition. *Science*, **166** : 837–847.

GILLE, R., et al. (1954) Le niveau intellectuel des enfants d'âge scolaire : la détermination des aptitudes ; l'influence des facteurs constitutionnels, familiaux, et sociaux. *Institut national d'études démographiques : travaux et documents*, **23** : 294.

GORDON, H., et al. (1970) Genetic and interracial aspects of hypertensive toxemia of pregnancy—A prospective study. *American journal of obstetrics and gynecology*, **107** : 254–262.

GORDON, J. E. (1969) Social implications of health and disease. *Archives of environmental health*, **18** : 216–234.

GRANT, M. W. (1964) Rate of growth in relation to birth rank and family size. *British journal of preventive and social medicine*, **18** : 35–42.

HARE, E. H. & SHAW, G. K. (1965) A study in family health : (1) Health in relation to family size. *British journal of psychiatry*, **111** : 461–466.

HARRINGTON, J. (1971) The effect of high infant and childhood mortality on fertility : The West African case. *Concerned demography*, **3** : 22–35.

HASSAN, S. (1966) *Influence of child mortality on population growth*. Ann Arbor, Michigan, University Microfilms.

HAY, S. & BARBANO, H. (1972) Independent effects of maternal age and birth order on the incidence of selected congenital malformations. *Teratology*, **6** : 271–279.

HEADY, J. A. & MORRIS, J. N. (1959) Social and biological factors in infant mortality : Variation of mortality with mother's age and parity. *Journal of obstetrics and gynaecology of the British Empire*, **66** : 577–593.

HEER, D. M. (1966a) Births necessary to assure desired survivorship of sons under differing mortality conditions. Paper presented to the Population Association of America, New York.

HEER, D. M. (1966b) Economic development and fertility. *Demography*, **3**(2): 423–444.

HEER, D. M. & SMITH, D. O. (1968) Mortality level, desired family size, and population increase. *Demography*, **5** : 104–121.

HEER, D. M. & WU, HSIN-YING (1975) The separate effects of individual child loss, perception of child survival and community mortality level upon fertility and family-planning in rural Taiwan with comparison data from urban Morocco. Paper presented at a Seminar on Infant Mortality in Relation to the Level of Fertility, Bangkok, Thailand, 6–12 May 1975.

HEUYER, G., et al. (1950) Le niveau intellectuel des enfants d'âge scolaire : une enquête nationale dans l'enseignement primaire. *Institut national d'études démographiques : travaux et documents*, **13** : 283.

HOLLEY, W. L., ROSENBAUM, A. L. & CHURCHILL, J. A. (1969) Effect of rapid succession of pregnancy. *In : Perinatal factors affecting human development*, Washington, Pan American Health Organization (Scientific Publication No. 185), pp. 41–44.

44

HUBBLE, D. (1966) Physical health and family planning—1. (*b*) Physical hazards of uncontrolled fertility for the child. *In :* Preventive medicine and family planning : Proceedings of the Fifth Conference of the Europe and Near East Region of the International Planned Parenthood Federation, Copenhagen.

HUGHES, E. (1923) Infant mortality, results of a field study in Gary, Indiana, based on births in one year. *Children's Bureau Publication* No. 112, pp. 44–45.

HUMERFELT, S. & WEDERVANG, F. (1957) A study of the influence upon blood pressure of marital status, number of children, and occupation. *Acta medica scandinavica*, **159** : 489–497.

IMMERWAHR, G. E. (1967) Survivorship of sons under conditions of improving mortality. *Demography*, **4** : 710–720.

ISRAEL, S. L. & BLAZAR, A. S. (1965) Obstetric behavior of the grand multipara. *American journal of obstetrics and gynecology*, **81** : 326–332.

ISRAEL, S. L. & DEUTSCHBERGER, J. (1964) Relation of the mother's age to obstetric performance. *Obstetrics and gynecology*, **24** : 411–417.

JAFFE, F. & POLGÁR, S. (1964) Medical indications for fertility control. Unpublished paper. Planned Parenthood—World Population.

KARN, M. N. & PENROSE, L. S. (1951) Birth weight and gestation time in relation to maternal age, parity and infant survival. *Annals of eugenics*, **16** : 147–164.

KESSNER, D. M. et al. (1973) *Infant death : an analysis by maternal risk and health care*, Washington, Institute of Medicine, National Academy of Sciences.

KINZEL, G. E. (1961) Enterocele : a study of 265 cases. *American journal of obstetrics and gynecology*, **81** (6) : 1166–74.

KNODEL, J. (1975) The influence of child mortality on fertility in European populations in the past : Results from individual data. Paper presented at a Seminar on Infant Mortality in Relation to the Level of Fertility, Bangkok, Thailand, 6–12 May 1975.

LAPHAM, R., WRIGHT, N. & QUANDT, A. (1975) The influence of special mortality reduction programs on fertility : An initial look at some empirical data and measurement problems. Paper presented at a Seminar on Infant Mortality in Relation to the Level of Fertility, Bangkok, Thailand, 6–12 May 1975.

LERY, A. & VALLIN, J. (1975) Attempt to estimate the over-fertility consecutive to the death of a young child. Paper presented at a Seminar on Infant Mortality in Relation to the Level of Fertility, Bangkok, Thailand, 6–12 May 1975.

LOBL, M., WELCHER, D. W. & MELLITS, E. D. (1971) Maternal age and intellectual functioning of offspring. *Johns Hopkins medical journal*, **198** : 347–357.

LOEB, J. (1965) Weight at birth and survival of newborn, by age of mother and total birth order : United States, early 1950. *Vital and health statistics*, Series 21, Number 5.

LOGAN, W. P. D. (1953) Marriage and childbearing in relation to cancer of the breast and uterus. *Lancet*, **265** : 1199–1202.

LUNDIN, F. E., JR, ERICKSON, C. C. & SPRUNT, D. H. (1964) *Socioeconomic distribution of cervical cancer*, Washington, Government Printing Office (Public Health Monograph No. 73.)

MACMAHON, B. et al. (1970) Age at first birth and breast cancer risk. *Bulletin of the World Health Organization*, **43** : 209–221.

MALIPHANT, R. G. (1949) The incidence of cancer of the uterine cervix. *British medical journal*, **1** : 978–982.

MATTHIESSEN, P. C. (1975) Influence of child mortality on fertility in the European demographic transition : Results from aggregate data. Paper presented at a Seminar on Infant Mortality in Relation to the Level of Fertility, Bangkok, Thailand, 6–12 May 1975.

MAY, D. A. & HEER, D. M. (1968) Son survivorship motivation and family size in India : A computer simulation. *Population studies*, **22** : 199–210.

MEHDI, Z., NAIDU, P. M. & GOPAL, R. V. (1961) Incidence and causes of perinatal mortality in Hyderabad, Andhra Pradesh, India. *Indian journal of medical research*, **49** : 897–946.

MIALL, W. E. (1959) Follow-up study of arterial pressure in the population of a Welsh mining valley. *British medical journal*, **2** : 1204–1210.

MIALL, W. E. et al. (1962) Factors influencing arterial pressure in the general population in Jamaica. *British medical journal*, **2** : 497–506.

MIALL, W. E. & OLDHAM, P. D. (1958) Factors influencing arterial blood pressure in the general population. *Clinical science*, **17** : 409–444.

MIDDLETON, G. D. & CAIRD, F. I. (1968) Parity and diabetes mellitus. *British journal of preventive and social medicine*, **22** : 100–104.

MILLIS, J. & SENG, YOU POH (1954) The effect of age and parity of the mother on birth weight of the offspring. *Annals of human genetics*, **19** : 58–73.

MORRIS, J. N. & HEADY, J. A. (1955) Social and biological factors in infant mortality. I. Objects and methods. *Lancet*, **1** : 343–349.

NAMBOODIRI, N. K. & BALAKRISHNAN, V. (1959) On the effect of maternal age and parity on the birth weight of the offspring (Indian infants). *Annals of human genetics*, **23** : 189–203.

NATIONAL CENTER FOR HEALTH STATISTICS (1972) *Parity and hypertension*, Washington, DC, US Department of Health, Education and Welfare (Vital and Health Statistics, Series 11, No. 38).

NATIONAL CENTER FOR HEALTH STATISTICS (1973) *A study of infant mortality from linked records by age of mother, total birth order, and other variables ; United States, 1960 live-birth cohort*, Washington, DC, US Department of Health, Education and Welfare (Vital and Health Statistics, Series 20, No. 14).

NATIONAL CENTER FOR HEALTH STATISTICS (1974) *Family background, early development, and intelligence of children 6–11 years, United States*, Washington, DC, US Department of Health, Education and Welfare (Vital and Health Statistics, Series 11, No. 142).

NELIGAN, G. & PRUDHAM, D. (1969) Norms for four standard developmental milestones by sex, social class and place in family. *Developmental medicine and child neurology*, **11** : 413–422.

NELSON, J. H. & SANDMEYER, M. W. (1958) A study of 812 grand multiparae. *American journal of obstetrics and gynecology*, **75** : 1262–1266.

NEWCOMBE, H. B. (1965) Environmental versus genetic interpretations of birth-order effects. *Eugenics quarterly*, **12** : 90–101.

NEWCOMBE, H. B. (1964) Screening for effects of maternal age and birth order in a register of handicapped children. *Annals of human genetics*, **27** : 367–382.

NEWCOMBE, H. B. & TAVENDALE, O. G. (1964) Maternal age and birth order correlations : Problems of distinguishing mutational from environmental components. *Mutation research*, **1** : 446–467.

NISBET, J. D. (1953) Family environment and intelligence. *Eugenics review*, **45** : 31–42.

NISBET, J. D. & ENTWISTLE, N. J. (1967) Intelligence and family size, 1949–1965. *British journal of educational psychology*, **37** : 188–193.

NORTMAN, D. (1974) Parental age as a factor in pregnancy outcome and child development. *In : Reports on Population/Family Planning*. New York, The Population Council.

NOVAK, E., JONES, G. & JONES, H. (1970) *Novak's textbook of gynecology*, 8th ed., Baltimore, Williams & Wilkins, pp. 268–271.

O'HARA, D. J. (1972) Mortality risks, sequential decisions on births, and population growth. *Demography*, 9 : 485–498.

OMRAN, A. R. (1971) *The health theme in family planning*. Chapel Hill, Carolina Population Center (Monograph No. 16).

O'SULLIVAN, J. B. & GORDON, T. (1966) *Childbearing and diabetes mellitus*, Washington, DC, US Department of Health, Education and Welfare (Vital and Health Statistics, Series 11, No. 21).

OXORN, H. (1955) Hazards of grand multiparity. *Obstetrics and gynecology*, 5 : 150–156.

PAN AMERICAN HEALTH ORGANIZATION (1971) *Inter-American investigation of mortality in childhood*, Washington, DC, PAHO.

PENROSE, L. S. (1933) The relative effects of paternal and maternal age in Mongolism. *Journal of genetics*, 27 : 219.

PENROSE, L. S. (1962) Paternal age in Mongolism. *Lancet*, 1 : 1101.

PENROSE, L. S. (1967) The effects of change in maternal age distribution upon the incidence of Mongolism. *Journal of mental deficiency research*, 11 : 54–57.

PETRY, J. A. & PEARSON, B. (1955) Obstetrical complications with grand multiparity. *Southern medical journal*, 48 : 820–826.

PYKE, D. A. (1956) Parity and the incidence of diabetes. *Lancet*, I (270) : 818–821.

RADOVIC, P. (1966) Frequent and high parity as a medical and social problem. *American journal of obstetrics and gynecology*, 94 : 583–585.

RECORD, R. G., MCKEOWN, T. & EDWARDS, J. H. (1969) The relation of measured intelligence to birth order and maternal age. *Annals of human genetics*, 33 : 61–69.

REED, E. W. & REED, S. C. (1965) *Mental retardation : A family study*, Philadelphia, Saunders.

RETHERFORD, R. D. (1975) The influence of child mortality on fertility : A review of mechanisms. Paper presented at a Seminar on Infant Mortality in Relation to the Level of Fertility, Bangkok, Thailand, 6–12 May 1975.

ROBERTS, D. F. & TANNER, R. E. S. (1963) Effects of parity on birth weight and other variables in a Tanganyika Bantu sample. *British journal of preventive and social medicine*, 17 : 209–215.

ROBERTSON, I. & KEMP, M. (1963) Child health and family size : A survey relating to the Cape coloured population of Cape Town in the years 1961–1962. *South African medical journal*, 37 : 888–893.

ROOPNARINESINGH, S., WEHBY, M. & MATADIAL, L. (1971) High parity in the Negro parturient. *Obstetrics and gynecology*, 38 : 690–692.

RUTSTEIN, S. O. (1971) The influence of child mortality on fertility in Taiwan : Study based on sample surveys conducted in 1967 and 1969. Thesis, University of Michigan.

SCHULTZ, T. A. (1973) The value of children : An economic perspective. *Journal of political economy*, 81 (No. 2, Part 2) : 2–13.

SCOTT, J. A. (1962) Intelligence, physique, and family size. *British journal of preventive and social medicine*, 16 : 165–173.

SCOTTISH COUNCIL FOR RESEARCH IN EDUCATION (1949) *The trend of Scottish intelligence*, London, University of London Press.

SELVIN, S. & GARFINKEL, J. (1972) The relationship between parental age and birth order with the percentage of low birth-weight infants. *Human biology*, 44 : 501–509.

SHAH, F. K. & ABBEY, H. (1971) Effects of some factors on neonatal and postneonatal mortality. *Milbank Memorial Fund quarterly*, 49 : 33–57.

SHAPIRO, S., LEVINE, H. S. & ABRAMOWICZ, M. (1970) Factors associated with early and late fetal loss. *In :* Proceedings of the 8th Annual Meeting of the AAPPP, 9–10 April 1970, Boston, Massachusetts, Excerpta Medica International Congress, Series No. 224.

SHIRODKAR, V. (1967) A new approach to the understanding of the anatomy and treatment of uterine prolapse. *In :* Marcus & Marcus, ed., *Advances in obstetrics and gynecology*, Vol. 1, Williams & Wilkins, pp. 567.

SIMPKISS, M. J. (1968) Birth weight, maternal age and parity among the African population of Uganda. *British journal of preventive and social medicine*, **22** : 234–237.

SMITH, A. & RECORD, R. G. (1955) Maternal age and birth rank in the aetiology of Mongolism. *British journal of preventive and social medicine*, **9** : 51–55.

SPENCE, J. et al. (1954) *A thousand families in Newcastle upon Tyne : An approach to the study of health and illness in children*, London, Oxford University Press.

SPICER, C. C. & LIPWORTH, L. (1966) Regional and social factors in infant mortality. *In : Studies on medical and population subjects*, No. 19. London, Her Majesty's Stationery Office.

SPIERS, P. S. (1972) Father's age and infant mortality. *Social biology*, **19** : 275–284.

STEVENSON, A. C. et al. (1966) Congenital malformations. *Bulletin of the World Health Organization*, **34** (suppl.) : 5–127.

STOECKEL, J. & CHOWDHURY, A. K. M. A. (1972) Neo-natal and post-neonatal mortality in a rural area of Bangladesh. *Population studies*, **26** (1) : 113–120.

SULLIVAN, J. (1972) The influence of demographic and socio-economic factors on infant mortality rates in Taiwan, 1966–1969. Unpublished manuscript prepared at the Population Council, New York, N.Y.

TANNER, J. M. (1968) Earlier maturation in man. *Scientific American*, **218** : 21–27.

TAYLOR, C. E. (1965) Health and population. *Foreign affairs*, April, pp. 475–486.

TYRONE, C. H. (1957) Procidentia of the uterus : experience with 166 cases. *Annals of surgery*, **145** : 963–65.

VEHASKARI, A., LAHTINEN, J. & TERHO, J. (1968) Hazards of grand multiparity. *Annales chirurgiae et gynaecologiae Fenniae*, **57** : 476–484.

WAHI, P. N., MALI, S. & LUTHRA, U. K. (1969) Factors influencing cancer of the uterine cervix in North India. *Cancer*, **23** : 1221–1232.

WAHL, C. W. (1956) Some antecedent factors in the family histories of 568 male schizophrenics of the United States Navy. *American journal of psychiatry*, **113** : 201–210.

WALDROP, M. F. & BELL, R. Q. (1966) Effects of family size and density on newborn characteristics. *American journal of orthopsychiatry*, **36** : 544–550.

WIENER, G. & MILTON, T. (1970) Demographic correlates of low birth weight. *American journal of epidemiology*, **91** : 260–272.

WOLFERS, D. & SCRIMSHAW, S. (1974) Child survival and interval between births in Guayaquil, Ecuador. Mimeographed paper.

WOODBURY, R. M. (1925) Causal factors in infant mortality, a statistical study based on investigations in eight cities. *Children's Bureau Publication*, No. 142, pp. 60–67.

WORLD HEALTH ORGANIZATION (1969) Special subject : Maternal mortality. *World health statistics report* **22** (6): 335–368.

WORLD HEALTH ORGANIZATION (1971) Special subject : Late foetal deaths per 1000 live births by age of mother and birth order, 1955–1957 and 1965–1967. *World Health Statistics Report* **24** (1): 42–55.

48

WORLD HEALTH ORGANIZATION (1974) Working paper No. 8 for the World Population Conference, 1974 : Health aspects of population trends and prospects. Geneva, World Health Organization.

WRAY, J. D. (1971) Population pressure on families : Family size and child spacing. *In : Rapid population growth*, Vol. II, prepared by a study committee of the Office of the Foreign Secretary, National Academy of Sciences, Baltimore, Johns Hopkins Press, pp. 403–461.

WRAY, J. D. & AGUIRRE, A. (1969) Protein-calorie malnutrition in Candelaria, Colombia : I. Prevalence ; social and demographic causal factors. *Journal of tropical pediatrics*, **15** : 76–98.

WYNDER, E. L. et al. (1954) A study of environmental factors in carcinoma of the cervix. *American journal of obstetrics and gynecology*, **68** : 1016–1052.

WYON, J. B. & GORDON, J. E. (1962) A long-term prospective-type field study of population dynamics in the Punjab, India. *In : Research in family planning*, ed. Clyde V. Kiser, pp. 17–32. Princeton, Princeton University Press.

YERUSHALMY, J. (1938) Neonatal mortality by order of birth and age of parents. *American journal of hygiene*, **28** : 244–270.

YERUSHALMY, J. (1939) Age of father and survival of offspring. *Human biology*, **11** : 342–356.

YERUSHALMY, J. (1945) On the interval between successive births and its effect on survival of infant—I. An indirect method of study. *Human biology*, **17** : 65–106.

YERUSHALMY, J. et al. (1956) Longitudinal studies of pregnancy on the island of Kauai, Territory of Hawaii—I. Analysis of previous reproductive history. *American journal of obstetrics and gynecology*, **71** : 80–96.

YERUSHALMY, J., PALMER, C. E. & KRAMER, M. (1940) Studies in childbirth mortality. II. Age and parity as factors in puerperal fatality. *Public health reports*, **55** : 1195–1220.

ZIEL, H. A. (1962) Grand multiparity—its obstetric implications. *American journal of obstetrics and gynecology*, **84** : 1427–1441.

Chapter Two

RESEARCH DESIGN
FOR THE COLLABORATIVE STUDIES

A. R. Omran, C. C. Standley and A. Kessler

THE RESEARCH PROBLEM AND OBJECTIVES

The Research Problem

As has been discussed in Chapter 1, several studies have indicated that the health of the family, especially of mothers and children, may be affected by certain components of family formation, particularly the age of the mother at pregnancy, pregnancy intervals, parity, and family size. However, most of the evidence for these relationships comes from Europe, the USA, and other economically and socially developed countries. The question remains whether the same relationships are to be found in the developing countries, where the environment is more hostile, the social and economic conditions poorer, and health care less adequate.

Because of the close association between unfavourable socio-environmental conditions and poor health, it is likely that the relationships between factors determining family formation and health would be different in the less developed countries. It is possible, for example, that when social and environmental conditions are bad, family formation effects may be obscured. It appears that under such conditions a mother cannot provide well for her children or care adequately for them, even if she has only a few. It is still relevant, nevertheless, to examine under such conditions the interaction between family formation and health of family members, especially mothers and children.

Finally, it is of interest to examine in less developed communities the possible impact that child loss early in the reproductive span of a woman may have on her subsequent fertility. This is of particular significance since it is generally believed that the level of fertility is closely associated with the level of childhood mortality, especially in infancy.

51

Specific Questions and Objectives of the Study

More specifically, the questions that required answers were:

1. Will high parity, large family size, and close spacing of pregnancies in the less developed countries be associated with:

(*a*) poor pregnancy outcome;

(*b*) high infant and childhood mortality and morbidity, especially from infectious diseases and undernutrition;

(*c*) poor physical development and lower intellectual achievement of children;

(*d*) poor maternal health, especially in regard to gynaecological and obstetrical problems?

2. Do pregnancies at an early or late maternal age have poorer pregnancy outcomes? Are they also associated with adverse effects on maternal and child health?

3. Does high child loss in the early stages of a woman's reproductive life lead to higher subsequent fertility?

4. Are the health effects of family formation the same among different socioeconomic groups? Are they the same among rural and urban groups and among various cultural subgroups living under similar socioeconomic conditions?

Under the auspices of the World Health Organization, a collaborative study was organized among research centres in several countries to investigate the above questions in different cultural settings. Each centre tested the study hypotheses in its own context; the findings cannot be extrapolated to a national context. The study was intended as a first step, possibly to be followed by more detailed investigations.

It was hoped, however, that it would, through the collection of local data, answer some questions of interest to those involved in policy formulation and implementation in both health and family planning programmes. Moreover, if different patterns of family formation were shown to affect significantly the health of mothers and children, this would prove a powerful argument for family planning for both the medical profession and for the public at large.

Some operational questions were also considered. The main ones were (*a*) whether it would be possible to use cross-culturally a unified research design and instruments, and (*b*) whether it would be possible to carry out, in some settings, physical and other examinations on samples of women and children or to obtain reliable answers to questions relating to many "personal" matters, such as family formation, health, and fertility behaviour.

Finally, another fundamental objective was institutional development, since WHO was interested in developing a network of research teams with competence in epidemiological studies in human reproduction.

RESEARCH HYPOTHESES *

Selection of Study Variables and Indices

The variables selected for study can be classified into 4 categories : (1) sociocultural variables, (2) family formation variables, (3) health variables, and (4) family planning behaviour variables. The variables are shown in Table 1.

TABLE 1. STUDY VARIABLES

I. SOCIOCULTURAL VARIABLES	II. FAMILY FORMATION VARIABLES	III. HEALTH VARIABLES	IV. FAMILY PLANNING BEHAVIOUR VARIABLES

Social class
Education of husband
Education of wife
Occupation of husband
Occupation of wife
Residence :
  urban/rural
Religion or caste
	Family size
	Age of mother
	Parity
	Gravidity
	Birth order
	Pregnancy order
	Birth interval
	Age at marriage
	Interval between marriage and first pregnancy
	Duration of marriage
	Family type : nuclear/extended
	Ideal family size
		A. *Pregnancy outcome*
		
		Abortion
		Stillbirth
		Live birth
		
		B. *Child health and development*
		
		Neonatal mortality
		Post-neonatal mortality
		Child mortality, 1–4 years
		Morbidity in children under 5 years : percentage with fever/diarrhoea in preceding month
		Health examination of children under 5 years :
		  weight
		  height
		  haemoglobin
		  medical diagnosis
		IQ of children aged 8–14 years
		
		C. *Maternal health*
		
		Weight/height
		Haemoglobin
		Blood pressure
		Gynaecological findings
		Feeling of poor health
		Lactation practices
			Family planning practices
			Ideal family size
			Attitudes toward contraception abortion sterilization
			Pregnancy interval preference
			Ideal age for boys or girls to marry
			Eligible women's opinions on health & family formation

Statement of the Research Hypotheses

Two overall hypotheses were considered :

1. Health risks for mothers and children increase with high frequency of pregnancies, large family size, short birth intervals, and too young or too old age of mother at the time of pregnancy.

2. Experience of child loss raises subsequent fertility.

---

* A glossary of key terms used in the study is provided on page 61.

RESEARCH DESIGN

Research Strategy

Since the collaborative studies were considered an initial step in a research programme, it was decided to start with the more feasible approaches to determining the existence of possible associations between patterns of family formation and health. Thus, a cross-sectional approach, with a pregnancy history component, was adopted to collect reproductive, health, economic, sociocultural, and demographic information. In addition to these core studies, which were followed by all collaborating centres, a two-year prospective study was undertaken in one country (India), a detailed nutritional study of children under two years of age was carried out in another (the Philippines); and a case-control infant mortality study was performed in a third (Lebanon).

Research Setting

Study population

In order to compare family formation and health patterns in two or more different population subgroups, each collaborating centre chose its subgroups (see sampling below) on the basis of either (a) *culture or religion* (for example, in India the subgroups chosen were Muslims and three subsects of Hindus), or (b) *residence* (for example, in the Philippines the subgroups chosen were urban and rural residents).

Sampling

Sampling technique

The choice of subgroups was decided upon by the collaborating centre, and the chosen samples were not necessarily intended to represent the national population.

In most centres, the sampling frame was based on local area maps or on a baseline census of households. In centres where cultural groups were considered, it was necessary that such groups be living in the same or adjacent areas under generally comparable conditions. In centres where subgroups represented residential or occupational groups, similar area samples were taken from each.

It should be noted, however, that some variation in sampling occurred between centres. The details of each centre's sample are found in the individual country reports. In each case, sampling was done by or in consultation with the team's statistician.

Determination of sample size

In determining sample size, one usually considers the frequencies of the most pertinent variables in the study. In this case, because of the multiplicity of variables and because of varying frequencies, infant mortality was chosen (a) because it was a very important variable in the study, and (b) because its frequency was relatively lower than that of many other indices in the study.

Calculations indicated that a sample size of 2000 women in each sub-group would be adequate and would allow 4 subclassifications (e.g., sub-classification by urban/rural residence and simultaneously by middle and low social status could be made). For the populations considered in the study, an estimate of 130 infant deaths per 1000 live births was used in calculating sample size. While allowing for a relative chance error of $\pm 15\%$ (or ± 19.5 per 1000 births), which represents a high level of precision in view of the hypothesized differences, the sample size needed to compare the infant mortality rates in the two subclassifications may be determined as follows. If p_1 and p_2 denote the sample estimates of infant mortality in the two subclassifications, then it is required that $\dfrac{p_1-p_2}{p} \leqslant 0.15$ with a 95% confidence coefficient. Under the assumption of equal infant mortality in the two subclassifications, $\dfrac{p_1-p_2}{\sqrt{p(1-p)\left(\dfrac{2}{N}\right)}}$ is approximately normally distributed, and one arrives at $N \geqslant \dfrac{2\,(1.96)^2\,(0.13)\,(0.87)}{(0.0195)^2}$ which gives 2285 births. Assuming a conservative average of 4 births per ever-married female, then 571 ever-married females are required, or 2285 ever-married females for each cultural or religious group comprising 4 sub-classifications. With a sample size of 2000 females, the size of the relative chance error that should be tolerated will be 22.23 per 1000 births, which gives a relative chance error of $\pm 17.1\%$. That is to say, a difference of more than ± 22.23 per 1000 births between any two subclassifications can be considered statistically significant at the 5% level.

Controls

In this study, the groups (and classes within each group) acted as controls for one another.

Study Components

The material for the collaborative study was obtained through : (a) house-hold surveys ; (b) structured interviews with married women under 45 years of age (referred to as eligible women or EWs) ; (c) medical examination of these women ; (d) paediatric examination of their children under 5 years of age ; and (e) IQ testing of children 8–14 years old.

55

Household survey

A household survey was done in each of the chosen areas according to the sampling design. A standardized household questionnaire was administered in order to obtain identification data for the household and information on its composition as well as demographic and social data. The questionnaire is shown in the Annex on page 539.

Eligible woman interview

Each eligible woman in the study sample was interviewed according to the standardized EW questionnaire, which takes approximately 45 minutes to one hour to administer. Some of the main areas covered by the EW questionnaire are : (*a*) demographic and social characteristics ; (*b*) pregnancy history with additional details for last pregnancy ; (*c*) mortality particulars, if applicable, for her dead children ; (*d*) selected morbidity particulars for children and mothers in the preceding month ; (*e*) health service utilization by family ; (*f*) perception of mortality and fertility and consciousness of change in each ; (*g*) concepts of " ideal family sizes ", best age at marriage, sex preference, etc. ; (*h*) knowledge, attitudes, and practice of contraception (KAP) , (*i*) attitudes toward abortion, sterilization, lactation, and family formation ; (*j*) fertility of EW's parents ; (*k*) attitudinal questions regarding childhood mortality and whether improvement in childhood survival would be taken into consideration in decision-making regarding family planning. The questionnaire, which is shown in the Annex (page 539), was slightly modified for the centres in Colombia, Egypt, Pakistan, and Syria, where the studies are still under way.

Paediatric examination of children under five

A physical examination was done on all children under 5 years of age belonging to the eligible women, or on samples of such children.[1] The examination included : (*a*) weight and height ; (*b*) physical abnormalities and diseases ; (*c*) history of illness and use of medical care in the preceding month ; and (*d*) haemoglobin level and stool examination for parasites.

Medical examination of the eligible women

The following information was collected for all or samples of the EW population : (*a*) weight and height ; (*b*) blood pressure ; (*c*) gynaecological examination ; (*d*) obstetric history ; and (*e*) haemoglobin level.

---

[1] In India, children 5–9 years of age were examined as well. Data from this group were excluded from this report.

Intelligence quotient of children aged 8–14 years

The Cattell & Cattell Culture-Fair Test designed for children 8–14 years of age was used in all centres. The scale chosen consists of 4 tests, with a time limit for each test. The raw scores from these tests were converted into standardized scores by using a conversion table provided in the test manual, which allowed for the age and sex of the child. The results were expressed as standardized IQ norms (with mean = 100 and standard deviation = 24.4).

Research Instruments

The household and eligible woman's questionnaires were developed by Dr Omran in consultation with the WHO Human Reproduction unit. These instruments were revised by teams of investigators from India, Iran, Lebanon, and Turkey during a conference held in Gandhigram, India, 1970. At the same meeting, the medical and other examination procedures were also standardized.

Training of interviewers and other personnel

Training of interviewers and other personnel was a crucial part of the preparation for the investigation and was conducted with the utmost care. Every effort was made to avoid creating interviewer bias, either by not discussing the hypotheses with the interviewers or, if the hypotheses were already known, by strongly emphasizing that the purpose of the study was to *test* rather than to verify these hypotheses. The interviewers were made completely familiar with the instruments (in the local language) and with the technique they were to use. Demonstration interviews, role-playing by interviewers and observations of interviews in a field situation were used as steps to train a new interviewer. Also, the first ten or so interviews of a new trainee were carefully scrutinized by a supervisor and errors in recording were pointed out and discussed.

Reliability checks

Because of the importance of the EW interviews in the whole study, reliability checks were introduced in order to test the recall consistency of the interviewees. This was done in two ways. Some questions concerning certain items in the pregnancy history chart were also included in other parts of the questionnaire and served as built-in reliability checks. Discrepancies were used for further probing until consistent responses were obtained. Secondly, each team was requested to re-interview at least 5% of the women as the study progressed ; for this purpose, factual items in the questionnaire rather than opinion questions were asked. The results were used to correct interviewing techniques. Thirdly, a very detailed list of consistency checks developed at the WHO International Reference

Centre for Epidemiological Studies in Human Reproduction at Chapel Hill (henceforth referred to as WHO-IRC), was applied in each centre for cleaning the data decks or tapes before these were sent to Geneva. Errors were corrected and in Geneva the same checks were also applied to gain further accuracy. This process took several months both at the centres and in Geneva.

Pretesting the instruments

The study instruments were carefully translated into the local language and dialect. Some of the items were independently retranslated into English as a test of accuracy, and necessary modifications were made. Pretesting of the translated instruments was carried out locally ; several women (about 10 in each cultural or residential group) were interviewed. These women had characteristics comparable to the study population but were not included in the actual study. Any ambiguity was eliminated from the instruments and culturally objectionable or easily misunderstood wording was altered.

Data Processing and Analysis

The questionnaires and other forms

Editing and coding of questionnaires and other data collection forms, subsequent transfer of data to punch cards and verification were done by the research team in each centre. The data were then transferred from the cards to computer tapes, either in Geneva or at the centre. Analysis was carried out in Geneva, in collaboration with the WHO-IRC.

Tabulation scheme

A tabulation scheme was developed when the study was designed. Volumes of dummy tables were prepared ; these were of 3 kinds : (*a*) descriptive tables ; (*b*) correlation tables ; and (*c*) tables designed to test the specific hypotheses.

Statistical analysis

The statistical methods used included : (*a*) descriptive statistics applied to frequency distribution, (*b*) the control or frequency table technique, widely used in epidemiology, where the relation of each of two independent variables to a dependent variable was examined in a simple fashion, and (*c*) tests of association and multivariate analysis.

ORGANIZATION OF THE STUDY

Coordination

The responsibility for planning, coordination and follow-up of the study was shared between the WHO Human Reproduction unit in Geneva and the WHO-IRC. Frequent site visits and consultations by Dr Omran, who acted as coordinator of the studies, were supplemented by 4 meetings of investigators, one in Gandhigram, India, in 1970 to review the research designs, protocols, and instruments, and one in Geneva in 1972 to evaluate progress and review plans for analysis. A third meeting was convened in 1974 at the University of Sussex, Brighton, England, to review the first drafts of the reports from 5 centres. The edited versions were discussed and finalized at the fourth meeting, held in Geneva in 1975.

Choice of the Collaborating Centres

With a provisional plan for the studies and after several site visits, 4 centres were initially involved in the studies : India, Iran, Lebanon, and Turkey. Owing to the interest they generated where there were on-going family planning programmes (Egypt, Pakistan, Philippines, and the province of Taiwan) and in countries with little or no official commitment to family planning (Colombia and Syria), the studies were rapidly extended and were, in fact, started in several countries at the request of the government.

The following is a list of collaborating institutions :

Colombia	School of Public Health, Medellín
Egypt	Institute of Public Health, Alexandria ; Department of Preventive Medicine, Assiut University
India	Gandhigram Institute of Rural Health and Family Planning, Madurai District, Tamil Nadu
Iran	School of Public Health, Teheran University
Lebanon	School of Public Health, American University in Beirut
Pakistan	National Institute of Fertility Studies, Karachi
Philippines	Institute of Public Health, University of the Philippines, Manila
Syria	Central Bureau of Statistics, Damascus
Taiwan [1]	Provincial Institute of Maternal and Child Health, Taichung
Turkey	Department of Community Medicine, Haceteppe University, Ankara

The present report includes the results of studies in 5 countries : India, Iran, Lebanon, Philippines, and Turkey. The results obtained in other countries will be published later.

---

[1] Withdrew from the study in 1972.

Study Organization in Each Centre

The head of the collaborating institution or agency selected a team of investigators and consultants and was officially responsible for the administration of the study on behalf of the institution. A field director was also named and became responsible for the field operation, record keeping, local analysis, etc. The composition of the research teams was multidisciplinary, including specialists in public health, biostatistics, obstetrics and gynaecology, paediatrics, and social sciences.

Organization of Data Analysis

As already indicated, data tapes or decks of punch cards were sent to Geneva for central analysis. Data were checked and corrected from the point of view of code range, consistency, and structure. Computer outputs were mailed back to the respective centres with copies to the International Reference Centre (IRC) at Chapel Hill. Summary tables were then prepared and sent to the IRC for further analysis and for statistical tests. The results were sent back to the countries along with comments on their interpretation.

Time Table

A detailed time table for the successive phases of the study was prepared and every effort was made to follow it. The usual length of the studies was 2 years, with one more year for analysis and write-up.

Writing of the Reports

The format for the reports was discussed and adopted at the second meeting of investigators in 1972. It was agreed that each centre would follow the same sequence in its data presentation; a final chapter would summarize the major findings from all centres and draw general conclusions. At the third meeting of investigators, when the draft reports were reviewed, some modification of the format was agreed upon, several new tables were requested, and it became obvious that considerable redrafting by the centres was needed to ensure balance and uniformity of presentation. These second drafts were edited by the WHO Human Reproduction unit and the International Reference Centre and sent back to the collaborating centres prior to the fourth meeting of investigators.

It must be emphasized that the reports published in this volume only make use of the data relating directly to the research hypotheses of this study. The data have been returned by WHO to the centres, who may wish to carry out additional analyses on their data to answer other questions.

GLOSSARY
Definitions of Terms as used in the Study

Abortion (fetal loss)—loss of the fetus or termination of pregnancy under seven months (28 weeks), including both induced and spontaneous abortions

Actual or achieved family size—number of children born to each eligible woman who are still living at the time of the survey

Age at marriage—in this study the term " age at marriage " is used synonymously with " age at consummation "

Birth order—the rank of an index live birth among other live births for each woman

Child loss—number of children born alive who died under 5 years of age

Childhood mortality—death of children (under 1 month, 1–11 months, under 1 year, under 5 years) per hundred reported live births per eligible woman

Eligible woman—woman under 45 years of age who was married at the time of the survey

Extended family—household including, in addition to nuclear family, relatives of husband or wife

Family size—see " actual or achieved family size "

Family structure—classification of family according to nuclear or extended family

Gravidity—number of pregnancies per woman

Household—those people living together in one dwelling (house, apartment, or room) sharing food and/or economically interdependent, including at least one eligible woman

Household head—person recognized by the members of a household as leader or economic provider based on economic, seniority, or other cultural considerations

Ideal family size—number of children considered by an interviewee to be desirable under circumstances similar to her own (see questionnaire)

Interval between marriage and conception—duration in months between the date of marriage and the beginning of the first pregnancy within the specified marriage

Maternal age—age of the eligible woman at termination of a given pregnancy (birth, abortion, stillbirth)

Nuclear family—family composed of husband, wife, and their unmarried offspring

Parity—number of children ever born alive or number of live births per woman

Ponderal index—an index of body bulk incorporating both height and weight

$$\text{ponderal index} = \frac{\text{height in inches}}{\sqrt[3]{\text{weight in pounds}}}$$

Preceding pregnancy interval—the interval (in months) between the termination of the preceding pregnancy and the termination of the given pregnancy (this definition automatically excludes the first pregnancy as a given pregnancy)

Pregnancy order—rank of index pregnancy among total pregnancies per woman

Pregnancy outcome—the result of a pregnancy including live birth, stillbirth, and abortion, whether induced or spontaneous

Pregnancy wastage—abortions and stillbirths combined

Social status—a composite score based on education and occupation of household head, family income, and average number of persons per room. The rating was done according to local standards and was relative within each area. Households were divided into high status, middle status, and low status according to a scheme attached to the questionnaire.

PART II. REPORTS FROM COLLABORATING CENTRES

Chapter One

STUDY AREAS AND POPULATION CHARACTERISTICS

INTRODUCTION

A. R. Omran

In this chapter, each of the collaborating centres describes the physical features of the area covered by its study, the transportation, medical, and other service facilities of the region, and the social, demographic, and/or cultural characteristics of the indigenous population. The general procedure of each centre was to select two or more cultural or residential groups that might differ in their patterns of family formation, but the method of selection varied from centre to centre. It was not possible to select areas that would necessarily be representative of the total population of a country, of a region within a country, or of a total cultural or residential group.

For most of the countries, the term " culture " is often used in preference to " religion ", since it encompasses a wider range of group traits. For example, in Beirut the two study groups were the Shiites and the Maronites, culturally distinct sects within the Muslim and Christian religions, respectively. In Teheran, the religious appellation " Muslim " is retained because the Muslims constitute a homogeneous cultural group there, but the other study group is referred to as " Armenian " because the Armenians are distinguished from other Christian sects by their ethnic origin. In the Gandhigram study, the Muslims, who have the highest fertility rate of the various religious groups in India, are presented as one group, the other consisting of three caste divisions within the Hindu religion, differing in their cultural practices and reproductive levels : the Scheduled Castes (who belong to the lowest social stratum and have the highest fertility), the Vellalas, and the Other Hindus (a mixture of all Hindu castes other than the Scheduled Castes and Vellalas) ; culturally and socially, the Vellalas and Other Hindus are intermediate in status between the Muslims and the Scheduled Castes, the Vellalas having a lower reproductive level than the Other Hindus. In the Philippines, where the population is predominantly Christian, and in Turkey, a Muslim nation, the place of residence rather than the religion was the variable used to differentiate the population groups.

To be eligible for inclusion in the study, a woman had to be under 45 years of age and married, with a husband present at the time of the study. This made it possible to cover nearly the full fertility span, except for the few women aged 45 or more who might yet be found to be fecund.

The social classification is a composite index based on the education and occupation of the head of the household (usually the spouse of the woman interviewed), the income of the family, and the number of individuals per room (an indication of the quality of housing). Because this index is " culture bound ", i.e., heavily influenced by local norms, an inter-country comparison of social status groups should not be attempted. Furthermore, as the classification index is only relative, it may not be representative of the general social status conditions of the country from which the specific area of study was chosen. So few high status households were included in the study that in all areas they were added to the middle status group.

A. GANDHIGRAM

K. A. Pisharoti & S. Gunasekaran

Introduction

This study was carried out during the years 1971–75 by the Gandhigram Institute of Rural Health and Family Planning in collaboration with the WHO Human Reproduction unit, Geneva, and the WHO International Reference Centre for Epidemiological Studies in Human Reproduction, Chapel Hill, NC, USA. The Institute is located in Tamil Nadu (formerly Madras) State in South India. The 41 million people in the area (1971 estimate) are 89% Hindu, 6% Christian, and 5% Muslim. The Hindu population is not a homogeneous group but consists of several castes, which vary considerably in economic, social, and cultural characteristics.

In order to examine the interaction between reproductive behaviour and health, the study population was chosen from the following 4 Indian subcultural groups, differentiated by their reproductive patterns : (1) Muslims, (2) Hindu Kongu Vellalas, (3) Hindu Scheduled Castes, and (4) all other Hindu castes except groups (2) and (3). For convenience, the 4 groups will be referred to throughout the report as Muslims, Vellalas, Scheduled Castes, and Other Hindus.

Muslims comprise several groups, engaged mostly in agriculture and also partly in trade. The Vellalas and Other Hindus are mainly landowning cultivators, while the Scheduled Castes, who belong to the lowest social stratum, are mainly agricultural labourers.

66

Muslims are characterized by relatively high fertility in comparison with other groups. Because of the differences in the cultural characteristics of the three Hindu groups, their reproductive patterns may also be expected to differ. Preliminary studies by the Gandhigram Institute indicated, for example, that the Vellalas had relatively lower fertility than other Hindus in the area. Christians were excluded from the study because of financial and time constraints.

Study Area

The study area is located on the border of Madurai and Coimbatore Districts, two very populous districts of Tamil Nadu State. This area was selected because it contains the 4 cultural groups chosen for the study, and is close to the Gandhigram Institute. Only rural populations were considered for the study, and 34 villages in the area were identified as containing the required number of eligible women. These villages were all located in the administrative jurisdiction of 4 community development blocks, namely Palani and Thoppampatti in Madurai District, and Madathukkulam and Dharapuram in Coimbatore District.

In general, there was little variation within the area in regard to geographic, climatic, and seasonal characteristics. Some features of the area are summarized below.

Transport. Roads suitable for motor traffic linked the 34 villages with the nearest town. Regular bus services were run by private and government enterprises on these routes.

Education. The area was served by 33 primary, 8 middle, and 7 high schools. Nearby towns had, in addition, 4 colleges, which provided undergraduate studies.

Sanitation. Sanitation in the villages was generally of a low standard. Housing conditions were poor. The water supply was obtained mainly from wells (tube or open), ponds, rivers, and overhead water tanks (in 10 villages). Only 1 village had a system of protected piped water supply. Electricity was available in all villages.

Occupation. Most of the working members of households were engaged in agriculture or cottage industry on a very small scale. The main crops in the area were rice, millet, cotton, and vegetables.

Social groups. Although Hindus were the predominant religious group in the area, the 34 villages in the study also had varying proportions of Muslims. The language of the people was Tamil, one of India's 13 major languages.

Health services. The study area was covered by 4 primary health centres (one centre per about 80 000 population) and 3 dispensaries (run by the Panchayat Unions). One 100-bed hospital was available in each of the nearby towns. A number of indigenous medical practitioners were widely used by the villages.

Data Collection Procedures

The sample size set for each cultural group was as follows :

Muslims	2000
Scheduled Castes	1000
Other Hindus	2000
Vellalas	1500

It was fixed sufficiently large to allow for within-group variation. The smaller sample size of 1000 eligible women for the Scheduled Castes was decided upon because of their greater economic and social homogeneity.

Discussions with health and community development personnel suggested that the required number of women could be found in 20 specified villages, which included concentrations of Muslims and Vellalas, the rarest members of the population sought. It was later found that 14 more villages were required to reach the target sample size.[1]

Because no systematic information existed on the cultural distribution of households, a preliminary enumeration of households was undertaken in each village, during which particulars of the caste and religion of the head of each household were collected.

In the first 20 villages, all the Muslim and Vellala households were visited, and all the eligible women in them were interviewed. For both the Scheduled Castes and the Other Hindus, the number of households exceeded the required targets; in each case, therefore, a random sample was taken, the size of which was proportional to the size of the group within the village. Thus, for both cultural groups the fraction sampled was identical for every village, although the fraction differed between the two cultures. All eligible women in the sampled households were interviewed. Households in the additional 14 villages were enumerated in a similar fashion to the initial 20 and screened to obtain the necessary number of eligible women. The fraction of each cultural group sampled depended upon the number of women still sought.

Ultimately, the following proportions of eligible women from each culture in the 34 villages were included :

Muslims	100%
Scheduled Castes	32%
Other Hindus	51%
Vellalas	100%

---

[1] This was partly due to emigration, but the main reason was that there were fewer eligible women in the first 20 villages than had been found in previous studies of other villages in the area. The number of refusals was negligible.

Organizational Features

Study headquarters. The headquarters of the field work was located in Palani town. From there, research teams were transported daily to the villages; some of the workers, particularly the interviewers, lived in the villages during the survey.

The interview survey. Thirty-nine female high school graduates were hired as interviewers, and 7 university graduates acted as their supervisors. All were adequately trained. The number of households and eligible women in each cultural group visited or interviewed is given in Table 1.A.1 (a).

Medical and psychological surveys. When the structured interview in each village had been completed, lists of eligible women, children under 5 years of age, children between 5 and 9 years, and children in the 8–14 age group were prepared. A team consisting of medical officers, laboratory technicians, IQ test administrators, and a health educator visited each village. The health educator prepared the village community well in advance of the arrival of the other members of the team. Physical examinations of women and children were carried out at a central place in each of the villages. Blood samples for the women and children under 5 years of age were collected at the time of the physical examination. Stool and blood samples for children of the 5–9 age group were collected during visits to each household included in the sample. The IQ test was administered to the 8–14 year old children either in school or in a central place in the village.

Duration of field work. The field work began in May 1971 and continued through August 1972.

Coverage. Little or no resistance was encountered in the interview survey. Because of traditional beliefs and unfounded fears, medical examinations and the collection of blood and stool specimens for laboratory work were not as successful. For the IQ testing, which used the Cattell & Cattell Culture-Fair Test, children who did not have regular schooling could not be included. Total coverage was nevertheless substantial; actual numbers are shown in Table 1.A.1 (b).

TABLE 1.A.1 (a). NUMBER OF HOUSEHOLDS AND NUMBER OF ELIGIBLE WOMEN INCLUDED IN EACH CULTURAL GROUP

Culture	Number of households	Number of eligible women
Muslim	1920	2005
Scheduled Castes	991	1021
Other Hindus	1919	1998
Vellala	1488	1517
Total	6318	6541

TABLE 1.A.1 (b). DETAILS OF COVERAGE FOR EACH STUDY COMPONENT

Type of field operation	Number in sample	Number interviewed or examined	Coverage (%)
Structured interview	6500	6541	100.0
Gynaecological examination of eligible women	6541	2430	37.2
Physical examination of children under 5 years of age	5705	2680	47.3
Psychological testing of children	5187	2464	47.5

Characteristics of the Study Population

The major characteristics of the 4 study groups are given in Table 1.A.2. These include social status and age structure, as well as occupation and education of the women and their husbands.

Social status. Using a social status scale (based on education and occupation of household head, annual family income, and average number of persons per room), women were classified as of high, middle, or low social status. Since there were so few women of " high " status (only 1% of the eligible women), this category was merged with the " middle " status group.

The Muslims had the highest proportion of women in the middle status group (70.6%), with the Other Hindus and Vellalas not far behind (67.6% and 64.2%, respectively). Among the Scheduled Castes, however, 70% of the women were in the low status group.

Age structure. Since the study population was rural, many women could not state their ages accurately. Therefore, from information on pregnancy intervals, age was estimated by building up the pregnancy history of each woman. The women in each of the 4 cultural groups were predominantly young, the mean ages at interview being between 27 and 29 years. The highest proportion of women under 20 years was observed for the Scheduled Castes (15.1%) and the lowest was for the Vellalas (only 6.5%). This was consistent with the mean ages of marriage of these two groups, which were 15.1 years for the Scheduled Castes and 17.3 years for the Vellalas. It was also noticeable that, while the proportion of women in the middle age range (20–34 years) was more or less the same for all cultural groups, there was a marked difference in the proportion of women in the age span 35–44 years. This proportion was lowest for the Scheduled Castes, which may indicate a higher death rate among women in this group.

Education. The women's educational level was low in all 4 groups. There were, in fact, relatively few women in the study who had been educated above the primary level. The proportion of women who were illiterate or

TABLE 1.A.2. CHARACTERISTICS OF THE STUDY POPULATION BY CULTURE AND SOCIAL STATUS (PERCENTAGE DISTRIBUTION)

Characteristic	Muslim			Scheduled Castes			Other Hindus			Vellala		
	Middle	Low	Total	Middle	Low	Total	Middle	Low	Total	Middle	Low	Total
Number of EW	1416	590	2005	306	715	1021	1351	647	1998	974	543	1517
Education of EW												
Illiterate + no school	79.8	89.6	82.7	91.2	98.8	96.5	74.0	92.6	80.0	85.0	96.3	89.0
Primary	19.9	10.2	17.0	8.5	1.3	3.4	22.4	7.3	17.5	15.0	3.5	10.9
Secondary	0.4	0.0	0.3	0.3	0.0	0.1	3.3	0.0	2.3	0.0	0.2	0.1
College or graduate	0.0	0.0	0.0	0.0	0.0	0.0	0.2	0.0	0.2	0.1	0.0	0.1
Education of EW's husband												
Illiterate + no school	27.8	65.5	38.9	55.3	93.5	81.9	35.8	79.0	49.8	42.6	85.5	58.0
Primary	64.2	31.7	54.7	40.5	6.4	16.4	51.6	20.1	41.4	52.1	13.6	38.3
Secondary	5.7	1.5	4.5	4.2	0.1	1.4	10.2	0.3	7.0	3.7	0.9	2.7
College or graduate	1.4	0.0	1.0	0.0	0.0	0.0	1.8	0.2	1.3	1.5	0.0	1.0
Occupation of EW												
Housewife	86.4	75.6	83.2	35.3	23.1	26.7	69.0	48.4	62.3	60.3	41.6	53.6
Clerical/professional	12.1	20.0	14.4	0.0	0.6	0.4	1.3	1.0	1.3	0.3	0.0	0.2
Agricultural/industrial	1.5	4.4	2.4	64.1	75.9	72.4	29.6	50.7	36.4	39.4	58.4	46.2
Janitorial/others	0.0	0.0	0.0	0.7	0.4	0.5	0.1	0.0	0.1	0.0	0.0	0.0
Occupation of EW's husband												
Unskilled worker	18.3	45.4	26.3	56.2	84.8	76.2	18.2	58.4	31.2	14.1	39.8	23.3
Skilled worker	6.6	1.7	5.1	13.1	0.8	4.5	33.3	9.3	25.5	4.2	0.9	3.0
Landowner	58.8	43.9	54.5	22.5	14.0	16.6	30.6	30.1	30.5	78.6	58.5	71.5
Professional/clerical	15.5	8.5	13.4	8.1	0.3	2.7	17.5	1.4	12.3	2.8	0.4	1.9
Supported by family	0.8	0.5	0.7	0.0	0.1	0.1	0.3	0.8	0.5	0.3	0.4	0.3
Family structure												
Nuclear	63.7	72.4	66.2	65.7	73.3	71.0	64.3	72.0	66.8	65.9	72.6	68.3
Extended	36.3	27.6	33.8	34.3	26.7	29.0	35.7	28.0	33.2	34.1	27.4	31.7
Age of EW												
< 20	14.3	12.4	13.8	17.0	14.3	15.1	12.1	9.6	11.3	6.8	5.9	6.5
20–24	22.6	21.0	22.1	23.2	22.6	22.8	20.2	16.8	19.1	23.3	18.0	21.4
25–29	20.6	23.7	21.5	25.5	23.7	24.2	21.9	27.2	23.6	22.6	27.3	24.3
30–34	18.4	21.2	19.2	16.3	21.2	19.8	18.2	21.1	19.1	22.9	23.0	22.9
35–39	14.9	14.4	14.8	10.2	14.6	13.2	16.3	15.6	16.1	15.7	16.8	16.1
40–44	9.2	7.3	8.6	7.8	3.6	4.9	11.3	9.7	10.8	8.7	9.0	8.8
Mean age of EW	28.2	28.3	28.3	27.1	27.5	27.3	29.0	29.2	29.1	29.2	29.7	29.4

who had received no formal schooling ranged from 80% of the Other Hindus to 97% of the Scheduled Castes, with Muslims (83%) and Vellalas (89%) in intermediate positions. The proportion who were illiterate or without schooling was higher for the low social status group (among whom it ranged from 90% for Muslims to 99% for Scheduled Castes) than for the middle status group (among whom it ranged from 74% for Other Hindus to 91% for Scheduled Castes).

In regard to education of the husband, Muslims had the lowest proportion of husbands with no formal education (39%), while the Scheduled Castes had the highest (82%). Again this proportion was low for the middle social status group (ranging from 28% for Muslims to 55% for Scheduled Castes) and high for the low status group (ranging from 66% for Muslims to 94% for Scheduled Castes). Although the educational level of wives was lower than that of husbands, there was a positive correlation (r = 0.37) between the level of the wife and that of her husband.

Perhaps the salient feature in this regard was the evidence that Scheduled Caste women, whatever their own educational experience, were more likely than others to be married to men with no schooling. By contrast, Muslim women were most likely to have husbands who had received some education.

Since so few of the women (or their husbands) received education above the primary level, the main interest lies in differences between those with no schooling and those who had attended primary schools.

Occupation. The distribution of women by occupation in the 4 cultural groups shows an interesting pattern. While the majority of women in the study as a whole were housewives, Muslim women had the lowest proportion employed outside the home (18%) followed by the Other Hindus (38%) and Vellalas (46%). More interesting was the extremely high proportion of women employed outside the home among the Scheduled Castes (73%). This is not to be taken as an index of modernization or prosperity; the women in this group were forced (by economic pressure) to work outside the home in low-paid jobs. Almost all the working Scheduled Caste women were engaged in agriculture. This was consistent with the social status distribution, since 70% of the Scheduled Caste women belonged to the low social status group.

The occupational distribution of husbands is also interesting and has cultural and social relevance. Scheduled Caste men were predominantly unskilled labourers (76%). Vellalas were mostly landowners (72%). Other Hindus were divided almost equally between skilled work, unskilled work and landownership but had the highest proportion of skilled labourers. More than half the Muslims (54%) were landowners; about one fourth (26%) were unskilled and 5% skilled labourers, while 13% were professional or clerical workers. A similar proportion of Other Hindus was in the professional/clerical category, while only negligible proportions of men from the other two groups held this type of position.

B. TEHERAN

V. Nahapetian

Introduction

This study was carried out by the School of Public Health of the University of Teheran, which has been investigating a number of public health topics. It has taken a particular interest in studies of culture and population dynamics and of family formation and family health. For this reason it was decided to include in the study two distinct cultural groups, the Muslim and the Christian Armenian communities, which live under comparable conditions in Teheran.

Muslims comprise about 99.8% of the 32 million people in Iran (1970 figures). The religious minorities in Iran are Christians, Jews, and Zoroastrians. The great majority of Christians are Armenians, whose number at the time of the study was estimated at 200 000, of whom 120 000 lived in Teheran. They have lived in the country for more than 350 years but have kept their own language, culture, and customs. Their children attend their own schools, where, besides the formal programme set by the Ministry of Education, they are taught the Armenian language, literature, and religion. Before this project started, the Iranian investigators had the impression that Armenian Christians (henceforth called Armenians) were less fertile than Muslims in Iran.

Study Area

A preliminary investigation in the city of Teheran revealed that 3 sections situated in the north-eastern part of the capital, Madjidiyeh, Heshmatiyeh, and Vahidiyeh, were appropriate for the collaborative study. These sections had well-defined boundaries, were relatively isolated from the main parts of the capital, and were composed of blocks inhabited by either purely Muslim, purely Armenian, or mixed communities, which were of either middle or low social status.

The 3 areas had good communication systems, with bus and taxi services and asphalt roads connecting them with the main part of the capital. They also used the central water supply of the capital, and there were several primary and secondary schools in these areas.

The health and medical needs of the population in these areas were provided either by private medical practitioners or by the medical facilities that operated in Teheran and were easily accessible to the residents of these areas.

Sampling

In August 1970, a preliminary enquiry was conducted in the selected sections to identify the blocks and houses that comprised each section and to determine which of the blocks were occupied entirely by Muslims or entirely by Armenians and which of them were occupied by a mixture of the two. The blocks necessary to obtain the target number of 4000 women (2000 in each cultural group) were then selected and marked on area maps.

In Madjidiyeh and Heshmatiyeh, all the blocks containing Armenian households (whether exclusively or in addition to Muslim households) were selected. For every exclusively Armenian block, an adjacent purely Muslim block was also selected. In Vahidiyeh the same procedure was followed, but only until the required number of eligible women had been found. It was decided to start the interviews from Madjidiyeh, to proceed to Heshmatiyeh and then to Vahidiyeh, and to visit all the households of the chosen blocks having one or more eligible women (married and aged between 15 and 44 years at the time of the interview). Since there were more Muslim households than Armenian in all 3 sections, the criterion for moving on from one section to another was the completion of interviewing Armenian households in each section.

It is important to mention that sampling was not planned to be representative of the population of Iran, or even of Teheran, but to cover populations of two cultural groups who were living close to each other in the area of study.

Ultimately, 4209 women were interviewed ; of these, 2115 were Muslim and 2094 were Armenian.

Data Collection Procedures

The household and eligible women's questionnaire forms, discussed at the Gandhigram conference of investigators, were reviewed and translated into Persian in December 1970. To pretest the questionnaires, interviews were carried out in 42 households selected at random from a similar population in another area of the city. The pretest showed that the questionnaires in their Persian forms were adequately clear and practical.

Six married women with secondary education were recruited to administer the questionnaires. The interviewers were trained for a period of one month ; the questionnaire forms were discussed with them in detail, and ample instructions were given to them on how to approach the families, how to phrase the questions (especially the delicate ones), how to probe for correct answers, and how to gain the confidence of the women to ensure full cooperation.

Since the instructions for completing the questionnaire forms as a whole were fairly simple and straightforward and the interviewers were competent, the training presented no problem. Results of an examination given at the end of the training programme and test interviews were very satisfactory.

An apartment was rented in the Madjidiyeh area, and clinics for gynaecological and paediatric examinations, as well as a small laboratory for taking blood, stool, and urine specimens, were established. A filing room was also available for the distribution and collection of questionnaire forms.

From the list prepared on the basis of the preliminary census of the area, a sublist of households was given to the interviewers each day. They visited the homes, interviewed the eligible women present, made appointments for later visits when the women were absent (usually on Fridays for working women), distributed containers for stool specimens, and arranged dates for the eligible women and their children to visit the clinic for various examinations.

Two physicians, one gynaecologist and one paediatrician, assisted by two nurses, carried out the gynaecological and paediatric examinations and measured heights, weights, and blood pressures.

On the predetermined day, the eligible women and their children under 5 years of age were brought to the clinic by a female member of the research team. To solve the problem of distance between the clinic and the homes of the eligible women and to ensure a complete coverage of the women and children to be examined, transportation to and from the clinic was provided by the project.

Since it was decided to examine 50% of the eligible women and their children under 5, a scheme was worked out by which appointments for women of every other block were given. This system yielded 2123 women for examination. All their children under 5 years of age were examined. These 1579 children comprised 45% of the total number of children under 5 years of age.

Coverage

During the first few days of data collection, some resistance to being interviewed and examined was observed by the interviewers. However, this reluctance gradually decreased, and the women became more and more willing and cooperative. During the entire period of the study, only 54 women (1.2%) refused to be interviewed and only 12 women (0.6%) refused to be examined. It should be mentioned that the free treatment provided for the women and children and the vitamin supplements they were given proved to be valuable inducements.

A total of 4209 eligible women in 4120 households were interviewed. The plan of action was so arranged that equal numbers of eligible women would be interviewed in each of the two cultures. The target of 50% of the women to be included in clinical studies was achieved, with 45% of the total preschool children being examined (Table 1.B.1).

TABLE 1.B.1. POPULATION AND COVERAGE

	Number interviewed	Medically examined	
		No.	%
Eligible women	4209	2123	50.48
Children under 5 years of age	3504	1579	45.06

Characteristics of the Study Population

Social status, age structure of the population, education, and occupation were the indices selected for comparing the Muslim and Armenian women and their husbands (Table 1.B.2). In addition, within each of the two religious groups, those of middle social status were compared with those of low social status. It should be noted that, by definition, all women in the sample were married.

Social status. As can be seem from Table 1.B.2, the distribution of the eligible women by social status differed in the two cultural groups, 54.2% of the Armenians being classified as of middle status compared with 45.8% of the Muslims. The difference in social status of the two cultural groups was significant ($P < 0.01$). According to the criteria used for social classification, only 9 Muslim women and 1 Armenian woman were of high social status. These women were grouped with those of middle status. It should be emphasized that the middle and low social classes identified in this study are not to be considered as representative of the middle and low social classes of Iran as a whole.

Age structure. The Muslim women as a whole were a few years younger on the average than the Armenian women, their mean ages being 27.6 and 30.6 years, respectively. Middle status women in both cultures were younger than low status women ; however, in both social status groups, Muslim women were younger than Armenian women. All these differences were statistically significant, with $P < 0.01$.

Education. There was little difference in educational levels achieved by Muslim and Armenian women. More than 50% of the middle status women and about 90% of the low status women in each cultural group were either illiterate or, if literate, had had no formal schooling. The proportion of women in each cultural group who had received no education was considerably higher among those of low social status than among those of middle social status. A comparison of each of the other educational categories showed middle status women as a whole to be better educated than their lower status counterparts, with no observable differences between cultural groups.

Characteristic	Muslim			Armenian		
	Middle	Low	Total	Middle	Low	Total
Number of EW	904	1211	2115	1071	1023	2094
Education of EW						
Illiterate + no school	52.6	90.2	74.1	53.9	89.9	71.6
Primary and some secondary	43.4	9.9	24.2	43.6	10.0	27.1
Secondary	3.8	0.0	1.6	2.3	0.0	1.2
College or graduate	0.3	0.0	0.1	0.1	0.0	0.0
Education of EW's husband						
Illiterate + no school	21.0	84.5	57.4	49.7	92.8	70.7
Primary and some secondary	62.4	15.4	35.5	45.4	7.1	26.7
Secondary	12.3	0.1	5.3	3.9	0.2	2.1
College or graduate	4.3	0.0	1.9	1.0	0.0	0.4
Occupation of EW						
Housewife	96.6	99.0	98.0	97.7	97.8	97.8
Clerical/professional	3.1	0.4	1.6	1.5	0.8	1.2
Agricultural/industrial	0.1	0.2	0.1	0.7	0.2	0.4
Janitorial/others	0.2	0.5	0.2	0.2	1.2	0.6
Occupation of EW's husband						
Unskilled worker	2.4	47.6	28.3	1.7	22.9	12.0
Skilled worker	39.8	32.2	35.5	81.8	63.5	72.9
Small businessman	14.6	14.6	14.6	8.6	10.3	9.3
Professional	42.9	4.3	20.8	7.9	1.0	4.5
Supported by family	0.2	1.3	0.9	0.0	2.3	1.1
Family structure						
Nuclear	85.6	83.6	84.5	66.9	67.4	67.1
Extended	14.4	16.4	15.5	33.1	32.6	32.9
Age of EW						
<20	18.9	10.0	13.8	6.6	4.0	5.4
20–24	28.5	25.3	26.7	26.4	12.4	19.6
25–29	20.4	21.7	21.1	24.2	16.8	20.6
30–34	14.4	21.6	18.5	19.6	25.9	22.7
35–39	9.7	12.1	11.1	10.7	22.6	16.5
40–44	8.1	9.3	8.8	12.4	18.2	15.3
Mean age of EW	26.7	28.3	27.6	28.9	32.2	30.6

In the study population, husbands were relatively better educated than their wives, although this advantage was more evident in the middle class. Muslim husbands were also better educated than Armenian husbands, a difference not observed among the women.

An association between the education of the spouses was observed, with Kendall's rank correlation coefficient equal to 0.49.

Occupation. An overwhelming majority of the women in each cultural and social status group were housewives. Only 2.1% of all the women worked outside the home. Since a total of only 90 women were engaged in work outside the home, this variable will not be considered in the remainder of this section.

There was a marked difference between the two cultural groups in the type of occupation followed by the husbands. Almost three-quarters of the Armenian husbands were skilled labourers; of the Muslim husbands, however, only just over one-third were skilled labourers, but more were unskilled, more were small businessmen, and more followed clerical or professional occupations.

Since one of the criteria for social classification was the occupation of the husband, one expects and finds that in both cultural groups among the middle status men higher proportions were in skilled and professional jobs or were owners of small businesses than among lower status men. Education and occupation of the husband were, as might be expected, closely correlated.

C. BEIRUT

H. Zurayk, C. Churchill, I. Lorfing and J. Azar

Introduction

This study was conducted by the School of Public Health of the American University of Beirut (AUB). The AUB School of Public Health has a major interest in research relating to human reproduction and family formation and in the course of other research projects has already become familiar with a considerable number of communities in the Lebanon.

Study Area

Since one of the procedures used in the collaborative studies was to compare two or more cultural or residential groups in regard to family formation and family health, two religious groups were chosen for the study: the Shiite Muslims and the Maronite Christians. The two groups have the Lebanese culture in common, but they differ in some ways. The following description, including a historical note, may clarify the distinction between the two groups.

The Maronites are Christians who owe allegiance to Rome but who have some special autonomies, which were granted by the Pope when the followers of St Maroun agreed to become part of the Roman Catholic Church. As such, they are subject to the Catholic Church discipline, which opposes artificial methods of contraception.

The Shiites are a Muslim subcultural group, which was established principally on the politics of the succession to the prophet Mohammad. Their pronounced reverence for Ali, a cousin and son-in-law of Mohammad, and his descendants distinguishes them from the other major subcultural group of Muslims, the Sunnis.

The Maronite and other Christian communities in Lebanon (e.g., the Greek Orthodox) are, for historical reasons, generally more prosperous and, by western standards, better educated than are the Muslims. The first schools that operated in Lebanon were run by the Maronite monks in the monasteries of Mount Lebanon, an area that is predominantly inhabited by Maronites. Then in the nineteenth century, French, English, and American Christian missions started schools in the city and these attracted Christian students. Consequently, Maronites and Christians in general received modern education considerably earlier than did the Muslims. This educational lag is being somewhat reduced now by the fact that public education is becoming more universal and has spread out from the cities into the rural areas. The Shiites, who have been predominantly a rural population, are now benefiting from the expanded system, with the result that their socioeconomic circumstances are improving.

This brief background will help to demonstrate that the difference between the two groups under study is not a simple one and that it has roots in historical, political, and cultural, as well as economic circumstances.

Sampling

The two groups were chosen because they happened to be present in the Beirut suburb of Mreyje, where the AUB School of Public Health has been maintaining a community health centre for several years. Because Mreyje by itself did not have a sufficiently large population to yield an adequate sample, the two adjacent communities of Chiah and Ghebeiri, where substantial numbers of both religious groups could be found, were added. The 3 towns are on the coastal plain, a few kilometres from the Mediterranean Sea and south of the capital, Beirut. It was decided to interview about equal numbers of women from each of the 3 towns.

Samples were drawn from comprehensive, detailed housing maps, which were available in the offices of a commercial research agency. The sampling and interviewing phase of the study was subcontracted to this agency under the close supervision of the AUB investigators. The maps were used as the sampling frame and a target of about 1500 eligible women in each of the religious groups was set.[1] Of the 3000 women who were to be interviewed, a target of 1000 was set for the physical examination; and of the children of the women interviewed, 1500 of those under 5 years of age were to receive a paediatric examination and 1000 of those aged 8–14 years were to receive intelligence testing.

In Mreyje, the town initially selected, all dwellings were visited and all eligible women found were interviewed. In Chiah and Ghebeiri, a

---

[1] This sample size is smaller than that in other countries because of financial constraints, particularly the high cost of project workers in Lebanon compared to other countries in the study.

two-stage procedure was used. A random sample of sections of each town was first drawn from the housing maps, and a random sample of dwellings, proportional to the density of the population within the sample sections, was selected. The listed dwellings were then visited in turn until the required number of women of each religion were found.

Random samples of the eligible women interviewed (500 from each religious group), together with their children under 5, were selected for physical examination. Since the refusal rate for the initial samples was high, additional women were approached, and the investigators finally accepted any of the interviewed women and their children who were willing to go to the examination centre (until the target numbers had been achieved).

Data Collection Procedures

The household and eligible women questionnaires were translated into Arabic and pretested in 1970. In the same year interviewers from the research agency were trained by the AUB investigators, and the field interviewing was started.

Examinations of women and children were conducted in the health centres of the three towns, with transportation provided to and from the centres. The women and children examined were drawn from the list of women who had already completed their interviews. Medical examinations were finished by the end of 1971. Abortive attempts were made to achieve the target for IQ testing of the women's children aged 8 to 14; however, the children were so widely scattered in schools in several towns and the testing conditions so bad that the results were discarded, and the IQ testing phase of the study was abandoned.

Coverage

As shown in Table 1.C.1, 1545 Shiite and 1459 Maronite women were interviewed, making a total of 3004 women. This represents 95% of the women contacted, or a refusal rate of 5%. For the gynaecological examination, 70% of the target sample size was achieved. Of their children sampled for paediatric examination, 80% of the target sample size was achieved.

The investigators had mixed feelings as regards the adequacy of these samples. It was felt to be quite an achievement to have reached so many women and children in these Lebanese towns, especially as their populations were in no way captive groups in continuous association with the AUB. Even in Mreyje, where the AUB community health centre was established, there were a number of doctors who were engaged in private practice and who drew a sizeable proportion of the population. In addition, Beirut and its specialists were close by. The situation in the other two towns was similar. Thus, every interview and/or examination conducted required persuasion.

TABLE 1.C.1. DETAILS OF SAMPLING COVERAGE

	Nos. in actual samples			Target totals	Total samples as percentages of targets
	Shiite	Maronite	Total		
Eligible women interviewed	1545	1459	3004	3000	100% [1]
Gynaecological examina-tion of eligible women	372	324	696	1000	70%
Paediatric examination of children under 5 years old	796	413	1209	1500	80%
IQ testing of children 8–14 years old [2]	208	195	403	1000	40%

[1] Despite a refusal rate of 5%, the target was met by extending the sampling area.
[2] This phase of the study was abandoned for reasons given in the text.

Although the sample sizes achieved represented a high proportion of the targets and although there was some overshooting in the sampling, the refusal rate must also be considered. For the interviewing, the refusal rate was 5%, but the medical examination encountered more resistance. Culturally, it is not easy to persuade Arab women (whether Shiite or Maronite) to submit to examination by strange doctors, especially when they see no medical purpose for it. More Maronite than Shiite women refused the examination, probably because they were more prosperous and more likely to have their own physician. The same observation applies to the paediatric examination. Because of this, some selective factors may have entered into the study.

It should also be noted that the sample area was not strictly typical of all Shiite and Maronite towns in Lebanon. The people in the 3 towns led a semi-urban existence. Earlier studies, one by Zurayk & Harfouche [1] (1970) in Mreyji and one by Churchill (unpublished) in Ghebeiri, indicated that a sizeable proportion of the population of these towns had been born elsewhere in Lebanon.

Despite these limitations, however, it is believed that the sample covered in the study represents the major traits of the Shiites and Maronites in the semi-urban area.

Characterististics of the Study Population

Social status, age structure, education and occupation are selected indices that compare the Shiite and Maronite women (and their husbands) within each religious group (Table 1.C.2). In addition, those belonging to the middle class are compared with those in the lower class. All women in the sample are, by definition, married.

---

[1] ZURAYK, H. C. & HARFOUCHE, J. K. Family health and population profile in a peri-urban setting, *Leb. Med. J.*, **22** : 3 (1970).

TABLE 1.C.2. CHARACTERISTICS OF STUDY POPULATION BY CULTURE
AND SOCIAL STATUS (PERCENTAGE DISTRIBUTION)

Characteristic	Shiite			Maronite		
	Middle	Low	Total	Middle	Low	Total
Number of EW	675	870	1545	864	595	1459
Education of EW						
Illiterate + no school	64.6	94.0	81.2	43.4	82.7	59.4
Primary	28.9	6.0	16.0	47.1	16.5	34.6
Secondary	5.3	0.0	2.3	8.2	0.8	5.2
College or graduate	1.1	0.0	0.6	1.2	0.0	0.7
Education of EW's husband						
Illiterate + no school	47.5	91.6	72.3	33.2	84.7	54.2
Primary	35.9	8.3	20.3	46.9	14.5	33.7
Secondary	8.3	0.1	3.7	15.2	0.8	9.3
College or graduate	8.3	0.0	3.7	4.7	0.0	2.8
Occupation of EW						
Housewife	92.4	97.5	95.3	91.4	95.8	93.2
Clerical/professional	6.5	1.3	3.6	6.9	2.4	5.1
Agricultural/industrial	0.4	0.9	0.7	1.0	0.5	0.8
Janitorial/others	0.5	0.2	0.4	0.5	1.3	0.8
Occupation of EW's husband						
Unskilled worker	12.3	53.4	35.5	4.3	26.6	13.4
Skilled worker	37.6	28.4	32.4	52.8	60.8	56.1
Landowner	27.2	14.3	20.0	20.1	8.9	15.5
Professional	21.2	0.8	9.7	22.2	1.7	13.9
Supported by family	1.8	3.0	2.5	0.6	2.0	1.2
Family structure						
Nuclear	81.9	90.3	86.7	82.8	90.9	86.1
Extended	18.1	9.7	13.3	17.2	9.1	13.9
Age of EW						
<20	7.7	7.0	7.3	2.8	2.7	2.7
20–24	22.5	20.7	21.5	15.7	12.1	14.3
25–29	20.9	25.5	23.5	22.7	19.5	21.4
30–34	18.7	21.8	20.5	18.6	25.7	21.5
35–39	14.8	14.6	14.7	18.8	22.9	20.4
40–44	15.4	10.3	12.6	21.4	17.1	19.7
Mean age of EW	29.9	29.2	29.5	32.1	32.2	32.1

Social status. Social status was determined by a social status scoring
system, which included education and occupation of the household head
and the annual family income.[1] The scale was both relative and culture-
bound and referred only to standards in the local Lebanese communities.
As there were small numbers in the high category (only 2%), this was
merged with the middle group. Thus, women are classified into middle
and low social status groups. The Maronites were somewhat better off
than the Shiites, with 59% and 44% respectively classified as of middle
status.

---

[1] Other centres in the study also included the average number of persons per room in their social status
scale.

Age structure. The Shiite women were a few years younger, on the average, than the Maronite women. The mean ages were 29 and 32 years, respectively. This was probably a reflection of the younger age at marriage for Shiites, as will be discussed later. Within each religious group, there was no difference in mean age by social class.

Education. Taking the two religious groups together, over 70% of the women were illiterate or, though literate, had received no formal schooling. In particular, the proportion having no education was much greater among Shiites than among Maronites; it was also greater among low status than among middle status women.

As might be expected in societies with strong patriarchal values, the husbands were relatively better educated than their wives, although this advantage was most marked in the middle status group. Even in this group, however, some 47% of the Shiite and 33% of the Maronite husbands had received no formal education. The correlation coefficient between the education of the husband and the education of the women was 0.6.

Occupation. Over 90% of the women in all groups, both Shiite and Maronite and both middle and low status, were housewives. In regard to husbands, the Shiites had a lower proportion than the Maronites in skilled and professional jobs. This may, however, reflect better educational opportunities.

D. MANILA

V. Balderrama-Guzman, S. Ignacio-Morelos and G. B. Roman

Introduction

This study was carried out between 1971 and 1975 by the Institute of Public Health, University of the Philippines, Manila. The two areas covered by the study were an urban area (Metropolitan Manila) and a rural area (Rizal province).

Study Area

The population of the Greater or Metropolitan Manila area and the surrounding provinces is racially homogeneous, of Malayan-Indonesian stock. For this reason, the grouping adopted for the purposes of this study was based mainly on the area of residence. The site chosen for the urban study was Pasay City, a part of Metropolitan Manila.

The estimated population of Pasay City (1970 census) was 205 212 and was predominantly young, with 36.4% under 15 years of age and only 2%

above 65. Although Pasay City was quite small in area, it was very thickly populated. Like other cities near Manila, for the past two decades it has had an influx of people from distant provinces of the Philippines and the rapid urbanization has brought concomitant health, social, and economic problems.

The literacy level was 90.2% for those aged 10 years and above, and although English was widely spoken, the dialect mostly used was Tagalog. There were a number of schools, both public and private, within the city and in Manila. The predominant religion was Roman Catholic. The city had such modern conveniences as paved roads, various means of transportation, electricity, piped water, telephones and other means of communication, and various recreational facilities. Health facilities and personnel were adequate. There were 4 private general hospitals, several small private clinics, and 9 government health centres, and the close proximity to Manila increased the accessibility of modern medical services.

The rural study was conducted in two towns (Baras and Morong) in the province of Rizal, which is situated in the south-western part of Luzon. Baras and Morong are adjacent towns of Rizal province and are about 51 and 42 kilometers respectively from Manila.

Since information specific to Baras and Morong was not available, a description of Rizal province, in which the two towns are located, will be given.

In 1970, the population of Rizal province was 2 819 045. Close to 31% of the population were under 10 years of age, about 22% were between 10 and 19 years of age and about 35% were between 20 and 44 years of age. For the entire Philippines, 47% of the population were in the age group 0–15 years.[1] The population density in Rizal province was 1529.7 persons per square kilometer. This was quite high compared with the Philippines as a whole, which had a density of 122.3 persons per square kilometer. However, the population density of Rizal province was low compared with that of Manila and neighbouring cities comprising the Metropolitan Manila area, which had a population density of 34 746 persons per square kilometer.

Over 90% of the population aged 10 years and over (in Rizal province as a whole) were literate. One out of 5 persons in the province graduated from high school or college. About 87% of the people in Rizal were Roman Catholic, with the remaining 13% belonging to the Aglipayan, Protestant, Iglesia ni Kristo, Buddhist, Muslim, and other religious sects. The main industries in Baras and Morong were farming, fishing, and pig and poultry raising. Around 71% of the rice fields were irrigated, enabling the farmers to have two harvests a year. A number of rice and corn mills operated in these towns; however, no large manufacturing establishments had at the time of the study been put up in the area.

---

[1] UNIVERSITY OF THE PHILIPPINES, POPULATION INSTITUTE, Philippine population—profiles, prospects and problems, Manila, 1970, p. 21.

Main roads within the town proper and those leading to adjacent barrios were paved with concrete or asphalt, while those in the remote barrios were still dirt. In addition to buses, jeepneys, and trucks owned by the inhabitants themselves or by other companies and individuals, the tricycle provided a convenient mode of transportation within the town. Motorized bancas, although utilized mainly for fishing, were also made available for transportation.

Provisions for health in Baras were limited to the health centre and its personnel, but in Morong there was a government emergency hospital and a privately owned hospital to supplement the services offered by the health centre. The proximity of these towns and the availability of transportation seemed to compensate for the apparent lack of health resources in Baras.

Opportunities for education were provided by public grade schools, public high schools, and parochial schools for grade pupils and secondary students. Those who desired to pursue a college education usually enrolled in the colleges and universities in Greater Manila.

Research Procedures

The study areas were chosen for practical reasons, such as accessibility, availability of suitable premises for carrying out the investigations, and the cooperativeness of local health service personnel.

Sampling. The target was to cover about 2000 married women under the age of 45 years in each of the urban and rural areas.

For the rural sample, every household with an eligible woman in Baras and in the adjacent barrios of Morong was included in the study. There seemed to be no marked sociocultural differences between the people in this part of Morong and their neighbours in Baras. 2200 eligible women were registered in the census, but only 1998 interviews were used. Those that yielded incomplete information were discarded.

The urban sample was drawn from San Roque, one of the 8 districts of the densely populated city of Pasay. The population density, demographic and sociocultural profiles, and economic features of San Roque were similar to those of the other 7 districts of Pasay City.

Each household with an eligible woman was included in the survey of the district. The total number of eligible women enumerated in the census described below was 2231. Only 2000 eligible women were available for interview at their homes.

In both areas, the target population for physical examinations was all women interviewed and their children under 5 years of age. (The children were also given a developmental test (Gesell), the results of which are not reported in this volume.) The women's children aged 8 to 14 years were given an IQ test (Cattell & Cattell Culture-Fair Test).

Data collection. The study was first discussed with local health personnel and, where appropriate, with leaders in the community. A census of all households was then carried out by the whole team, during the course of which the questionnaire was pretested. Subsequently, all eligible women found during the census who were available were interviewed by a team of 5 graduate interviewers. At the end of each interview, a record card was made out for the informant showing the number of her children under 5 years of age, and spaces were left for checking as each subsequent examination or test was completed.

The eligible woman was also instructed to go with her children to the health centre the following day for physical examination, and she was provided with a sufficient number of containers for urine and stool specimens, which she was asked to bring with her. Transportation, where necessary, was provided.

Difficulties encountered. The main difficulties encountered in the study may be categorized into :

(1) Factors that hindered accessibility of the population, such as interference with household chores and occupation (planting and harvesting rice), physical distance, and inability to pay for transportation. The last two problems were resolved by providing transportation for the subjects.

(2) Customs and cultural practices : Women, particularly from the rural area, were very reluctant to submit to gynaecological examination. People did not see why they should visit a doctor unless they felt ill, and certain religious sects prohibited blood examination.

(3) Ignorance, misconception, and misinformation : There was fear of blood extraction by both the eligible women and their children. Despite the efforts of the team members to correct the misconception, rumours that blood extracted from subjects was mixed in containers and sold to hospitals in Manila existed. Some people believed in witchcraft and did not want to submit their specimens (blood, stool, and urine) because they believed the specimens could be used for witchcraft purposes.

(4) Weather : Heavy rain and monsoon contributed to the reluctance of the mothers to go to the clinic, particularly if they had to bring along their children.

Response rates. Response rates at the main stages of the inquiry are shown in Table 1.D.1. Details of the results of each type of examination are shown in Chapters 5 and 6.

Characteristics of the Study Population

Table 1.D.2 compares the social status, occupation, education and age structure of the rural and urban women and their husbands.

TABLE 1.D.1. POPULATION COVERAGE

Stage of study	Rural			Urban		
	Registered population = 100%	Persons interviewed or examined		Registered population = 100%	Persons interviewed or examined	
		No.	%		No.	%
Interview	2200	1998	91	2231	2000	90
Physical examination						
Women	1998	1484	74	2000	1434	72
Children under 5	2750	1791	65	3119	1907	61
IQ test						
Children aged 8–14	2252	1397	63	1661	750	45

Social status. There was some difference in social status distribution for the two residential groups. In the total sample, only 80 women belonged to the high social status group and they were added to the middle status group. This formed the predominant group in both areas, constituting 88.7% of the urban sample and 80.4% of the rural sample. Because some of the variables studied may be influenced by social status, the latter will be controlled for whenever feasible in this report.

It should be mentioned that the 1961 Philippine Bureau of Census and Statistics figures were used because the 1971 data were not available until July 1973. The 1961 figures showed that the average family income was 1804 pesos or US $286 per annum. The distribution of the family income was as follows :

Low income group	(under 500 to 2999 pesos p.a.) (or under $79 to $476 p.a.)	—	86.8%
Middle income group	(3000 to 9999 pesos p.a.) (or $476.2 to $1587 p.a.)	—	11.8%
Upper income group	(10 000 pesos & over) (or $1587.3 & over)	—	1.5%

Age structure. The standard population composition used for any area in the Philippines is as follows :

Years	*Years*
0– 4	45–49
5– 9	50–54
10–14	55–59
15–19	60–64
20–24	65–69
25–29	70–74
30–34	75–79
35–39	80 &
40–44	above

TABLE 1.D.2. CHARACTERISTICS OF STUDY POPULATION BY CULTURE
AND SOCIAL STATUS (PERCENTAGE DISTRIBUTION)

Characteristic	Rural			Urban		
	Middle	Low	Total	Middle	Low	Total
Number of EW	1606	392	1998	1774	226	2000
Education of EW						
Illiterate + no school	37.6	68.7	43.7	16.6	49.2	20.2
Primary	38.9	27.0	36.6	60.1	47.8	58.7
Secondary	9.3	2.8	8.0	15.6	2.2	14.1
College or graduate	14.2	1.5	11.8	7.7	0.8	6.9
Education of EW's husband						
Illiterate + no school	15.4	75.0	27.1	7.9	57.5	13.5
Primary	39.5	14.0	34.5	52.2	30.5	49.7
Secondary	21.4	7.9	18.7	27.1	9.7	25.1
College or graduate	23.7	3.1	19.7	12.7	2.2	11.5
Occupation of EW						
Housewife	81.3	92.1	83.4	90.2	93.8	90.6
Clerical/professional	5.5	0.0	4.5	0.6	0.0	0.4
Agricultural/industrial	5.6	1.6	4.8	2.5	0.4	2.3
Others	7.5	6.4	7.4	6.7	5.8	6.5
Occupation of EW's husband						
Unskilled worker	33.1	82.7	42.8	26.9	82.7	33.2
Skilled worker	49.5	10.2	41.8	66.7	13.3	60.7
Landowner	3.5	2.8	3.5	1.5	2.2	1.5
Professional	10.3	0.3	8.4	3.7	0.8	3.5
Supported by family	3.5	4.1	3.6	1.0	0.9	0.9
Family structure						
Nuclear	66.6	63.5	66.0	80.6	77.9	80.2
Extended	33.4	36.5	34.0	19.4	22.1	19.7
Age of EW						
<20	4.7	6.1	5.0	8.3	4.9	7.9
20–24	17.5	17.1	17.4	25.5	17.3	24.5
25–29	24.1	21.4	23.6	24.1	25.7	24.3
30–34	24.4	21.4	23.8	20.5	25.2	21.0
35–39	17.8	20.7	18.4	14.0	18.1	14.5
40–44	11.5	13.3	11.9	7.5	8.8	7.6
Mean age of EW	30.4	30.8	30.5	28.4	30.0	28.6

Education. The proportion of women who were illiterate or who
received no formal education was considerably higher in the rural than in
the urban area (43.7% compared with 20.2%). Although urban women
were better educated than the rural women in general, 11.8% of the rural
women achieved a college or higher education, compared with only 6.9%
of the urban women. The same pattern was observed for the education of
the women's husbands, although the husbands' education was generally
higher than that of their wives. As expected, the findings also demonstrated
a substantial difference by social status. In both the rural and urban areas
and for both the women and their husbands, the proportion who were
illiterate or had no schooling was greater among the low social status

group, while the proportion with a college education was greater among the middle status group.

It is interesting to note that the proportions both of the women and of their husbands who had attended college was high for a developing country, reflecting what has often been referred to as the Filipinos' passion for education. Implied in this is the desire for a degree and subsequent entrance into the ranks of the white collar workers or the professions, which are considered prestigious occupations in the country.

It is also important to explain the higher proportion of college educated women and husbands in the rural area. The rural family that is able to send one of its members to college enjoys high regard and prestige. In addition, a college education confers added economic security and power on a person living in a rural community. Rural families are also more closely-knit than their urban counterparts. It is customary in the rural areas to pool the resources of the parents and those of the comparatively affluent relatives to enable them to send some of their children to college, even if the parents are obliged to make great sacrifices.

Since the absolute numbers, as well as the proportions, of women and their husbands who had attended college were considerable, it was both practical and useful to examine the relationship between family formation variables and the whole range of educational attainment.

E. ANKARA

N. H. Fişek, K. Sümbüloglu, D. Benli and M. Bertan

Introduction

The Community Medicine Department of Hacettepe University was responsible for the Turkish study. The Etimesgut Health District, which has been a research area for the Department of Community Medicine for several years, was chosen as the area in which to study the relationship between family formation and family health. The data were collected and analysed between 1971–75.

Study Area

The Etimesgut District is located to the west of the city of Ankara and includes 83 villages and 2 towns. The surface area of the district, which is predominately mountainous, is 640 square miles, with an average of 7.4 square miles per village. Three major highways and the Ankara-Istanbul railroad pass through the district, and road conditions are quite satisfactory. Almost all the villages are accessible by car, although the district is covered with snow for an average of 16 days a year.

In 1971, when this research project was launched, the population of the district was 60 724. The age distribution showed a relatively young population, with 42.2% under 15 years and only 3.9% aged 65 years and over. The demographic profile of the district (1971) was much more favourable than that of Turkey as a whole (1967), as shown below.

	Etimesgut (1971) [1]	Turkey (1967) [2]
Crude death rate per 1000 population	7.1	15.0
Crude birth rate per 1000 population	31.9	40.0
Infant mortality rate per 1000 live births	87.6	153.0
Life expectancy males	62.50	55.84
Life expectancy females	67.50	58.49

The district had an out-migration rate of 4.9% and an in-migration rate of 21.7%.

The females in the fertile age group (15–44 years) constituted 20.8% of the district population and of these "fertile age" females, some 67% were married (72.3% in the villages and 60.2% in the towns).

The district had one sugar factory, one cement factory, and a few small plants. Most people living in the towns worked in these factories or plants or in the city of Ankara. The predominant occupation of the heads of families, especially those in the villages, was agriculture. For the district as a whole, 70% of the family heads were farmers. The great majority of the houses, especially in the villages, were adobe buildings. In the villages, 90% of the houses had animal quarters compared to 21% in the towns. Nearly two-thirds of the houses had either closed tank toilet facilities in the yard or properly built toilets within the house. Fountains and wells, many of which were contaminated, were the usual source of water in the villages. The 2 towns had piped water supply systems.

Health services in the area were provided by the Etimesgut Health District, which was composed of 7 health units, 30 health stations and a 50-bed rural hospital. Since the district was part of the National Health Services, residents were able to obtain general practitioner and visiting nurse services, drugs, hospital care, and all preventive care, including periodic check-ups, free of charge. In addition, people could choose to go to private physicians. All residents had individual health cards where preventive measures, examinations, diagnoses, and treatments were recorded. The unit doctor, public health nurses, and midwives visited the villages and homes on a fixed schedule. In addition, auxiliary nurse midwives visited homes in their zone regularly and reported births, deaths, and migration, and male public health nurses visited each house in their zone twice a year to correct the household forms.

---

[1] Annual Report of the Etimesgut Rural Health District, 1971.

[2] SCHOOL OF PUBLIC HEALTH, MINISTRY OF HEALTH OF TURKEY. Turkish Demographic Survey, 1966–1967.

Sampling

Since almost all the residents of the area were Muslims, the type of residence was used to differentiate 2 groups for the study. The study area was therefore divided into 2 strata, rural and semi-urban, and each stratum was further divided into sub-strata according to the number of children and number of rooms in each household. The maps and records for the district households were used as the sampling frame. Sampling procedures for the semi-urban and rural areas were identical, samples within the sub-strata being selected systematically.

The total number of households in the district was 10 287. For this study 5010 households were initially chosen, 2236 from the semi-urban and 2774 from the rural areas. Of these, 4329 households were visited for interviews, including 1855 in semi-urban and 2474 in rural areas. The coverage for interviews was therefore 86.4% (83.0% in semi-urban and 89.2% in rural areas). Of the chosen households 320 (6.4%) had migrated, 350 (7.0%) were absent on repeated visits, and 11 (0.2%) refused to be visited.

In the households that were visited, there were 3785 eligible women, of whom 3675 (97.7% in semi-urban and 96.2% in rural) were interviewed.

For the gynaecological examination, 633 households were selected randomly from among the main sample of households of 2 of the 7 health centres (one from the semi-urban and one from the rural area). The total numbers of households and eligible women examined are shown in Table 1.E.1.

TABLE 1.E.1. NUMBER OF HOUSEHOLDS AND OF ELIGIBLE WOMEN SELECTED FOR GYNAECOLOGICAL EXAMINATION

Area	No. of households	No. of EW in households	No. of EW examined	% examined
Semi-urban	321	305	271	88.9
Rural	300	300	261	87.3
Total	621	605	532	88.0

The sampling procedures followed were the same as for the interview sample.

For the paediatric examination, sub-samples of 25% of the main samples were chosen at random ; this procedure yielded 1346 children from the semi-urban area and 1346 from the rural area. Again, sampling procedures followed were the same as for the interview sample. A total of 2110 children (80%) were examined. Complete physical examinations, including laboratory examinations such as the haemoglobin test, urine analysis, stool examination and cultures, were made when possible.

All children attending school were given IQ tests (Cattell & Cattell Culture-Fair Test), and the tests of the children belonging to the households in the main sample were analysed separately.

Interview Procedure

Thirty-six female interviewers from the schools of Nursing and of Home Economics and Administration of the Hacettepe University interviewed the heads of households and the eligible women. Interviewers were divided into 7 teams and each team was assigned to one health centre, where the members of the team were accommodated. There was one supervisor in each team, and all teams were regularly supervised by the chief supervisor.

Characteristics of the Study Population

The urban and semi-urban areas were compared by social status, age structure, education, and occupation of the population (Table 1.E.2).

Social status. Because of small numbers of eligible women in the high social status group (11 rural and 63 semi-urban women), this group was combined with the middle status group.

Table 1.E.2 shows that the rural area had a larger proportion of low social status families than the semi-urban area (21.6% compared with only 5.0%, respectively). As will be seen later, persons in the semi-urban area were somewhat better off than their rural counterparts. In fact, 94.9% of all semi-urban women were classified as middle class ; therefore, control for social status in the semi-urban group will give very little information.

Age structure. There was very little difference in the ages of the eligible women in the two residential groups, the mean ages of both the rural and urban women being 30.3. Small differences were also found by social status.

Education. The educational status of the women and their husbands is shown in Table 1.E.2. About one-half of the semi-urban and two-thirds of the rural women were either illiterate or had received no formal education. The majority of the remaining women had had primary education, with only 0.9% of the rural women and 5.8% of the semi-urban women achieving secondary or higher education. There were no women with college education in the rural area, while in the semi-urban area 0.3% of the women attended college (but all these women were from the high social status group).

Many more husbands than women received formal education, although 20.4% of the urban and 35.0% of the rural men received none. In general, the rural and low status husbands were less likely to have received formal schooling than the others.

Occupation. Since 94.6% of the women (93.6% in rural and 96.1% in semi-urban areas) were classified as housewives, the occupation of the women will not be used as an independent variable in the analysis of Turkish data.

TABLE 1.E.2. CHARACTERISTICS OF STUDY POPULATION BY RESIDENCE
AND SOCIAL STATUS (PERCENTAGE DISTRIBUTION) *

Characteristic	Rural			Semi-urban		
	Middle	Low	Total	Middle	Low	Total
Number of EW	1599	440	2039	1555	81	1636
Education of EW						
Illiterate + no school	61.9	74.0	65.0	50.3	79.0	52.0
Primary	36.9	25.0	34.5	43.3	21.0	42.2
Secondary or higher	(1.0)	—	(0.9)	6.1	—	5.8
Education of EW's husband						
Illiterate + no school	27.3	63.4	35.0	17.8	69.0	20.4
Primary	67.6	35.4	60.6	59.5	(28.4)	57.9
Secondary or higher	4.7	—	3.9	17.9	—	17.2
College or graduate	(0.4)	—	(0.3)	5.1	—	4.5
Occupation of EW						
Housewife	93.8	92.7	93.6	96.1	95.1	96.1
Clerical/professional	(1.0)	—	(0.9)	1.7	1.2	1.7
Others	5.2	6.8	5.5	2.2	—	2.2
Occupation of EW's husband						
Unskilled worker	11.7	22.3	14.0	21.5	48.1	22.9
Skilled worker	13.1	(3.4)	11.0	36.8	(11.1)	35.5
Small landowner/shopkeeper	67.4	69.1	67.7	12.1	(18.5)	12.4
Clerical/professional	5.4	(1.4)	4.6	26.8	—	25.7
Supported by family	2.4	(3.8)	2.7	2.8	(18.5)	3.5
Family structure						
Nuclear	45.3	49.3	46.2	69.3	58.0	68.7
Extended	54.7	50.7	53.8	30.7	42.0	31.3
Age of EW						
<20	8.4	7.0	8.1	7.0	(9.9)	7.2
20–24	20.4	16.1	19.5	19.7	(14.8)	19.6
25–29	17.0	17.3	17.1	18.2	(14.8)	18.0
30–34	20.3	21.8	20.6	22.0	(23.4)	22.1
35–39	22.6	23.2	22.8	20.6	(23.4)	20.7
40–44	11.2	14.5	11.9	12.2	(13.6)	12.3
Mean age of EW	30.1	31.1	30.3	30.3	30.8	30.3

* Percentages in parentheses refer to fewer than 25 EW.

In regard to the occupation of the husbands, both skilled and unskilled workers were more prevalent in the semi-urban than in the rural area, with unskilled workers more common among the low status men and skilled workers more common among middle status men of both residential areas. In contrast, the majority of the husbands (68%) were small landowners in rural areas compared with only 12% in the semi-urban area.

Chapter Two

FAMILY FORMATION
AND SOCIAL CHARACTERISTICS

INTRODUCTION

A. R. Omran, C. C. Standley and M. R. Bone

Patterns of family formation differ from culture to culture and from place to place. The aim of this chapter is to identify those social variables that are strongly associated with patterns of family formation, so that they can be taken into account when health patterns are examined in subsequent chapters.

Six characteristics of family formation are discussed here in the context of the cultural (or residential) situation and social status.

(*a*) *Family structure*. This refers to the membership of the family. A nuclear family consists of a father and mother and their children who are unmarried at the time of the survey. If in-laws, married children and/or other blood relatives live in the same family unit, then the family is described as an extended one.

Though no significant variations in family structure were found among the study groups, this does not imply that the structure of a family fails to influence family formation. Such an influence may have been present but may have been masked by the fact that the main criterion for classifying a family was the physical situation. Thus, an interfering mother-in-law who lived round the corner would have been excluded from consideration because the family was defined as physically nuclear, though socially extended. The survey was not, however, designed for an in-depth sociological inquiry into family network influences, and hence, this variable is rarely used in the analysis.

(*b*) *Age at marriage*. In this study age at marriage must always refer to the age of consummation of marriage because of the prevalence of " arranged " marriages in certain cultures, including those arranged for children not yet of marital age. There is a pronounced negative association between the age at marriage and fertility; this makes it important to consider intergroup variations and variations over time. Within each group, the age at marriage is examined in terms of education, occupation, and social status.

(*c*) *Gravidity.* This denotes the number of pregnancies per woman up to the time of the survey. In a comparative study such as this, age-specific figures must be used. The number of pregnancies up to the age of 40 to 44 years comes close to being a measure of the completed fertility of a woman and is frequently used as such in this report.

Though the gravidity figures are based upon a detailed pregnancy history obtained from each woman, the possibility of underreporting cannot be excluded, since the history of an older woman covers some 30 years. Also, some pregnancies ending in abortion, stillbirth, or even the death of a young child, may have been suppressed for psychological reasons.

(*d*) *Parity.* This is defined as the number of live births per woman until the time of the survey. In the present study, age-specific parity is used. Like gravidity, parity at the age of 40 to 44 years is often taken as an approximation to completed parity, even though children might occasionally be born to older women. While parity is definitely more reliable than gravidity, the possibility of underreporting cannot be excluded.

(*e*) *Family size.* This indicates the number of living children a woman had at the time of the survey.

(*f*) *Ideal family size.* This indicates a woman's estimate of the optimal family size for a family with economic and social traits similar to her own. Though this is a theoretical index and is therefore vulnerable to inaccuracies related to the education and other social situations of the eligible woman, it is nevertheless valuable as a reflection of cultural and social variations in the different groups.

A. GANDHIGRAM

R. S. Kurup and S. Gunasekaran

Family Structure

About one-third of the women in the study were living in extended families. The highest proportion of nuclear families was found among the Scheduled Castes (71%) and the lowest among the Muslims (66%). Nuclear families were also slightly more common among low status than among middle status women, the proportions for both cultures being about 73% and 65%, respectively. It is possible that the families of low social status tend to disintegrate as a result of the economic pressures involved in maintaining a large family.

Age at Marriage

Age at marriage is both a social characteristic and a family formation variable. In earlier times, and even during the early years of this century, marriage took place before the bride had attained puberty. There was, however, another ceremony *(shantimuhoortham)* at which the marriage would be consummated and the couple would begin to live as husband and wife. In this report, age at marriage refers to the age at consummation. In most cases the *shantimuhoortham* ceremony had taken place on the day of marriage, but in a negligible proportion of cases, it had occurred 3 months after marriage. However, the age at marriage may, in some cases, be less than the age prescribed by law for females to marry, namely 16 years.

Among the study population, there were evident cultural differences in the average age at which women married. At one extreme, Vellala women married at a mean age of 17.3 years, while at the other extreme Scheduled Caste women married at 15.1 years (Fig. 2.A.1). The proportion of women marrying under the age of 20 ranged from 96% among the Muslims and Scheduled Castes to 91% among the Other Hindus and 82% among the Vellalas (Table 2.A.1).

Although few women in the study had been educated above the primary level, there was a positive relationship between age at marriage and education. Those with secondary education had a significantly higher age at marriage than those with only primary education, the means being 20.3 and 16.6 years respectively. On the average, women with no schooling married at a lower age than those with a primary education. For all cultural groups combined, 92% of the women who were illiterate or had no schooling married under the age of 20 years, as compared with 89% for those with a primary education and 39% for those with a secondary education.

Within each cultural group, no consistent differences were found in the mean age at marriage by women's occupation (Table 2.A.1).

Gravidity

The pattern of pregnancy experience among the different cultural groups is given in Table 2.A.2 according to social status. The data should be viewed with caution, since there may have been selective underreporting of pregnancies. The mean number of pregnancies per woman was generally highest for Muslims and lowest for Vellalas, with intermediate values for Scheduled Castes and Other Hindus (Fig. 2.A.2, a, b). By the age of 40–44 years, Muslim women had had, on the average, 6.58 pregnancies, compared with only 4.13 pregnancies for Vellala women. Women in the Scheduled Castes and Other Hindu cultural groups experienced 5.74 and 5.40 pregnancies, respectively (Fig. 2.A.1). Further inspection of the age-specific mean pregnancies indicated that among women under 30 years of age, it was the women in the Scheduled Caste group who had the highest mean number of pregnancies; however, in older age groups, the Muslims had the highest numbers.

TABLE 2.A.1. PERCENTAGE DISTRIBUTION OF ELIGIBLE WOMEN
BY AGE AT MARRIAGE AND SOCIAL CHARACTERISTICS *

Characteristic	Percentage of eligible women who married at age :						Number (all ages)
	10–14	15–19	20–24	25–29	30–34	35–44	
Culture and social status							
Muslim							
Middle	29.6	66.4	3.9	0.1	0.0	0.1	1415
Low	35.1	61.0	3.5	0.2	0.2	0.0	590
Total	31.2	64.8	3.8	0.1	0.1	0.1	2005
Scheduled Castes							
Middle	37.2	59.9	2.6	0.4	0.0	0.0	306
Low	41.2	55.8	2.9	0.2	0.0	0.0	715
Total	40.0	57.0	2.8	0.2	0.0	0.0	1021
Other Hindus							
Middle	24.2	65.8	9.2	0.5	0.3	0.1	1351
Low	29.1	64.5	6.1	0.3	0.0	0.0	647
Total	25.8	65.4	8.1	0.4	0.2	0.1	1998
Vellala							
Middle	0.8	71.8	18.7	0.7	0.0	0.0	974
Low	10.9	72.3	16.2	0.6	0.0	0.0	543
Total	9.6	72.0	17.8	0.6	0.0	0.0	1517
Education of EW							
Muslim							
Illiterate + no schooling	31.4	64.5	3.9	0.2	0.0	0.1	1654
Primary	24.3	71.3	4.1	0.3	0.0	0.0	341
Secondary	(0.0)	(50.0)	(33.3)	(0.0)	(16.7)	(0.0)	6
College + college graduate	—	—	—	—	—	—	0
Scheduled Castes							
Illiterate + no schooling	39.5	56.9	3.5	0.1	0.0	0.0	980
Primary	22.9	74.3	0.0	2.9	0.0	0.0	35
Secondary	(0.0)	(0.0)	(100.0)	(0.0)	(0.0)	(0.0)	1
College + college graduate	—	—	—	—	—	—	0
Other Hindus							
Illiterate + no schooling	28.4	64.9	6.3	0.3	0.0	0.1	1590
Primary	14.3	71.9	12.6	0.6	0.6	0.0	349
Secondary	2.2	37.0	52.2	6.5	2.2	0.0	46
College + college graduate	(0.0)	(33.3)	(66.7)	(0.0)	(0.0)	(0.0)	3
Vellala							
Illiterate + no schooling	9.3	71.5	18.6	0.5	0.0	0.1	1350
Primary	8.5	71.5	18.8	1.2	0.0	0.0	165
Secondary	(0.0)	(0.0)	(100.0)	(0.0)	(0.0)	(0.0)	1
College + college graduate	(0.0)	(100.0)	(0.0)	(0.0)	(0.0)	(0.0)	1
Occupation of EW							
Muslim							
Housewife	28.8	66.6	4.3	0.2	0.1	0.1	1665
Clerical/professional	36.8	61.1	1.7	0.3	0.0	0.0	288
Agricult./janit./industrial	33.3	56.3	10.4	0.0	0.0	0.0	48
Others	—	—	—	—	—	—	0
Scheduled Castes							
Housewife	37.9	55.5	6.6	0.0	0.0	0.0	273
Clerical/professional	(50.0)	(50.0)	(0.0)	(0.0)	(0.0)	(0.0)	4
Agricult./janit./industrial	39.2	58.2	2.3	0.3	0.0	0.0	744
Others	—	—	—	—	—	—	0
Other Hindus							
Housewife	21.1	69.6	8.9	0.2	0.2	0.1	1239
Clerical/professional	(16.7)	(75.0)	(8.3)	(0.0)	(0.0)	(0.0)	24
Agricult./janit./industrial	32.9	58.3	8.0	0.7	0.1	0.0	724
Others	(0.0)	(0.0)	(0.0)	(100.0)	(0.0)	(0.0)	1
Vellala							
Housewife	8.9	72.3	18.2	0.5	0.0	0.1	813
Clerical/professional	(0.0)	(66.7)	(33.3)	(0.0)	(0.0)	(0.0)	3
Agricult./janit./industrial	9.7	70.5	19.1	0.7	0.0	0.0	701
Others	—	—	—	—	—	—	0

* Percentages in parentheses refer to fewer than 25 EW.

98

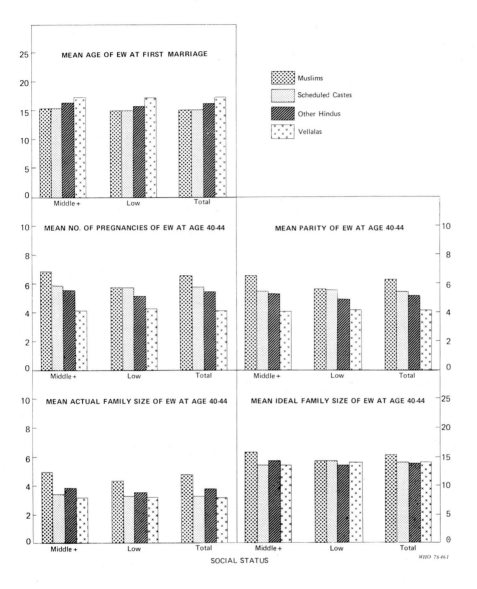

FIG. 2.A.1. FAMILY FORMATION BY SOCIAL CHARACTERISTICS

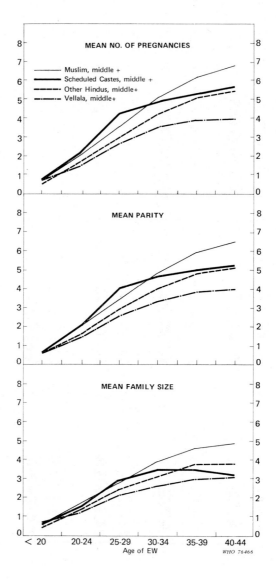

FIG. 2.A.2b. FERTILITY VARIABLES SPECIFIC FOR AGE BY CULTURE FOR WOMEN OF LOW SOCIAL STATUS

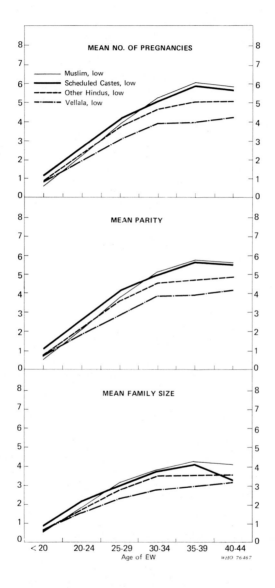

TABLE 2.A.2. MEAN GRAVIDITY BY AGE OF ELIGIBLE WOMEN,
CULTURE, AND SOCIAL STATUS

Culture and social status	Mean gravidity at age :						Number (all ages)
	<20	20–24	25–29	30–34	35–39	40–44	
Muslim							
Middle	0.69	2.13	3.67	5.08	6.21	6.85	1415
Low	0.62	2.15	3.85	5.26	6.05	5.74	590
Total	0.67	2.13	3.73	5.14	6.16	6.58	2005
Scheduled Castes							
Middle	0.75	2.14	4.22	4.94	5.35	(5.75) [a]	306
Low	1.06	2.62	4.16	5.11	5.86	5.73	715
Total	0.95	2.48	4.18	5.07	5.74	5.74	1021
Other Hindus							
Middle	0.63	1.78	3.07	4.28	5.15	5.54	1351
Low	0.81	2.20	3.73	4.68	5.05	5.08	647
Total	0.68	1.90	3.32	4.43	5.12	5.40	1998
Vellala							
Middle	0.77	1.57	2.72	3.52	3.97	4.06	974
Low	0.75	1.09	3.04	3.98	3.99	4.24	543
Total	0.77	1.67	2.85	3.69	3.98	4.13	1517

[a] Refers to fewer than 25 EW.

The cultural differences persisted after controlling for social status, which had a small and rather inconsistent influence. Muslim women aged 40–44 who were of middle social status had a higher mean gravidity than those of low status. A similar but smaller difference was also observed among the Other Hindus ; little difference by social status was found among Vellalas or Scheduled Castes.

Parity

Taking as index the age-specific number of live births, Vellala women had the lowest parity on the average, just as they had the lowest gravidity. Muslim women, on the other hand, had the highest parity, especially among those aged 30 and over. For women under the age of 30, it was the Scheduled Castes that had the highest parity (Table 2.A.3 and Fig. 2.A.2 a, b).

Within each cultural group, social status was associated with small differences in parity in one direction or the other. Among the Scheduled Castes and the Vellalas, the mean parity of women of low social status in the age groups above 30 was higher than that of women in the middle status group. For Muslims and other Hindus, the opposite tendency was noted, but the differences by social status were not significant (Fig. 2.A.1 and 2.A.2 a, b).

Mean parity increased progressively with increasing age, although the rate of increase varied from one cultural group to another. Vellalas had the highest mean parity for marriages of less than 5 years, but by 15 years

TABLE 2.A.3. MEAN PARITY BY AGE OF ELIGIBLE WOMEN AND SOCIAL CHARACTERISTICS *

Characteristic	Mean parity at age :						Number (all ages)
	<20	20–24	25–29	30–34	35–39	40–44	
Culture and social status							
Muslim							
Middle	0.65	2.05	3.50	4.89	6.00	6.55	1415
Low	0.59	2.06	3.75	5.06	5.75	5.60	590
Total	0.63	2.05	3.58	4.95	5.93	6.32	2005
Scheduled Castes							
Middle	0.67	2.03	4.03	4.74	5.03	(5.38)	306
Low	1.05	2.51	4.03	4.95	5.63	5.50	715
Total	0.92	2.36	4.03	4.90	5.49	5.44	1021
Other Hindus							
Middle	0.59	1.69	2.98	4.07	4.90	5.27	1351
Low	0.71	2.17	3.60	4.55	4.77	4.86	647
Total	0.62	1.83	3.21	4.24	4.86	5.15	1998
Vellala							
Middle	0.77	1.55	2.67	3.47	3.92	4.00	974
Low	0.75	1.88	2.97	3.89	3.92	4.20	543
Total	0.77	1.65	2.79	3.62	3.92	4.07	1517
Education of EW							
Muslim							
Illiterate + no schooling	0.65	2.10	3.57	4.97	5.93	6.30	1658
Primary	0.61	1.87	3.62	4.92	5.96	(6.48)	341
Secondary	(0.00)	1.67	—	(2.00)	—	—	6
College + college graduate	—	—	—	—	—	—	0
Scheduled Castes							
Illiterate + no schooling	0.93	2.43	4.07	4.92	5.50	5.39	985
Primary	(0.86)	(1.53)	(3.00)	(3.67)	(5.00)	(8.00)	35
Secondary	—	—	(0.00)	—	—	—	1
College + college graduate	—	—	—	—	—	—	0
Other Hindus							
Illiterate + no schooling	0.69	1.94	3.31	4.34	4.82	5.07	1599
Primary	0.47	1.62	2.95	3.89	5.11	5.53	350
Secondary	(0.20)	(1.10)	(1.92)	(2.17)	(3.67)	—	46
College + college graduate	—	(0.33)	—	—	—	—	3
Vellala							
Illiterate + no schooling	0.79	1.70	2.78	3.63	3.90	4.04	1350
Primary	(0.65)	1.36	2.85	3.54	(4.19)	(4.50)	165
Secondary	—	(0.00)	—	—	—	—	1
College + college graduate	—	(0.00)	—	—	—	—	1
Education of EW's husband							
Muslim							
Illiterate + no schooling	0.70	2.23	3.74	4.91	6.12	6.66	779
Primary	0.57	1.95	3.49	4.98	5.78	6.24	1096
Secondary	(0.90)	1.82	(3.57)	(4.71)	(5.88)	(4.50)	90
College + college graduate	(0.50)	(2.50)	(3.00)	(3.80)	—	(5.00)	20

* Numbers in parentheses refer to fewer than 25 EW.

TABLE 2.A.3.* *(continued)*

Characteristic	Mean parity at age :						Number (all ages)
	<20	20–24	25–29	30–34	35–39	40–44	
Education of EW's husband (cont.)							
Scheduled Castes							
Illiterate + no schooling	0.95	2.41	4.00	4.94	5.59	5.60	837
Primary	0.81	2.25	4.21	4.67	(5.06)	(5.29)	170
Secondary	(0.50)	(1.67)	(3.67)	—	(3.50)	(0.00)	14
College + college graduate	—	—	—	—	—	—	0
Other Hindus							
Illiterate + no schooling	0.73	1.92	3.28	4.42	5.02	4.99	994
Primary	0.60	1.84	3.21	4.16	4.68	5.57	827
Secondary	(0.39)	1.53	2.79	3.27	(4.82)	(4.11)	140
College + college graduate	(0.25)	(1.11)	(2.00)	(5.00)	(4.50)	(7.00)	26
Vellala							
Illiterate + no schooling							
Primary	0.80	1.75	2.94	3.69	4.01	4.11	879
Secondary	0.70	1.56	2.50	3.54	3.83	4.08	581
College + college graduate	(1.00)	(1.00)	(3.00)	(3.22)	(3.00)	(4.67)	41
	—	(1.57)	(4.00)	(3.33)	(3.00)	(2.00)	15
Occupation of EW							
Muslim							
Housewife	0.60	2.05	3.55	4.92	5.93	6.61	1668
Clerical/professional	(1.00)	2.15	3.83	5.17	5.79	(4.65)	289
Agricultural/industrial	(0.71)	(1.56)	(2.33)	(4.20)	(6.50)	(4.83)	48
Janitorial/others	—	—	—	—	—	—	0
Scheduled Castes							
Housewife	1.14	2.29	3.76	5.08	4.81	(4.45)	273
Clerical/professional	—	—	(5.50)	(3.00)	(7.00)	—	4
Agricultural/industrial	0.79	2.40	4.08	4.85	5.70	5.72	739
Janitorial/others	—	—	(5.00)	(6.00)	(4.00)	—	5
Other Hindus							
Housewife	0.59	1.78	3.34	4.28	4.72	5.26	1245
Clerical/professional	(0.25)	(1.00)	(3.17)	(6.00)	(4.80)	(4.67)	24
Agricultural/industrial	0.75	1.94	3.00	4.16	5.05	5.00	728
Janitorial/others	—	—	(1.00)	—	—	—	1
Vellala							
Housewife	0.81	1.59	2.79	3.60	4.01	4.04	813
Clerical/professional	—	—	—	(3.00)	(6.50)	—	3
Agricultural/industrial	0.68	1.73	2.79	3.64	3.79	4.11	701
Janitorial/others	—	—	—	—	—	—	0

* Numbers in parentheses refer to fewer than 25 EW.

of marriage they had the lowest mean parity. Muslims, on the other hand, had a higher parity than other groups only in marriages of 15 or more years' duration.

As already indicated, very few women in any cultural group advanced past a primary level of education, and among the Scheduled Castes, only 35 women achieved even this level. The relationship between mean age-specific parity and educational level was not consistent. Excluding the Scheduled Castes, young women (less than 35 years of age) in the 3 other cultural groups who had had a primary education experienced lower mean parities than those who were illiterate or with no schooling. For older women, the reverse was true (Table 2.A.3).

In general, there was an inverse relationship between education of the husband and parity (Table 2.A.3). With few exceptions, the more education a man had, the fewer births his wife was likely to experience.

In regard to occupation of the eligible woman, no distinct pattern was discernible (Table 2.A.3).

Family Size

This index reflects both parity and child mortality. Table 2.A.4 shows that Muslims had the largest families (4.78 children for mothers aged 40–44). Whereas the second highest parities were found among women of the Scheduled Castes, the second largest mean family sizes were found among Other Hindus, the Scheduled Castes being in third place and the smallest family size (3.19 children at age 40–44) being registered for the Vellalas.

As in the case of parity, middle status Muslim women had larger families at most age groups than Muslim women of low social status. The same was true for women aged 40–44 among the Scheduled Castes and Other Hindus. For younger women there was a tendency, though not a consistent one, for family size to bear an inverse relationship to social status (Fig. 2.A.1 and 2.A.2 a, b).

It was evident that women who had had a secondary or higher education had smaller families than those who had not (Table 2.A.4). It will be recalled, however, that very few of the women had attended secondary schools; consequently, it becomes of more interest to know whether women with primary education had smaller families than those who had received no formal schooling. The evidence from the different cultural groups was conflicting and there seemed to be no reason to conclude that the kind of education predominantly available (namely primary) had a consistent effect on family size.

Table 2.A.5 shows mean family size by age at marriage. It is apparent that, for each cultural group, when the age at interview was held constant, the earlier a woman had married, the more children she was likely to have. Two exceptions to this were Other Hindus and Vellalas in the 40–44 year age group, where women who had married between the ages of 10 and 14 years had a smaller mean family size than those who had married at

105

Characteristic	Family size at age :						Number (all ages)
	<20	20–24	25–29	30–34	35–39	40–44	
Culture and social status							
Muslim							
Middle	0.60	1.74	2.83	3.98	4.67	4.92	1415
Low	0.51	1.76	3.12	3.81	4.25	4.33	590
Total	0.57	1.75	2.92	3.93	4.55	4.78	2005
Scheduled Castes							
Middle	0.58	1.51	2.95	3.52	3.55	(3.38)	306
Low	0.83	2.02	2.95	3.63	4.08	3.27	715
Total	0.75	1.86	2.95	3.60	3.96	3.32	1021
Other Hindus							
Middle	0.47	1.38	2.42	3.16	3.83	3.84	1351
Low	0.56	1.64	2.77	3.47	3.54	3.54	647
Total	0.50	1.46	2.55	3.27	3.74	3.76	1998
Vellala							
Middle	0.65	1.27	2.17	2.77	3.07	3.19	974
Low	0.66	1.53	2.32	2.79	2.98	3.18	543
Total	0.65	1.35	2.23	2.78	3.03	3.19	1517
Education of EW							
Muslim							
Illiterate + no schooling	0.59	1.76	2.90	3.89	4.51	4.84	1658
Primary	0.55	1.68	3.01	4.20	4.93	(4.29)	341
Secondary	(0.00)	(1.67)	—	(2.00)	—	(1.50)	6
College + college graduate	—	—	—	—	—	—	0
Scheduled Castes							
Illiterate + no schooling	0.76	1.90	2.97	3.61	3.94	3.23	985
Primary	(0.57)	(1.35)	(2.80)	(3.33)	(5.00)	(4.00)	35
Secondary	—	—	(0.00)	—	—	—	1
College + college graduate	—	—	—	—	—	—	0
Other Hindus							
Illiterate + no schooling	0.54	1.52	2.58	3.26	3.65	3.63	1599
Primary	0.40	1.40	2.52	3.45	4.37	4.38	350
Secondary	(0.20)	(0.90)	(1.83)	(2.00)	(3.33)	—	46
College + college graduate	—	(0.33)	—	—	—	—	3
Vellala							
Illiterate + no schooling	0.65	1.38	2.19	2.75	2.97	3.10	1350
Primary	(0.65)	1.23	2.55	3.53	(3.94)	(4.30)	165
Secondary	—	(0.00)	—	—	—	—	1
College + college graduate	—	(1.00)	—	—	—	—	1
Occupation of EW							
Muslim							
Housewife	0.56	1.77	2.90	3.96	4.57	5.06	1668
Clerical/professional	(0.76)	1.70	3.13	3.90	4.53	(3.35)	289
Agricultural/industrial	(0.57)	(1.22)	(1.50)	(3.00)	(4.10)	(2.50)	48
Janitorial/others	—	—	—	—	—	—	0
Scheduled Castes							
Housewife	0.98	1.89	2.84	3.92	3.38	(2.18)	273
Clerical/professional	—	—	(5.00)	(3.00)	(7.00)	—	4
Agricultural/industrial	0.60	1.85	2.95	3.52	4.11	3.64	739
Janitorial/others	—	—	(4.00)	(4.00)	(4.00)	—	5
Other Hindus							
Housewife	0.49	1.42	2.65	3.43	3.67	3.80	1245
Clerical/professional	(0.25)	(0.25)	(2.50)	(4.00)	(2.80)	(4.00)	24
Agricultural/industrial	0.55	1.55	2.39	3.01	3.85	3.67	728
Janitorial/others	—	—	(1.00)	—	—	—	1
Vellala							
Housewife	0.76	1.36	2.29	2.75	3.18	3.23	813
Clerical/professional	—	—	—	(3.00)	(4.50)	—	3
Agricultural/industrial	0.42	1.34	2.16	2.81	2.87	3.14	701
Janitorial/others	—	—	—	—	—	—	0

* Numbers in parentheses refer to fewer than 25 EW.

TABLE 2.A.5. MEAN FAMILY SIZE BY AGE OF ELIGIBLE WOMEN, CULTURE AND AGE AT MARRIAGE *

Age at marriage	Mean family size at age of EW						Number (all ages)
	<20	20–24	25–29	30–34	35–39	40–44	
Muslim							
<15	0.9	2.3	3.4	4.0	4.9	5.1	553
15–19	0.5	1.6	2.8	4.0	4.4	4.7	1123
20–24	—	0.7	1.6	(2.8)	(3.8)	(3.2)	62
25–44	—	—	(0.0)	(2.3)	—	(0.0)	3
Scheduled Castes							
<15	1.2	2.4	3.4	3.8	4.1	(4.0)	372
15–19	0.5	1.6	2.8	3.5	4.0	2.9	512
20–24	—	(0.4)	(1.4)	(2.4)	(2.6)	(3.7)	26
25–44	—	—	(1.0)	—	(1.0)	—	2
Other Hindus							
<15	0.9	1.8	2.8	3.8	3.9	3.6	458
15–19	0.4	1.5	2.6	3.2	3.8	3.9	1143
20–24	—	0.6	1.6	2.9	2.8	(3.2)	138
25–44	—	—	(0.5)	(1.0)	(2.8)	(2.0)	11
Vellala							
<15	(1.4)	2.4	2.4	3.2	3.7	(3.0)	136
15–19	0.6	1.4	2.3	2.8	3.0	3.3	1003
20–24	—	0.8	1.8	2.2	2.8	2.9	244
25–44	—	—	(0.5)	(2.0)	(3.0)	(5.0)	10

* Numbers in parentheses refer to fewer than 25 EW. Dashes represent 5 or fewer EW.

15–19 years. It is nevertheless evident that even after controlling for age at marriage cultural differences persist; Muslim women who had married before the age of 20 and who were aged 30 or over at the time of the interview had larger families on the average than the corresponding women in the other cultural groups.

Ideal Family Size

Each woman was asked what she considered to be the ideal number of children for a family in similar circumstances to her own. The majority of women stated that an ideal number of children would be between 5.5 and 6.6 (Table 2.A.6). In each social status group, Muslim women preferred a larger family size than women in the other 3 groups. Within each group, only small differences by social status were observed (Fig. 2.A.1).

Except among the Muslims, where there was some fluctuation, the mean ideal family size increased steadily with the parity of the woman interviewed, but was not consistently related to the parity of her mother. Again, with the exception of the Muslims, the ideal family size generally increased with the age of the woman.

107

TABLE 2.A.6. MEAN IDEAL FAMILY SIZE BY POPULATION CHARACTERISTICS *

Characteristic	Muslim			Scheduled Castes		
	Middle	Low	Total	Middle	Low	Total
Residence/social status	6.63	6.45	6.58	5.91	5.66	5.74
Parity						
0	6.69	6.23	6.55	6.07	5.34	5.61
1	5.90	6.34	6.02	5.46	5.22	5.32
2	5.99	5.75	5.93	5.18	5.45	5.36
3	5.91	6.15	5.98	5.61	5.43	5.48
4	7.12	6.36	6.90	5.42	5.53	5.50
5	6.79	6.97	6.84	7.53	5.77	6.16
6 and over	7.40	6.93	7.25	6.36	6.26	6.29
Parity of EW's mother						
1	—	—	—	—	—	—
2	7.13	6.04	6.80	(5.44)	5.13	5.21
3	6.20	6.30	6.23	(6.28)	5.65	5.79
4	6.55	6.84	6.64	5.21	5.38	5.33
5	6.91	6.33	6.75	5.88	5.65	5.71
6	6.40	6.26	6.36	6.25	5.82	5.91
7	6.95	6.90	6.93	6.10	5.62	5.79
8	6.41	6.63	6.47	5.77	5.66	5.70
9	6.26	6.14	6.23	6.41	5.87	6.08
10 and over	6.78	6.35	6.65	5.66	6.03	5.90
Education of husband						
Illiterate + no schooling	6.71	6.54	6.63	6.20	5.69	5.79
Primary	6.62	6.34	6.57	5.52	5.33	5.46
Secondary	6.53	(6.44)	6.52	(5.85)	—	(5.71)
College + college graduate	(6.40)	—	(6.40)	—	—	—
Education of EW						
Illiterate + no schooling	6.67	6.45	6.60	5.97	5.68	5.76
Primary	6.51	6.50	6.50	5.31	(4.44)	5.09
Secondary	(5.00)	(5.00)	5.00	(5.00)	—	(5.00)
College + college graduate	—	—	—	—	—	—
Occupation of EW						
Housewife	6.58	6.42	6.54	5.79	5.62	5.69
Clerical/professional	7.09	6.75	6.95	—	(5.75)	(5.75)
Agricultural/industrial	(6.00)	5.65	5.81	5.97	5.67	5.75
Janitorial/others	—	—	—	(6.50)	(6.33)	(6.40)
Age of EW						
<20	6.32	6.84	6.46	5.87	5.88	5.88
20–24	6.58	6.40	6.53	6.07	5.41	5.61
25–29	6.33	6.54	6.40	5.88	5.49	5.62
30–34	6.88	6.28	6.69	5.80	5.79	5.79
35–39	7.09	6.34	6.87	5.68	5.94	5.88
40–44	6.69	6.40	6.62	(6.13)	5.69	5.90

* Numbers in parentheses refer to fewer than 25 EW.

TABLE 2.A.6.* *(continued)*

Characteristic	Other Hindus			Vellala		
	Middle	Low	Total	Middle	Low	Total
Residence/social status	5.63	5.73	5.66	5.44	5.84	5.58
Parity						
0	5.01	5.48	5.12	5.34	5.40	5.36
1	5.45	5.08	5.35	5.17	5.62	5.33
2	5.14	5.72	5.30	5.30	5.65	5.41
3	5.64	5.61	5.63	5.32	6.13	5.59
4	5.57	5.92	5.70	5.53	5.71	5.61
5	6.16	5.67	5.99	5.59	6.03	5.78
6 and over	6.44	6.18	6.35	6.38	6.27	6.34
Parity of EW's mother						
1	—	—	—	—	—	—
2	5.31	6.03	5.59	6.21	5.42	5.91
3	5.80	5.14	5.60	5.57	5.37	5.51
4	5.51	5.40	5.47	5.46	5.86	5.63
5	5.68	6.01	5.80	5.32	5.65	5.45
6	5.54	5.49	5.53	5.36	5.99	5.60
7	5.66	5.88	5.73	5.28	5.71	5.42
8	5.79	6.27	5.94	5.15	6.24	5.50
9	5.54	5.52	5.54	5.30	(5.50)	5.37
10 and over	5.64	5.80	5.68	5.65	(9.64)	6.62
Education of husband						
Illiterate + no schooling	5.83	5.79	5.81	5.46	5.86	5.67
Primary	5.57	5.55	5.56	5.40	5.76	5.45
Secondary	5.39	(4.50)	5.38	5.64	(4.80)	5.54
College + college graduate	5.12	(4.00)	5.08	(5.60)	—	(5.60)
Education of EW						
Illiterate + no schooling	5.70	5.79	5.74	5.45	5.86	5.61
Primary	5.50	5.04	5.44	5.35	(5.37)	5.35
Secondary	4.96	(4.00)	4.93	—	(4.00)	(4.00)
College + college graduate	(4.00)	—	(4.00)	(5.00)	—	(5.00)
Occupation of EW						
Housewife	5.52	5.84	5.60	5.40	5.88	5.53
Clerical/professional	(5.61)	(5.17)	(5.50)	(5.00)	—	(5.00)
Agricultural/industrial	5.89	5.64	5.77	5.49	5.81	5.63
Janitorial/others	(6.00)	—	(6.00)	—	—	—
Age of EW						
<20	5.11	5.56	5.23	5.58	6.09	5.74
20–24	5.57	5.73	5.62	5.35	5.98	5.54
25–29	5.52	5.68	5.58	5.24	5.89	5.50
30–34	5.73	5.56	5.67	5.49	5.77	5.59
35–39	5.73	5.80	5.75	5.63	5.75	5.68
40–44	6.18	6.33	6.23	5.55	5.59	5.57

* Numbers in parentheses refer to fewer than 25 EW.

Actual family size	Percentage of EW choosing ideal family size of:								Number of women
	0–3	4	5	6	7	8	9	10 and over	
Muslim									
0	0.7	38.8	20.8	24.6	6.2	4.8	1.4	2.8	289
1	3.7	38.4	21.4	29.5	2.2	3.0	0.4	1.5	271
2	0.0	30.4	29.6	30.4	4.8	3.0	0.3	1.5	335
3	0.0	6.6	43.6	37.4	6.6	4.0	0.4	1.5	273
4	0.4	10.8	11.9	55.8	8.6	8.2	1.1	3.3	269
5	0.0	11.4	11.4	33.8	29.9	9.5	0.5	3.5	201
6 and over	0.0	5.1	10.6	31.4	10.2	23.1	8.2	11.4	255
Total	0.7	21.2	22.1	34.5	8.8	7.6	1.7	3.5	1893
Scheduled Castes									
0	0.0	35.4	31.3	25.9	5.4	1.4	0.0	0.7	147
1	0.6	36.9	25.0	33.1	1.9	0.6	0.6	1.2	160
2	0.0	34.6	28.8	30.9	3.7	0.5	0.5	1.0	191
3	0.5	9.4	40.3	35.6	11.0	2.6	0.5	0.0	191
4	0.0	7.4	17.4	60.4	10.7	3.4	0.7	0.0	149
5	0.0	4.4	17.8	38.9	33.3	1.1	1.1	3.3	90
6 and over	0.0	10.1	12.8	39.2	8.9	16.5	3.8	8.9	79
Total	0.2	21.6	26.8	37.1	9.1	2.8	0.8	1.5	1007
Other Hindus									
0	1.3	38.6	24.5	30.1	3.9	1.0	0.3	0.3	306
1	2.0	41.5	26.3	24.3	4.2	1.7	0.0	0.0	354
2	0.0	37.3	27.2	26.9	7.0	0.8	0.0	0.8	383
3	0.6	14.0	41.4	34.5	6.8	1.5	0.0	1.2	336
4	0.4	14.1	21.8	54.0	6.9	2.4	0.0	0.4	248
5	0.0	14.6	17.5	33.3	29.8	3.5	0.6	0.6	171
6 and over	0.0	8.9	23.4	36.1	8.9	15.8	1.9	5.1	158
Total	0.7	27.0	27.2	33.0	8.1	2.8	0.3	0.9	1956
Vellala									
0	0.0	37.1	27.5	31.7	2.4	1.2	0.0	0.0	167
1	1.0	39.5	24.8	29.6	3.9	0.3	0.3	0.6	311
2	0.0	36.8	25.9	32.3	3.7	0.7	0.0	0.5	402
3	0.6	11.3	47.3	32.9	5.5	1.8	0.0	0.6	328
4	0.0	13.7	12.5	60.1	8.9	4.2	0.0	0.6	168
5	1.4	10.8	21.6	29.7	33.8	2.7	0.0	0.0	74
6 and over	2.6	7.9	21.1	15.8	5.3	36.8	2.6	7.9	38
Total	0.5	27.2	28.7	34.4	6.1	2.4	0.1	0.7	1488

The relationship between education of the eligible woman and ideal family size was not clear in any cultural group. Even though the largest ideal family size in each cultural and social status group was chosen by those women who were illiterate or with no schooling, the differences in the mean ideal family sizes stated by women of any two educational levels were small. The relationship between education of the husband and ideal family size was, however, generally negative, the differences between educational categories again being small. In regard to occupation, among Muslim women agricultural or industrial workers chose the lowest ideal family size, followed by housewives and then clerical and professional workers. Among Scheduled Castes, Other Hindus and Vellalas, none of which had enough clerical or professional workers to make comparisons meaningful, housewives had lower ideal family sizes than did those in agricultural and industrial occupations.

There was a significant positive association (r = 0.39) between the eligible woman's opinion of ideal family size and her own actual family size (Table 2.A.7). This association was to be expected, however, because people try to rationalize their own fertility pattern when expressing their ideal family size. Despite this, the majority of women with 6 or more children chose 6 or fewer children as ideal.

B. TEHERAN

V. Nahapetian, B. D. Navidi-Kasmaii and A. R. Omran

Family Structure

The analysis showed that 84.5% of the Muslim families and 67.1% of the Armenian families were nuclear. Within each cultural group, there was no significant difference between the two social status groups. The distinction between the two family types in this population is made only in terms of living arrangements and does not signify any cultural difference. For this reason, the variable will not be used in any later analysis.

Age at Marriage

On the average, Muslim women married earlier (at 15.9 years of age) than Armenian women (17.8 years). It is striking to notice that 30% of the Muslims compared with only 5% of the Armenians married as early as 10–14 years of age. Within each cultural group, the lower status women married at a slightly earlier age than did the middle status women (Table 2.B.1 and Fig. 2.B.1).

In general, the more education the woman had received, the later she married : those with primary education or no schooling married, on the average, between the ages of 16.3 and 17.3, while those with secondary or higher education married around or after 21 years of age. Differences in age at marriage associated with different educational levels were found in both cultural groups. For Muslim women, 93.4% of those who had had no formal schooling and 90.0% of those with primary or some secondary education married before they were 20 years old ; only 50% of those with

Characteristic	Percentage of eligible women who married at age :						Number (all ages)
	10–14	15–19	20–24	25–29	30–34	35–44	
Culture and social status							
Muslim							
Middle	24.5	65.2	9.2	1.0	0.1	0.0	904
Low	33.0	60.3	5.7	0.6	0.3	0.1	1211
Total	29.4	62.4	7.2	0.8	0.2	0.0	2115
Armenian							
Middle	3.5	73.4	20.5	2.0	0.7	0.0	1071
Low	7.4	74.0	17.0	1.4	0.2	0.0	1023
Total	5.4	73.7	18.8	1.7	0.4	0.0	2094
Education of EW							
Muslim							
Illiterate + no schooling	33.5	59.9	5.7	0.6	0.0	0.1	1567
Primary	18.6	71.4	9.2	0.6	0.2	0.0	511
Secondary	2.9	47.1	41.2	8.8	0.0	0.0	34
College + college graduate	0.0	(100.0) [a]	0.0	0.0	0.0	0.0	3
Armenian							
Illiterate + no schooling	6.9	74.0	17.6	1.1	0.4	0.0	1498
Primary	1.8	75.6	19.7	2.5	0.5	0.0	569
Secondary	0.0	12.0	76.0	12.0	0.0	0.0	26
College + college graduate	0.0	0.0	0.0	(100.0) [a]	0.0	0.0	1

[a] Refers to fewer than 25 EW.

secondary education married before this age. For Armenian women, the percentages were 80.9, 77.4, and 12.0, respectively. Apparently, primary education, as opposed to no education, made only a small difference to the age at which women married. This is relevant because the great majority of women who had received some education did not pass beyond the primary stage. Relevant also is the observation that education affected family formation through the age at marriage only if it was continued at least to the secondary level.

Gravidity

As expected, mean gravidity increased with age for all groups (Table 2.B.2). At each age group, Muslims had a higher mean gravidity than did Armenians, and in each cultural group, middle status women had lower mean gravidity than did low status women (Fig. 2.B.2).

The gravidity for the age group 40–44 provides an approximate measure of the completed marital fertility for that cohort, and the difference in gravidity by social status was found to be the same for both cultural groups.

Culture and social status	Mean gravidity at age :						Number (all ages)
	<20	20–24	25–29	30–34	35–39	40–44	
Muslim							
Middle	0.83	2.00	3.44	5.12	5.98	6.97	904
Low	1.00	2.72	4.35	6.04	7.27	8.12	1211
Total	0.90	2.39	3.98	5.73	6.78	7.67	2115
Armenian							
Middle	0.72	1.51	2.78	3.83	4.48	5.39	1071
Low	0.63	1.94	3.35	4.97	5.98	6.72	1023
Total	0.69	1.64	3.01	4.46	5.49	6.17	2094

Thus, the average number of pregnancies for Muslim women in this age group was 7.67, compared with 6.17 for Armenian women, and in both cultural groups, the mean number of pregnancies of low status women aged 40–44 exceeded the mean number for the middle status women of this age (Fig. 2.B.1).

Parity

On the average, Muslim women in each age group had more live births than did Armenian women in the same social class (Table 2.B.3 and Fig. 2.B.2). At age 40–44 years, Muslim women had an average of one more live birth than did the Armenian women, their mean parities being 6.50 and 5.45 respectively. In both cultural groups, the middle status women had a lower mean parity than did the low status women (Fig. 2.B.1).

Among both Muslims and Armenians, women and their husbands who had received primary education experienced lower mean parities (specific for age) than their counterparts who were illiterate or had received no formal education (Table 2.B.3). Still lower mean parities were observed among those who had progressed beyond a primary education, but their numbers were too small to permit valid conclusions to be drawn. While the mean parity of the woman, when controlled for age, is found to decrease with an increase in both her own educational level and that of her husband, it is her own educational level that has the greater influence.

As might be expected, both the total mean parity and the age-specific mean parity increased with the duration of marriage in each cultural and social status group.

Family Size

Differences between mean parity and mean family size result from child loss, which is higher among Muslims and in the low social status group (Table 2.B.4). At age 40–44, Muslim women had an average

113

FIG. 2.B.1. FAMILY FORMATION BY SOCIAL CHARACTERISTICS

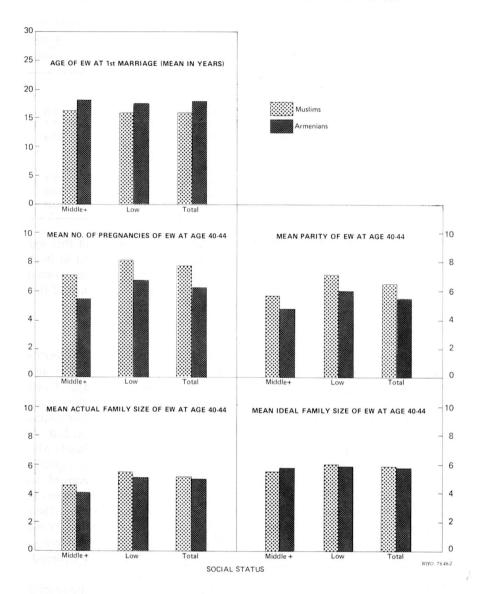

family size of 5.03, compared with 4.59 for an Armenian family (Fig. 2.B.1). However, the relationship of family size to social and demographic characteristics followed a similar pattern to the relationship of parity to these characteristics. For each age group, mean family size was larger among Muslims than among Armenians, and this relationship held even after controlling for social status (Fig. 2.B.2).

114

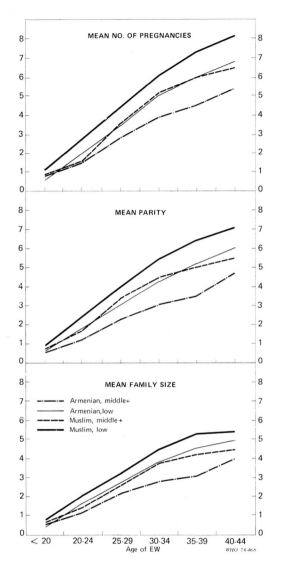

FIG. 2.B.2. FERTILITY VARIABLES SPECIFIC FOR AGE
BY CULTURE AND SOCIAL STATUS

MEAN NO. OF PREGNANCIES

MEAN PARITY

MEAN FAMILY SIZE

Armenian, middle+
Armenian, low
Muslim, middle+
Muslim, low

< 20   20-24   25-29   30-34   35-39   40-44
Age of EW   WHO 76468

    The earlier a woman had married, the more children she was likely to
have compared with other women of the same age (Table 2.B.5). Among
women who had married at the same ages, however, Armenians had smaller
families than did Muslims, the difference being greatest for older women.
    There were significant negative associations between family size and
education of the women in all age groups except 40–44, where the associ-

115

Characteristic	Mean parity at age :						Number (all ages)
	<20	20–24	25–29	30–34	35–39	40–44	
Culture and social status							
Muslim							
Middle	0.70	1.77	3.00	4.52	5.07	5.58	904
Low	0.89	2.48	3.97	5.43	6.48	7.10	1211
Total	0.78	2.15	3.57	5.13	5.95	6.50	2115
Armenian							
Middle	0.62	1.30	2.38	3.08	3.54	4.69	1071
Low	0.54	1.85	3.05	4.34	5.23	5.99	1023
Total	0.59	1.47	2.65	3.78	4.67	5.45	2094
Education of EW							
Muslim							
Illiterate + no schooling	0.86	2.39	3.89	5.36	6.25	6.79	1567
Primary	0.67	1.82	3.10	4.30	4.59	(4.91)	611
Secondary	—	(0.90)	(1.64)	(3.00)	(3.33)	—	34
College + college graduate	—	—	(2.00)	—	—	(1.50)	3
Armenian							
Illiterate + no schooling	0.59	1.73	2.82	3.95	4.79	5.54	1498
Primary	0.61	1.34	2.49	3.23	(3.27)	(4.22)	569
Secondary	—	(0.60)	(1.00)	(2.20)	(2.00)	(3.50)	26
College + college graduate	—	—	—	—	(4.00)	—	1
Education of husband							
Muslim							
Illiterate + no schooling	0.88	2.41	3.97	5.25	6.29	6.86	1214
Primary	0.61	2.02	3.36	5.08	5.64	5.91	750
Secondary	(1.33)	1.50	2.41	(3.93)	(5.40)	(5.29)	112
College + college graduate	(1.50)	(1.36)	(1.90)	(3.00)	(4.50)	(6.50)	39
Armenian							
Illiterate + no schooling	0.56	1.71	2.79	3.89	4.81	5.50	1478
Primary	0.61	1.30	2.58	3.46	4.10	5.46	531
Secondary	(0.50)	(1.26)	(1.13)	(2.67)	(4.00)	(4.60)	51
College + college graduate	—	(0.50)	(1.00)	(3.00)	—	(3.67)	10

* Numbers in parentheses refer to fewer than 25 EW.

ation was also negative but not significant. There was also a significant inverse association between family size and husband's education in all age groups, including 40–44.

Ideal Family Size

Each woman was asked what she considered to be the ideal number of children for a family in similar circumstances to her own. The majority of women stated that an ideal number of children would be around 5

TABLE 2.B.4. MEAN FAMILY SIZE BY AGE OF ELIGIBLE WOMEN
AND SOCIAL CHARACTERISTICS *

Characteristic	Mean family size at age :						Number (all ages)
	<20	20–24	25–29	30–34	35–39	40–44	
Culture and social status							
Muslim							
Middle	0.62	1.54	2.64	3.85	4.30	4.53	904
Low	0.79	2.16	3.27	4.48	5.27	5.35	1211
Total	0.69	1.88	3.01	4.27	4.91	5.03	2115
Armenian							
Middle	0.59	1.23	2.25	2.89	3.16	4.03	1071
Low	0.51	1.77	2.78	3.86	4.60	4.98	1023
Total	0.56	1.40	2.47	3.43	4.12	4.59	2094
Education of EW							
Muslim							
Illiterate + no schooling	0.75	2.02	3.19	4.41	5.12	5.18	1567
Primary	0.60	1.62	2.68	3.58	3.91	4.42	611
Secondary	—	(0.90)	(1.57)	(2.86)	(3.00)	—	34
College + college graduate	—	—	(2.00)	—	—	1.50	3
Armenian							
Illiterate + no schooling	0.57	1.63	2.58	3.55	4.22	4.63	1498
Primary	0.56	1.26	2.33	2.96	3.11	(4.00)	569
Secondary	—	(0.60)	(1.00)	(2.00)	(2.00)	(3.50)	26
College + college graduate	—	—	—	—	(4.00)	—	1

* Numbers in parentheses refer to fewer than 25 EW.

TABLE 2.B.5. MEAN FAMILY SIZE BY AGE OF ELIGIBLE WOMEN,
CULTURE, AND AGE AT MARRIAGE *

Age at marriage	Mean family size at age :						Number (all ages)
	<20	20–24	25–29	30–34	35–39	40–44	
Muslim							
<15	1.0	2.5	3.6	4.8	5.4	5.4	617
15–19	0.6	1.8	3.0	4.2	4.9	5.1	1312
20–24	—	0.6	1.7	3.1	3.3	(4.7)	151
25 and over	—	—	(0.5)	(2.0)	(1.8)	(2.5)	22
Armenian							
<15	(1.2)	2.4	2.9	(4.1)	4.6	5.0	113
15–19	0.5	1.6	2.7	3.7	4.4	4.7	1543
20–24	—	0.7	1.8	2.8	3.4	4.0	394
25 and over	—	—	(0.5)	(1.0)	(1.8)	(2.8)	44

* Numbers in parentheses refer to fewer than 25 EW.

TABLE 2.B.6. MEAN IDEAL FAMILY SIZE BY POPULATION CHARACTERISTICS *

Characteristic	Muslim			Armenian		
	Middle	Low	Total	Middle	Low	Total
Culture/social status	4.98	5.40	5.22	4.99	5.29	5.14
Parity						
0	4.67	5.17	4.83	4.50	4.69	4.55
1	4.57	4.95	4.73	4.51	4.58	4.53
2	4.87	5.02	4.94	4.84	4.85	4.85
3	5.07	5.22	5.16	5.10	5.08	5.09
4	5.27	5.47	5.40	5.43	5.33	5.37
5	5.00	5.54	5.38	5.57	5.52	5.53
6 and over	5.63	5.77	5.73	6.14	5.73	5.81
Parity of EW's mother						
1	—	—	—	—	—	—
2	(5.00)	(5.91)	(5.48)	(5.53)	(5.70)	5.63
3	5.27	5.29	5.28	5.33	5.40	5.37
4	4.84	5.45	5.19	4.89	5.15	5.02
5	4.86	5.61	5.25	4.93	5.13	5.03
6	4.86	5.17	5.01	4.83	5.32	5.06
7	4.97	5.33	5.18	5.02	5.32	5.16
8	5.03	5.51	5.30	4.96	5.26	5.09
9	5.10	5.38	5.26	5.02	5.33	5.18
10 and over	4.97	5.39	5.22	5.03	5.29	5.17
Education of husband						
Illiterate + no schooling	5.17	5.44	5.40	5.07	5.32	5.23
Primary	4.95	5.18	5.01	4.93	4.86	4.92
Secondary	4.91	(4.00)	4.90	4.95	(5.00)	4.95
College + college graduate	4.59	—	4.59	(4.50)	—	(4.50)
Education of EW						
Illiterate + no schooling	5.18	5.43	5.35	5.13	5.32	5.25
Primary	4.78	5.09	4.85	4.85	5.00	4.88
Secondary	4.50	—	4.50	4.60	—	4.60
College + college graduate	(4.00)	—	(4.00)	(5.00)	—	(5.00)
Occupation of EW						
Housewife	4.99	5.40	5.23	5.00	5.30	5.14
Clerical/professional	4.46	(4.60)	4.48	(5.06)	(4.75)	(4.96)
Agricultural/industrial	(6.00)	(6.00)	(6.00)	(4.23)	(5.00)	(4.56)
Janitorial/others	(5.50)	(5.20)	(5.29)	(4.50)	(5.17)	5.07
Age of EW						
<20	4.74	5.12	4.90	4.51	4.98	4.68
20–24	4.84	5.15	5.01	4.63	4.83	4.70
25–29	5.01	5.41	5.24	4.97	5.01	4.98
30–34	5.05	5.55	5.38	5.17	5.30	5.24
35–39	5.34	5.44	5.40	5.20	5.51	5.41
40–44	5.37	5.94	5.72	5.59	5.65	5.62

* Numbers in parentheses refer to fewer than 25 EW.

(Table 2.B.6). Only small differences in the ideal family size were observed by culture or social status (Fig. 2.B.1).

Although there was some fluctuation among Muslim women, the mean ideal family size of each cultural group increased with the parity of the woman interviewed but was not as consistently related to the parity of her mother. Ideal family size also increased steadily with the age of the women, from 4.90 to 5.72 children for Muslim women and from 4.68 to 5.62 children for Armenian women (Fig. 2.B.2).

There was a negative relationship between ideal family size and education of the woman, and a negative relationship between ideal family size and the husband's education was also observed although it was not as clear or consistent.

There was a positive correlation between ideal and achieved family size, with Pearson's correlation coefficient equal to 0.27 for Muslim women and 0.44 for Armenian women. It is interesting, however, that the number of children most women considered ideal was higher than the number of living children they actually had at the time of the interview (Table 2.B.7), the exception being those having an actual family size of 6 or greater, who preferred family sizes closer to their own.

TABLE 2.B.7. PERCENTAGE DISTRIBUTION OF IDEAL FAMILY SIZE
BY ACTUAL FAMILY SIZE

Actual family size	Percentage of EW choosing ideal family size of :								Number of women
	0–3	4	5	6	7	8	9	10 and over	
Muslim									
0	1.3	49.3	25.6	18.8	2.2	0.9	0.4	1.3	223
1	1.2	49.4	19.6	26.8	0.9	1.2	0.3	0.6	332
2	0.2	43.3	21.5	30.0	2.2	2.2	0.5	0.0	404
3	0.3	21.2	41.9	31.8	1.9	2.4	0.0	0.5	377
4	0.3	28.4	7.5	57.2	2.6	3.3	0.7	0.0	306
5	0.5	28.9	23.2	21.6	20.1	4.6	0.5	0.5	194
6 and over	0.0	22.9	22.2	35.1	2.5	11.1	3.2	2.9	279
Total	0.5	34.8	23.5	32.5	3.7	3.5	0.8	0.8	2115
Armenian									
0	0.5	59.6	24.0	15.8	0.0	0.0	0.0	0.0	183
1	1.4	55.7	27.3	14.9	0.0	0.0	0.0	0.7	289
2	0.5	41.2	34.8	23.5	0.0	0.0	0.0	0.0	434
3	0.5	12.5	59.8	26.0	0.5	0.7	0.0	0.0	415
4	0.0	22.5	9.3	67.6	0.5	0.0	0.0	0.0	364
5	0.0	18.7	28.5	27.1	23.4	2.3	0.0	0.0	214
6 and over	0.0	17.9	11.8	49.2	2.1	13.3	3.6	2.1	195
Total	0.4	31.4	30.6	32.6	2.8	1.6	0.3	0.3	2094

C. BEIRUT

C. Churchill, I. Lorfing, H. Zurayk and J. Azar

Family Structure

Over 80% of the families in the study were nuclear. This proportion did not vary between the cultural groups but, in each group, it was somewhat greater among those of low social status. However, family structure was not found to be an important variable in our analysis and will not be referred to again in this section.

Age at Marriage

This is one of the key variables in family formation. On the average, Shiite women married earlier than Maronite women (at a mean age of 18.5 and 20.2 years respectively, Fig. 2.C.1). Two-thirds of the Shiite women were under 20 years when they first married, compared with about one-half of the Maronite women. Among the social variables, the woman's education and occupation seemed to be important correlates of age at marriage (Table 2.C.1). In each cultural group, the more education the woman had received the later she married. It is apparent, nevertheless, that primary level education, as opposed to no schooling, made only a small difference to the age at which women married. This is relevant because the great majority of women who had received any education had not passed beyond the primary stage. Relevant also is the probability that education affects family formation through age at marriage only if it is continued at least to secondary level.

In regard to occupation, women in the housewife category married at a younger age than those in the professional and clerical group. Although the latter group was relatively small, it was striking that 28% of Maronite and 25% of Shiite women classified as professional and clerical married before the age of 20 years compared with 50% and 70% respectively for housewives.

Gravidity

As was to be expected, mean gravidity increased steadily with age for all groups (Table 2.C.2 and Fig. 2.C.2). While there was little or no difference (r = 0.049) by social status within each culture group, Shiite women reported more pregnancies per woman than did Maronite women for each age group. The mean gravidity for the age group 40–44, was 9.7 for Shiites and 6.5 for Maronites, giving a significant mean difference of 3 pregnancies per woman (Fig. 2.C.1).

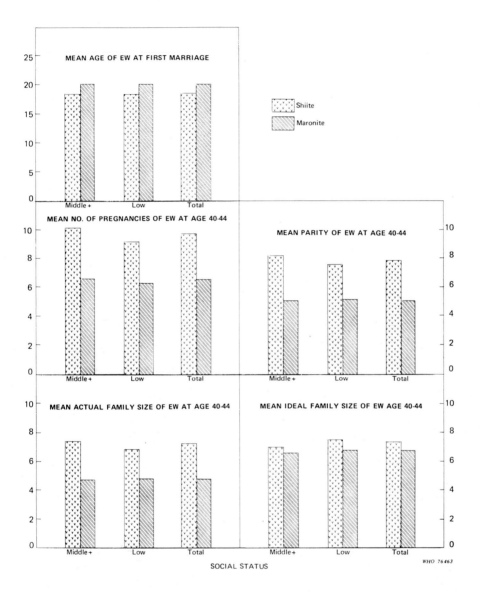

FIG. 2.C.1. FAMILY FORMATION BY SOCIAL CHARACTERISTICS

MEAN AGE OF EW AT FIRST MARRIAGE

Shiite

Maronite

MEAN NO. OF PREGNANCIES OF EW AT AGE 40-44

MEAN PARITY OF EW AT AGE 40-44

MEAN ACTUAL FAMILY SIZE OF EW AT AGE 40-44

MEAN IDEAL FAMILY SIZE OF EW AGE 40-44

SOCIAL STATUS

WHO 76463

121

Characteristic	Percentage of eligible women who married at age :						Number (all ages)
	10–14	15–19	20–24	25–29	30–34	35–44	
Culture and social status							
Shiite							
Middle	7.1	61.8	25.0	5.2	0.6	0.3	675
Low	8.6	59.3	25.9	5.3	0.8	0.1	870
Total	8.0	60.4	25.5	5.2	0.7	0.2	1545
Maronite							
Middle	3.2	43.4	40.9	10.8	1.6	0.1	864
Low	4.0	48.2	32.3	12.8	2.4	0.3	595
Total	3.6	45.4	37.4	11.6	1.9	0.2	1459
Education of EW							
Shiite							
Illiterate + no schooling	8.8	60.5	24.5	5.3	0.7	1.6	1254
Primary	4.5	64.8	25.9	4.9	—	—	247
Secondary	2.8	36.1	50.0	5.6	5.6	—	36
College + college graduate	—	(25.0)	(50.0)	(12.5)	—	(12.5)	8
Maronite							
Illiterate + no schooling	4.1	47.5	33.7	12.1	2.3	0.2	867
Primary	3.0	44.0	41.2	10.5	1.2	0.2	505
Secondary	1.3	32.9	50.0	13.2	2.6	—	76
College + college graduate	—	(27.3)	(63.6)	(9.9)	—	—	11
Occupation of EW							
Shiite							
Housewife	7.9	62.2	24.4	5.0	0.5	0.1	1472
Clerical/professional	5.3	19.6	51.8	14.3	7.1	1.8	56
Agricult./janit./industrial	(23.1)	(53.8)	(23.1)	—	—	—	13
Others	(25.0)	—	(75.0)	—	—	—	4
Maronite							
Housewife	3.7	46.3	36.9	11.1	1.8	0.2	1360
Clerical/professional	1.3	27.0	44.6	21.6	5.4	—	74
Agricult./janit./industrial	(4.5)	(45.5)	(40.9)	(9.1)	—	—	22
Others	—	(66.7)	(33.3)	—	—	—	3

* Numbers in parentheses refer to fewer than 25 EW.

Parity

On the average, the Shiite women had more live births than the Maronite women for each age group and in each social status (Table 2.C.3 and Fig. 2.C.2). At age 40–44 years, Shiite women had almost 3 live births more than the Maronites (Fig. 2.C.1). Some differences by social class were observed, particularly among the Maronites.

The mean parity specific for age varied inversely with the educational level of the woman ; thus, the more education a woman had, the fewer births she was likely to experience. For women aged 40–44 years, there was, on the average, one birth fewer for those who had a primary or higher education compared with those with no formal schooling in each cultural group. A similar pattern was observed for the husband's education.

In regard to occupation, among both Shiites and Maronites housewives experienced higher parity than those engaged in professional and clerical jobs. Because of the small numbers of non-housewives, however, no valid conclusions can be drawn.

Both total mean parity and age-specific mean parity increased steadily with the duration of marriage in every social status and cultural group.

TABLE 2.C.2. MEAN GRAVIDITY BY AGE OF ELIGIBLE WOMEN, CULTURE, AND SOCIAL STATUS

Culture and social status	Mean gravidity at age :						Number (all ages)
	<20	20–24	25–29	30–34	35–39	40–44	
Shiite							
Middle	0.88	2.59	4.02	6.28	7.99	10.16	675
Low	1.13	2.60	4.89	6.44	7.80	9.16	870
Total	1.02	2.59	4.55	6.37	7.88	9.69	1545
Maronite							
Middle	(0.54) [a]	1.67	3.09	4.22	5.95	6.60	864
Low	(1.12) [a]	2.33	3.72	5.23	6.41	6.28	595
Total	0.77	1.89	3.32	4.71	6.16	6.49	1459

[a] Refers to fewer than 25 EW.

Family Size

Family size is a function of parity and child loss. The values for family size are usually smaller than those for parity, depending on the magnitude and distribution of child loss. Apparently, Shiite women experienced slightly higher child loss than the Maronite women. At age 40–44, Shiite women had an average family size of 7.1, compared with a family size of 4.7 for Maronite women (Fig. 2.C.1). Because of the relatively small magnitude of child loss, however, family size was related to the various social and

FIG. 2.C.2. FAMILY FORMATION BY CULTURE AND SOCIAL STATUS

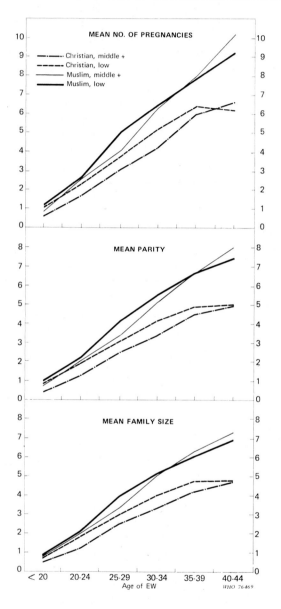

MEAN NO. OF PREGNANCIES

—·—·— Christian, middle +
— — — Christian, low
———— Muslim, middle +
———— Muslim, low

MEAN PARITY

MEAN FAMILY SIZE

Age of EW

WHO 76469

TABLE 2.C.3. MEAN PARITY BY AGE OF ELIGIBLE WOMEN
AND SOCIAL CHARACTERISTICS *

Characteristic	Mean parity at age :						Number (all ages)
	<20	20–24	25–29	30–34	35–39	40–44	
Culture and social status							
Shiite							
Middle	0.77	2.12	3.40	5.26	6.78	8.13	675
Low	0.98	2.27	4.15	5.58	6.68	7.51	870
Total	0.88	2.20	3.86	5.46	6.72	7.85	1545
Maronite							
Middle	(0.46)	1.32	2.58	3.47	4.51	5.01	864
Low	(0.88)	1.90	3.05	4.24	5.01	5.08	595
Total	0.63	1.52	2.75	3.85	4.74	5.03	1459
Education of EW							
Shiite							
Illiterate + no schooling	0.94	2.30	4.08	5.65	7.11	7.91	1254
Primary	0.74	2.13	3.34	4.16	(4.18)	(6.38)	247
Secondary	(0.67)	1.27	2.64	(2.25)	(3.00)	—	36
College + college graduate	—	—	(1.60)	—	(1.50)	—	8
Maronite							
Illiterate + no schooling	(0.75)	1.87	3.29	4.23	4.94	5.30	867
Primary	(0.58)	1.34	2.33	3.33	4.27	4.11	505
Secondary	(0.67)	(1.13)	2.12	(2.62)	(3.90)	(4.13)	76
College + college graduate	—	(0.50)	(1.67)	(3.00)	(4.50)	—	11
Education of husband							
Shiite							
Illiterate + no schooling	0.97	2.34	4.10	5.71	7.06	8.04	1118
Primary	0.82	2.16	3.72	4.89	5.89	(6.84)	314
Secondary	(0.25)	(1.67)	(2.33)	(3.13)	(5.38)	(5.75)	57
College + college graduate	(0.67)	(1.53)	(1.93)	(3.75)	(2.71)	(5.0)	56
Maronite							
Illiterate + no schooling	(0.69)	1.78	3.12	4.28	4.99	5.11	791
Primary	(0.61)	1.40	2.53	2.53	4.36	5.03	491
Secondary	(0.50)	(1.32)	2.34	2.57	(4.04)	(4.71)	136
College + college graduate	—	(0.50)	(2.19)	(3.20)	(4.50)	(3.71)	41
Occupation of EW							
Shiite							
Housewife	0.88	2.24	3.96	5.54	6.88	7.85	1472
Clerical/professional	—	(1.09)	(2.35)	(2.56)	(3.33)	(7.57)	56
Agricultural/industrial	—	(2.00)	(3.50)	(5.50)	(8.00)	(8.33)	9
Janitorial/others	—	(2.00)	(1.00)	—	(3.00)	(8.00)	6
Maronite							
Housewife	0.63	1.57	2.85	3.88	4.78	5.05	1360
Clerical/professional	—	(0.60)	(1.86)	(3.43)	(4.13)	(4.71)	74
Agricultural/industrial	—	—	(2.00)	(3.67)	(3.00)	(6.50)	12
Janitorial/others	—	—	—	(3.25)	(4.33)	(4.25)	13

* Numbers in parentheses refer to fewer than 25 EW.

Characteristic	Mean family size at age :						Number (all ages)
	<20	20–24	25–29	30–34	35–39	40–44	
Culture and social status							
Shiite							
Middle	0.77	2.05	3.32	5.06	6.33	7.38	675
Low	0.89	2.15	3.91	5.21	6.09	6.78	870
Total	0.83	2.10	3.68	5.15	6.20	7.10	1545
Maronite							
Middle	(0.46)	1.28	2.53	3.37	4.28	4.69	864
Low	(0.75)	1.86	3.01	4.05	4.74	4.75	595
Total	0.58	1.48	2.71	3.70	4.49	4.71	1459
Education of EW							
Shiite							
Illiterate + no schooling	0.91	2.21	3.87	5.31	6.52	7.16	1254
Primary	0.65	2.05	3.25	4.03	4.18	5.75	247
Secondary	(0.67)	(1.27)	(2.54)	(2.25)	(3.00)	—	36
College + college graduate	—	—	(1.60)	—	(1.50)	—	8
Maronite							
Illiterate + no schooling	(0.75)	1.83	3.23	4.04	4.67	4.96	867
Primary	0.50	1.29	2.29	3.25	4.07	3.86	505
Secondary	(0.67)	(1.12)	2.11	(2.57)	(3.90)	(3.75)	76
College + college graduate	—	(0.50)	(1.67)	(3.00)	(4.50)	—	11
Occupation of EW							
Shiite							
Housewife	0.83	2.14	3.77	5.24	6.33	7.08	1472
Clerical/professional	—	(1.09)	(2.30)	(2.33)	(3.22)	(7.29)	56
Agricultural/industrial	—	(2.00)	(3.00)	(4.50)	(7.00)	(8.00)	11
Janitorial/others	—	(2.00)	(1.00)	—	(3.00)	(7.00)	6
Maronite							
Housewife	0.58	1.53	2.81	3.73	4.52	4.73	1360
Clerical/professional	—	(0.60)	(1.86)	(3.14)	(4.00)	(4.50)	74
Agricultural/industrial	—	—	(1.80)	(3.67)	(3.00)	(5.00)	12
Janitorial/others	—	—	—	(3.25)	(4.33)	(4.25)	13

* Numbers in parentheses refer to fewer than 25 EW.

demographic characteristics in a pattern similar to that for parity (Table 2.C.4 and Fig. 2.C.2). This means that a Maronite woman aged 40–44 would have reared 2.4 fewer children than a Shiite woman. No social class difference was apparent among the Maronites and only a small difference among the Shiites.

Mean family size varied inversely with the woman's level of education, so that the higher the educational level achieved by a woman, the smaller family she was likely to have.

For each age group (except Shiites aged 40–44, among whom no difference by occupation existed), housewives had a higher mean family size than those engaged in clerical and professional work.

The earlier a woman had married, the more children she was likely to have compared with others of the same age (Table 2.C.5). Among women who had married at the same ages, however, Maronite women had smaller families than did Shiites, the differences being greatest for elder women.

TABLE 2.C.5. MEAN FAMILY SIZE BY AGE OF ELIGIBLE WOMEN, CULTURE, AND AGE AT MARRIAGE *

Age at marriage	Mean family size at age :					Number (all ages)
	<20	20–24	25–29	30–34	35–39	
Shiite						
<15	(1.4)	3.9	(6.0)	(6.8)	(6.9)	123
15–19	0.7	2.3	4.2	5.9	7.2	932
20–24	—	0.8	2.3	4.4	5.6	393
25 and over	—	—	(0.7)	2.4	3.0	95
Maronite						
<15	(1.1)	(3.4)	(5.0)	(4.7)	(5.4)	52
15–19	0.5	1.8	3.4	4.4	5.1	662
20–24	—	0.6	1.9	3.6	4.6	545
25 and over	—	—	(0.8)	2.1	3.0	200

* Numbers in parentheses refer to fewer than 25 EW.

Ideal Family Size

Women were asked what they considered to be the ideal number of children for a family in similar circumstances to their own. The answers reveal some interesting features.

The average number of children considered ideal by women was about 6 (Table 2.C.6), with no or little variation by culture, social class, woman's occupation, or parity of the woman's mother. In each cultural group, younger women preferred smaller families than older ones, although the

TABLE 2.C.6. MEAN IDEAL FAMILY SIZE BY POPULATION CHARACTERISTICS *

Characteristic	Shiite			Maronite		
	Middle	Low	Total	Middle	Low	Total
Culture/social status	6.3	6.6	6.5	6.2	6.3	6.2
Parity						
0	5.7	5.7	5.7	5.6	5.6	5.6
1	5.7	5.9	5.8	5.5	5.5	5.5
2	5.8	6.3	6.0	5.7	5.6	5.7
3	5.9	6.3	6.1	6.1	6.1	6.1
4	6.2	6.5	6.4	6.2	6.3	6.3
5	6.4	6.8	6.6	6.6	6.5	6.5
6 and over	7.1	7.3	7.2	7.2	7.3	7.3
Parity of EW's mother						
1	—	—	—	—	—	—
2	(7.0)	(7.8)	(7.3)	(7.6)	(6.0)	(6.9)
3	(6.5)	(6.8)	6.6	5.8	(5.8)	5.8
4	(6.2)	7.1	6.7	6.3	6.5	6.3
5	6.7	6.7	6.7	6.1	6.2	6.1
6	6.3	7.0	6.7	6.0	6.1	6.1
7	6.1	6.5	6.3	6.0	6.6	6.2
8	6.2	6.5	6.4	6.2	6.3	6.2
9	6.1	6.8	6.5	6.3	6.2	6.3
10 and over	6.4	6.6	6.5	6.4	6.4	6.3
Education of husband						
Illiterate + no schooling	6.7	6.7	6.7	6.4	6.3	6.4
Primary	6.1	6.2	6.1	6.0	6.2	6.1
Secondary	6.0	(5.0)	6.0	6.0	(6.2)	6.0
College + college graduate	5.6	—	5.6	6.2	—	6.2
Education of EW						
Illiterate + no schooling	6.6	6.7	6.7	6.5	6.4	6.4
Primary	5.9	6.0	5.9	5.9	6.0	5.9
Secondary	5.5	—	5.2	6.0	(6.0)	6.0
College + college graduate	(5.4)	—	(5.4)	(6.5)	—	(6.5)
Occupation of EW						
Housewife	6.4	6.6	6.5	6.2	6.3	6.2
Clerical/professional	5.4	(8.2)	6.0	6.2	(6.4)	6.2
Agricultural/industrial	(6.7)	(7.5)	(7.3)	(6.7)	(6.7)	(6.7)
Janitorial/others	(5.5)	(6.5)	(5.8)	(5.4)	(6.8)	(6.2)
Age of EW						
<20	6.0	5.7	5.8	(5.7)	(5.7)	5.7
20–24	6.0	6.3	6.1	5.8	5.8	5.8
25–29	6.0	6.5	6.3	5.9	6.0	5.9
30–34	6.2	7.0	6.7	6.2	6.3	6.2
35–39	7.0	6.9	6.9	6.5	6.7	6.6
40–44	6.9	7.4	7.2	6.5	6.8	6.6

* Numbers in parentheses refer to fewer than 25 EW.

number of children preferred by women less than 25 years old differed by only about 1 child from the number preferred by women over 40.

A positive correlation existed between ideal family size and women's parity. There was also a small decline in ideal family size for each group with increasing educational achievement, the greatest reduction occurring for those with primary education compared with those who were illiterate or had had no schooling.

There was also a positive correlation between ideal and achieved family size. Pearson's correlation coefficient was 0.40 for Shiites and 0.49 for Maronites. It is interesting, however, that the number of children most women considered ideal was higher than the number of living children they actually had at the time of interview (Table 2.C.7), the exception being the grand multiparas (those having an actual family size of 8 and over) who preferred family sizes close to their own.

TABLE 2.C.7. PERCENTAGE DISTRIBUTION OF IDEAL FAMILY SIZE
BY ACTUAL FAMILY SIZE

Actual family size	Percentage of EW choosing ideal family size of :								Number of women
	0–3	4	5	6	7	8	9	10 and over	
Shiite									
0	3.5	12.4	22.8	46.9	6.9	6.2	0.7	0.7	145
1	0.7	10.6	19.7	54.2	6.3	4.9	2.8	0.7	142
2	1.0	5.7	19.7	58.5	6.2	6.2	0.0	2.6	193
3	0.5	1.9	19.0	57.3	13.7	3.8	1.4	2.4	211
4	0.6	0.6	7.1	65.5	15.5	4.8	2.4	3.6	168
5	1.0	2.0	9.8	34.3	35.8	10.3	3.9	2.9	204
6 and over	1.2	2.3	7.3	30.7	14.3	26.3	5.8	12.0	482
Total	1.1	4.1	13.3	45.8	14.8	12.4	3.1	5.3	1545
Maronite									
0	2.5	10.1	26.1	48.7	7.6	5.0	0.0	0.0	119
1	2.5	12.3	25.8	49.7	7.1	2.6	0.0	0.0	155
2	0.9	6.3	20.2	65.5	5.4	1.8	0.0	0.0	223
3	0.4	0.8	15.4	67.7	8.5	5.4	0.4	1.5	260
4	0.4	1.8	4.3	71.1	12.1	8.9	1.1	0.4	280
5	1.4	1.9	6.7	39.7	35.4	13.9	1.0	0.0	209
6 and over	1.4	1.4	3.3	27.7	10.8	36.6	9.4	9.4	213
Total	1.1	4.0	13.0	54.7	12.7	11.0	1.8	1.7	1459

D. MANILA

V. Balderrama-Guzman, G. B. Roman and S. Ignacio-Morelos

Family Structure

The majority of families in the study were classified as nuclear. This proportion varied considerably by residence : 66.0% of the rural families were nuclear compared with 80.2% of the urban families. There was also a slight variation (around 3%) by social status, the middle status women being more frequently found in nuclear households. However, family structure was not found to be an important variable in our analysis and will not be discussed further.

Age at Marriage

There was very little variation in mean age at first marriage, either by residence or by social status (see Fig. 2.D.1). Women in all groups married at a mean age of about 20 years. Somewhat larger differences in age at marriage were found when education was considered. Looking at the percentage distribution (Table 2.D.1), it can be seen that the age at marriage increased gradually with the education level of the women in both the rural and the urban areas. The proportion of rural women marrying under age 20 decreased from about 54% for those with primary or less education to 38.7% for those with secondary education and to 22.6% for those with college or higher education. A similar pattern was discerned for urban women. It is apparent that only secondary or higher education was associated with a higher age at marriage.

In regard to occupation, the pattern was somewhat more varied. In the rural area, women who were housewives or who worked in agricultural or industrial occupations married at about the same age. Women in these occupations married at a lower age than women in the clerical and professional occupations. In the urban area, the housewives married earlier than those in industrial occupations, who in turn married younger than those in clerical and professional occupations. The associations between age at marriage, the woman's education and occupation, and the husband's occupation were significant (P < 0.001).

Gravidity

Table 2.D.2, which gives gravidity specific for age, shows that gravidity increased steadily with age, as would be expected. There were no substantial differences between residential groups in the average number of pregnancies,

130

FIG. 2.D.1. FAMILY FORMATION BY SOCIAL CHARACTERISTICS

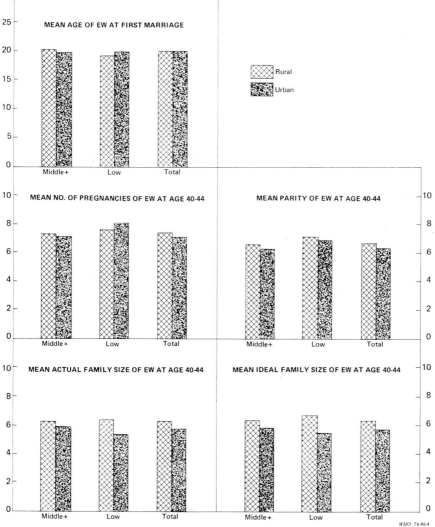

TABLE 2.D.1. PERCENTAGE DISTRIBUTION OF ELIGIBLE WOMEN
BY AGE AT MARRIAGE AND SOCIAL CHARACTERISTICS *

Characteristic	Percentage of eligible women who married at age :						Number (all ages)
	10–14	15–19	20–24	25–29	30–34	35–44	
Residence and social status							
Rural							
Middle	2.0	44.2	41.3	9.8	2.3	0.4	1606
Low	3.6	55.3	34.4	7.7	0.8	0.3	392
Total	2.3	45.9	39.9	9.4	2.0	0.4	1998
Urban							
Middle	3.2	47.6	36.6	10.2	2.0	0.3	1774
Low	1.8	52.2	35.0	9.7	0.9	0.4	226
Total	3.0	48.1	36.4	10.1	1.9	0.3	2000
Education of EW							
Rural							
Illiterate + no schooling	3.8	48.8	39.1	6.8	0.9	0.7	873
Primary	1.5	51.8	35.7	8.8	1.9	0.3	731
Secondary	1.2	37.5	46.2	10.6	4.4	0.0	160
College + college graduate	0.0	22.6	52.1	20.5	4.7	0.0	234
Urban							
Illiterate + no schooling	4.9	50.6	31.6	9.4	2.5	1.0	405
Primary	3.2	51.1	35.0	8.8	1.8	0.2	1174
Secondary	1.4	40.1	43.3	13.1	2.1	0.0	282
College + college graduate	0.0	32.4	48.2	18.0	0.7	0.7	139
Occupation of EW							
Rural							
Housewife	2.3	48.4	39.4	8.0	1.4	0.4	1667
Clerical/professional	0.0	5.6	48.3	36.0	10.1	0.0	89
Agricultural/industrial	2.1	43.3	39.2	10.3	5.2	0.0	97
Others	3.4	44.1	41.4	8.3	2.1	0.7	145
Urban							
Housewife	3.1	49.4	35.7	9.7	1.8	0.3	1813
Clerical/professional	(0.0)	(30.0)	(30.0)	(40.0)	(0.0)	(0.0)	10
Agricultural/industrial	0.0	28.3	54.7	15.1	0.0	1.9	53
Others	4.0	39.5	39.5	12.1	4.0	0.8	124

* Percentages in parentheses refer to fewer than 25 EW.

but the middle status group reported fewer pregnancies per woman than the lower status group. In the age group 40–44, it was found that, in the middle status group, rural women had 0.24 more pregnancies than urban women, whereas in the low status group, urban women had 0.47 more pregnancies than rural women (Fig. 2.D.1).

TABLE 2.D.2. MEAN GRAVIDITY BY AGE OF ELIGIBLE WOMEN, RESIDENCE, AND SOCIAL STATUS *

Residence and social status	Mean gravidity at age :						Number (all ages)
	<20	20–24	25–29	30–34	35–39	40–44	
Rural							
Middle	0.64	1.88	3.20	4.55	6.07	7.34	1606
Low	(0.75)	2.09	3.79	5.35	6.75	7.63	392
Total	0.67	1.92	3.31	4.69	6.22	7.41	1998
Urban							
Middle	0.97	1.94	3.09	4.45	6.04	7.10	1774
Low	(0.91)	2.46	4.00	4.81	6.61	(8.10)	226
Total	0.96	1.98	3.20	4.50	6.12	7.23	2000

* Numbers in parentheses refer to fewer than 25 EW.

Parity

As would be expected, the pattern for parity was similar to that for gravidity (Table 2.D.3 and Fig. 2.D.2). There was no clear and consistent difference in average parity between women from the urban and those from the rural area, but those of middle social status experienced fewer births than those of low social status.

Mean age-specific parity was inversely related to education in both residential areas. That is, the more education a woman had, the fewer births she was likely to experience. It is interesting to note, however, that college educated women over 40 years of age in each area experienced higher parities on the average than women in the same age group with a secondary education (6.11 compared with 4.78 in the rural area and 6.00 compared with 5.36 in the urban area, see Fig. 2.D.1).

In general, the same inverse relation between education and parity was evident when considering the education of the husband. In every age group in both residential areas, wives of college educated men had the lowest mean parities, followed by those with a secondary education.

The women in the rural area who were in clerical or professional occupations (although few in number) had the lowest mean parity in each age group. Women in agricultural or industrial occupations had a lower parity on the average than either housewives or women in " other " occupations.

133

TABLE 2.D.3. MEAN PARITY BY AGE OF ELIGIBLE WOMEN
AND SOCIAL CHARACTERISTICS *

Characteristic	Mean parity at age :						Number (all ages)
	<20	20–24	25–29	30–34	35–39	40–44	
Residence and social status							
Rural							
Middle	0.56	1.69	2.97	4.24	5.47	6.62	1606
Low	(0.58)	1.85	3.48	5.11	6.00	7.15	392
Total	0.57	1.72	3.06	4.40	5.58	6.74	1998
Urban							
Middle	0.89	1.74	2.79	4.09	5.50	6.34	1774
Low	(0.73)	2.28	3.64	4.54	5.98	(7.00)	226
Total	0.88	1.78	2.89	4.15	5.57	6.42	2000
Education of EW							
Rural							
Illiterate + no schooling	(0.92)	1.87	3.37	4.70	6.11	6.90	873
Primary	0.49	1.77	3.20	4.25	5.57	6.82	731
Secondary	(0.11)	1.58	2.87	4.19	4.91	(4.78)	160
College + college graduate	(0.60)	1.37	2.12	3.73	3.90	(6.11)	234
Urban							
Illiterate + no schooling	1.07	2.03	3.08	4.63	6.09	6.76	405
Primary	0.89	1.84	2.96	4.12	5.56	6.40	1174
Secondary	(0.33)	1.50	2.79	3.69	5.03	(5.36)	282
College + college graduate	(0.80)	1.43	2.43	3.95	4.36	(6.00)	139
Education of husband							
Rural							
Illiterate + no schooling	(0.90)	1.78	3.55	4.77	5.72	7.35	541
Primary	0.59	1.85	3.17	4.43	5.98	6.94	690
Secondary	(0.45)	1.80	3.00	4.30	5.31	5.66	374
College + college graduate	(0.15)	1.42	2.53	3.85	4.97	5.57	393
Urban							
Illiterate + no schooling	(1.05)	2.02	3.18	4.07	5.58	6.85	271
Primary	0.87	1.87	2.92	4.37	6.04	6.51	995
Secondary	0.84	1.66	2.87	3.98	4.96	5.75	503
College + college graduate	(0.77)	1.50	2.62	3.76	4.81	(6.71)	231
Occupation of EW							
Rural							
Housewife	0.58	1.77	3.13	4.55	5.70	6.91	1667
Clerical/professional	—	(1.17)	1.65	(2.60)	(4.14)	(5.00)	89
Agricultural/industrial	—	(1.47)	2.93	(3.91)	(4.59)	(5.15)	96
Others	(0.00)	(1.29)	3.74	4.17	5.95	(7.23)	146
Urban							
Housewife	0.87	1.79	2.93	4.12	5.60	6.62	1813
Clerical/professional	—	(1.50)	(2.25)	—	—	—	10
Agricultural/industrial	(1.00)	(1.00)	(2.50)	(4.50)	(5.20)	(4.67)	46
Others	(1.00)	(1.92)	2.65	4.36	5.48	(5.23)	131

* Numbers in parentheses refer to fewer than 25 EW.

In the urban area, however, where only about 9% of the women were employed outside the home, no clear relationship between parity and occupation was found.

As might be expected, both total mean parity and age-specific mean parity increased with duration of marriage in each residential area and in each social status group.

Family Size

Since family size (number of children still living at the time of the interview) is a function of parity and child loss, it can be expected that the figures for family size will be smaller than those for parity. Indeed, the patterns of family size by age of eligible women, residence, and social status were very similar to those for parity and gravidity (Table 2.D.4 and Fig. 2.D.1 and 2.D.2). However, the low status women did not have a consistently higher family size. This difference between parity and family size was almost certainly due to the greater child loss among low status women. (Child loss will be discussed further in a later chapter of this report.)

The relationship between family size and the woman's education was not as consistent as that between parity and education, but in general mean family size was inversely related to education.

In regard to the women's occupation, it is hard to perceive a definite trend when all the age groups are considered. Looking at women aged 40–44, however, it can be seen that among rural women, housewives and those in " other " occupations had the largest mean family size (6.4), while those in clerical and professional and in agricultural and industrial occupations had a lower mean family size (4.7). Among the urban women, the housewives had the largest family size (5.9).

The later a woman married, the smaller her family was likely to be compared with others of the same age at interview. It will be recalled that about half the women in both areas had married before the age of 20 years. In both residential areas, those aged 35–39 who had married between the ages of 20 and 24 years had, on the average, one fewer child than those who had married between 15 and 19 years of age. Within each age-at-marriage group, there was little difference in family size between urban and rural women.

Ideal Family Size

Each woman was asked what she considered to be the ideal number of children for a family in similar circumstances to her own. The majority of women stated that an ideal number of children would be between 5 and 6 (Table 2.D.6). In each social status group, rural women gave a larger ideal family size than urban women. Also, in each area, women of low social status gave a slightly larger ideal family size than

FIG. 2.D.2. FERTILITY VARIABLES SPECIFIC FOR AGE
BY RESIDENCE AND SOCIAL STATUS

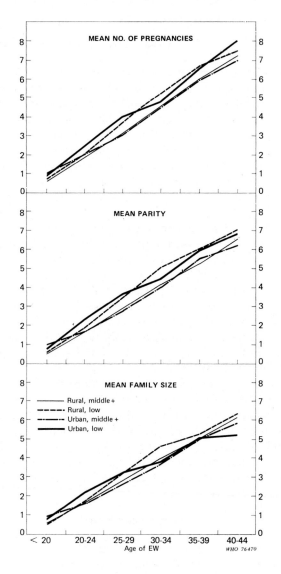

MEAN NO. OF PREGNANCIES

MEAN PARITY

MEAN FAMILY SIZE

Rural, middle+
Rural, low
Urban, middle +
Urban, low

Age of EW

WHO 76470

136

Characteristic	Mean family size at age :						Number (all ages)
	<20	20–24	25–29	30–34	35–39	40–44	
Residence and social status							
Rural							
Middle	0.55	1.60	2.77	3.97	5.06	6.21	1606
Low	(0.50)	1.75	3.18	4.67	5.26	6.31	392
Total	0.54	1.63	2.84	4.10	5.10	6.23	1998
Urban							
Middle	0.82	1.60	2.62	3.72	4.96	5.80	1774
Low	(0.80)	2.18	3.28	3.86	5.07	5.25	226
Total	0.82	1.65	2.71	3.74	4.98	5.73	2000
Education of EW							
Rural							
Illiterate + no schooling	(0.88)	1.72	3.12	4.33	5.50	6.34	873
Primary	0.46	1.67	2.98	3.96	5.13	6.38	731
Secondary	(0.11)	1.58	2.62	4.08	4.53	(4.67)	160
College	(0.60)	1.43	2.63	(4.10)	(3.85)	(7.60)	105
College graduate	—	(1.24)	1.64	(3.00)	3.75	(5.14)	129
Urban							
Illiterate + no schooling	1.04	1.87	2.79	3.90	5.13	5.86	405
Primary	0.81	1.69	2.78	3.75	5.07	5.74	1174
Secondary	(0.33)	1.41	2.69	3.48	4.67	(5.07)	282
College	(0.80)	1.35	2.59	(3.59)	(4.17)	(5.25)	109
College graduate	—	—	(1.85)	(3.75)	(2.50)	(6.25)	30
Occupation of EW							
Rural							
Housewife	0.55	1.67	2.92	4.23	5.18	6.39	1667
Clerical/professional	—	(1.17)	1.52	(2.55)	(4.05)	(4.82)	89
Agricultural/industrial	—	(1.40)	2.57	(3.78)	(2.29)	(4.69)	96
Others	—	(1.21)	3.45	3.85	5.44	(6.54)	146
Urban							
Housewife	0.81	1.65	2.74	3.71	5.03	5.90	1813
Clerical/professional	—	(1.50)	(2.13)	—	—	—	10
Agricultural/industrial	(1.00)	(1.00)	(2.40)	(4.40)	(4.80)	(4.33)	46
Others	(0.67)	(1.77)	2.57	3.86	4.62	(4.54)	131

* Numbers in parentheses refer to fewer than 25 EW.

TABLE 2.D.5. MEAN FAMILY SIZE BY AGE OF ELIGIBLE WOMEN,
RESIDENCE, AND AGE AT MARRIAGE *

Age at marriage	Mean family size at age :					Number (all ages)
	<20	20–24	25–29	30–34	35–39	
Rural						
<15	(1.0)	(2.8)	(4.5)	(6.4)	—	46
15–19	0.5	2.0	3.7	5.3	6.2	918
20–24	—	0.9	2.4	3.7	4.9	798
25 and over	—	—	0.9	2.1	3.1	236
Urban						
<15	(0.9)	(2.4)	(4.2)	(5.6)	(6.2)	61
15–19	0.8	1.9	3.5	4.6	6.3	963
20–24	—	1.0	2.4	3.8	4.8	728
25 and over	—	—	1.1	2.0	3.2	248

* Numbers in parentheses refer to fewer than 25 EW.

women of middle social status. However, these differences by residence and social status were not large (Fig. 2.D.1).

In both residential areas, the mean ideal family size increased almost steadily with the parity of the woman interviewed, but it was not as consistently related to the parity of her mother. The mean ideal family size also increased steadily with the age of the women, from 5.2 to 6.4 children in the rural area and from 4.9 to 5.8 children in the urban area (Fig. 2.D.2).

The relationship between education and ideal family size was not clear in either residential area. The differences in mean ideal family size for any two educational levels of either the woman or her husband were small. In regard to occupation, women in the rural area chose a mean ideal family size of about 5.8, except for those engaged in " other " occupations, whose mean ideal family size was 6.0. In the urban area, the mean ideal family size for housewives was 5.4, while for all other occupational categories, it was 5.7.

There was a significant positive association ($r = 0.374$) between a woman's opinion of ideal family size and her own actual family size (Table 2.D.7). This association is to be expected, however, because people try to rationalize their own fertility pattern when stating their ideal family size. Despite this, the majority of women with 6 or more children chose 6 or fewer children as the ideal number.

TABLE 2.D.6. MEAN IDEAL FAMILY SIZE BY POPULATION CHARACTERISTICS *

Characteristic	Rural			Urban		
	Middle	Low	Total	Middle	Low	Total
Residence/social status	5.8	6.0	5.8	5.4	5.5	5.4
Parity						
0	5.3	5.1	5.3	4.8	(5.5)	4.8
1	5.1	5.6	5.1	4.9	4.9	4.9
2	5.3	5.3	5.3	5.2	(4.8)	5.2
3	5.6	5.5	5.6	5.5	5.4	5.5
4	5.9	6.3	6.0	5.9	5.7	5.8
5	6.3	6.3	6.3	5.9	5.8	5.9
6 and over	6.5	6.7	6.5	5.9	5.7	5.8
Parity of EW's mother						
1	—	—	—	—	—	—
2	5.9	(5.9)	5.9	5.4	(4.8)	5.3
3	6.0	(6.7)	6.2	5.5	(5.5)	5.5
4	5.8	(5.9)	5.8	5.3	(5.5)	5.3
5	5.8	6.1	5.9	5.4	5.5	5.4
6	5.9	5.8	5.8	5.3	5.2	5.3
7	5.6	6.1	5.7	5.4	(5.5)	5.4
8	5.9	6.0	5.9	5.5	5.4	5.5
9	5.8	6.0	5.9	5.4	5.7	5.5
10 and over	5.8	6.2	5.9	5.4	5.6	5.4
Education of husband						
Illiterate + no schooling	5.8	6.2	6.0	5.4	5.6	5.5
Primary	5.8	5.7	5.8	5.4	5.3	5.4
Secondary	5.9	5.7	5.9	5.4	5.5	5.4
College+ college graduate	5.7	(5.4)	5.7	5.5	(5.0)	5.5
Education of EW						
Illiterate + no schooling	5.9	6.2	6.0	5.5	5.7	5.5
Primary	5.7	5.8	5.8	5.4	5.3	5.4
Secondary	5.8	5.6	5.7	5.4	(5.6)	5.4
College + college graduate	5.7	(5.0)	5.7	5.4	(6.0)	5.4
Occupation of EW						
Housewife	5.8	6.0	5.8	5.4	5.5	5.4
Clerical/professional	5.8	—	5.8	(5.7)	—	(5.7)
Agricultural/industrial	5.7	(6.5)	5.8	5.7	(5.0)	5.7
Others	5.9	6.4	6.0	5.7	(5.7)	5.7
Age of EW						
<20	5.1	5.3	5.2	4.9	5.1	4.9
20–24	5.4	5.5	5.4	5.1	5.1	5.1
25–29	5.6	6.0	5.7	5.5	5.6	5.5
30–34	5.9	6.2	5.9	5.6	5.8	5.6
35–39	6.2	6.2	6.2	5.8	5.4	5.7
40–44	6.3	6.7	6.4	5.8	5.5	5.8

* Numbers in parentheses refer to fewer than 25 EW.

Actual family size	Percentage of EW choosing ideal family size of :								Number of women
	0–3	4	5	6	7	8	9	10 and over	
Rural									
0	0.6	34.1	14.0	45.7	3.7	0.6	0.6	0.6	164
1	1.6	32.8	20.2	41.1	3.2	0.8	0.0	0.4	253
2	0.0	25.5	19.1	50.3	2.2	2.5	0.0	0.3	314
3	0.0	3.5	41.1	47.5	4.1	2.8	0.0	0.9	316
4	0.0	4.6	1.8	82.6	5.7	3.9	0.0	1.4	281
5	0.0	7.8	11.7	42.0	29.0	9.5	0.0	0.0	231
6 and over	0.0	5.5	9.8	53.3	7.7	14.8	3.2	5.7	439
Total	0.3	14.3	17.0	52.6	7.6	5.9	0.8	1.8	1998
Urban									
0	3.8	38.3	29.5	25.1	2.7	0.5	0.0	0.0	183
1	7.1	34.2	25.5	28.8	2.7	1.4	0.3	0.0	368
2	0.0	31.3	21.3	42.6	3.0	1.8	0.0	0.0	399
3	0.0	7.9	42.6	42.6	3.9	2.7	0.0	0.3	331
4	0.0	7.0	10.3	75.2	2.1	4.5	0.8	0.0	242
5	0.0	13.2	21.3	40.8	18.4	6.3	0.0	0.0	174
6 and over	0.0	11.2	17.5	55.4	4.6	8.9	1.7	0.7	303
Total	1.6	21.0	24.4	44.2	4.5	3.5	0.4	0.1	2000

E. ANKARA

K. Sümbüloglu, M. Bertan and N. H. Fişek

Family Structure

The proportion of nuclear families (husband, wife, and unmarried children) was higher in semi-urban than in rural areas (68.7% compared with 46.2%, respectively ; see Chapter 1, Table 1.E.2). In the rural areas, there was very little difference between the family structures of the middle and low social status women : in the middle status group 43.5% of the women lived in a nuclear family, compared with 49.3% in the low status group. Family structure was not, however, found to be an important variable in our analysis and will not be referred to further in this section.

Age at Marriage

In Turkey men and women under 18 years of age marry only with the consent of their parents. However, parents usually permit their daughters to marry before they reach 18. As seen in Table 2.E.1, 9.4% of the rural

Characteristic	Percentage distribution of eligible women at age :						Number (all ages)
	10–14	15–19	20–24	25–29	30–34	35–44	
Residence and social status							
Rural							
Middle	9.1	77.5	12.6	(0.7)	0.0	—	1599
Low	10.5	69.5	18.7	(1.1)	0.0	—	440
Total	9.4	75.8	13.9	(0.8)	0.0	—	2039
Semi-urban							
Middle	9.0	73.1	16.3	1.4	0.3	0.1	1555
Low	(18.5)	67.9	(9.9)	—	0.0	0.0	81
Total	9.4	72.8	16.0	1.5	0.2	0.1	1636
Education of EW							
Rural							
Illiterate + no schooling	10.8	72.9	15.0	(1.1)	0.0	—	1317
Primary	7.0	81.7	11.2	—	0.0	0.0	703
Secondary	—	(50.0)	(44.4)	0.0	0.0	0.0	19
College + college graduate	—	—	—	—	—	—	0
Semi-urban							
Illiterate + no schooling	13.4	73.3	11.7	(1.2)	—	0.0	846
Primary	5.8	75.4	17.8	(0.9)	0.0	—	691
Secondary	—	52.6	40.0	(6.3)	0.0	0.0	95
College + college graduate	0.0	0.0	—	—	—	0.0	4

* Percentages in parentheses refer to fewer than 25 EW.

and semi-urban women married before they reached 15 years of age. Of the rural and semi-urban women, 85.2% and 82.2%, respectively, married before 20 years of age. On the average, there was very little difference in the marriage ages of women in the two residential groups, the mean age at marriage of rural women being 17.3 years and that of the semi-urban women 17.5 years (Fig. 2.E.1). In the rural areas, low status women seemed to have married slightly later than middle status women. Of the low status women, 19.8% married after age 20, compared with only 13.3% of those in the middle status group.

While age at marriage rose with each educational level of the EW, it should be noted that primary school education increased the mean age at marriage very little above that of the " no schooling " group. Secondary education, on the other hand, seemed to be more relevant. Only 12.9%

141

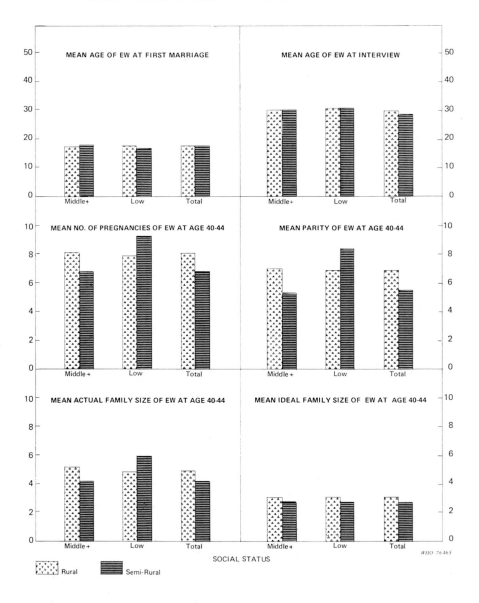

FIG. 2.E.1. FAMILY FORMATION BY SOCIAL CHARACTERISTICS

of those who had had no formal schooling and 18.7% of those with primary education married after age 20 in the semi-urban areas, compared with 46.3% of those with secondary education. The same pattern appeared in the rural areas, but those with secondary education were very few.

Gravidity

As expected, mean gravidity increased steadily with age in all groups (Table 2.E.2), except among semi-urban, low status women in age group 35–39, whose mean gravidity was lower than that of women aged 30–34 having the same residence and social status. For each age group the mean number of reported pregnancies was higher for rural women than for urban women. The mean gravidity for the age group 40–44, which provides an approximate measure of completed marital fertility, was 8.1 for rural women compared with only 6.9 for the corresponding semi-urban women, a difference of slightly more than 1 pregnancy (Fig. 2.E.1). Among the rural women, it was found that for each age group the difference in mean gravidity between the middle social status group and the low social status group was quite small and that the trend by age was very inconsistent (Fig. 2.E.2).

TABLE 2.E.2. MEAN GRAVIDITY BY AGE OF ELIGIBLE WOMEN, RESIDENCE, AND SOCIAL STATUS *

Residence and social status	Mean gravidity at age :						Number (all ages)
	<20	20–24	25–29	30–34	35–39	40–44	
Rural							
Middle	0.80	2.18	4.34	6.32	7.45	8.14	1599
Low	0.65	2.62	4.75	5.81	7.73	7.90	440
Total	0.77	2.26	4.43	6.20	7.51	8.07	2039
Semi-urban							
Middle	0.70	2.15	3.83	5.38	6.31	6.77	1555
Low	(0.63)	(1.58)	(3.75)	(6.79)	(6.31)	(9.27)	81
Total	0.70	2.12	3.83	5.45	6.31	6.91	1636

* Numbers in parentheses refer to fewer than 25 EW.

Parity

On the average, in each age group rural women had more live births than semi-urban women (Table 2.E.3 and Fig. 2.E.2). At age 40–44 years rural women had a mean parity of 7.0, compared with a mean parity of 5.6 for semi-urban women, an average difference of 1.4 live births. In general, however, middle status women in the age span 20–29 had a lower mean parity than their low status counterparts. After the age of

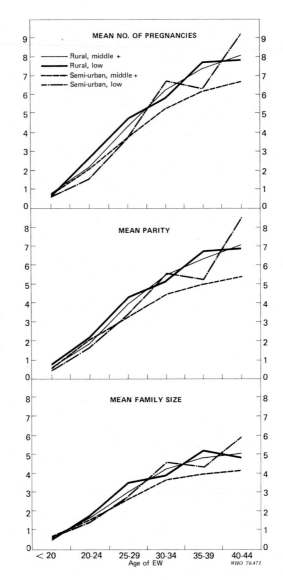

TABLE 2.E.3. MEAN PARITY BY AGE OF ELIGIBLE WOMEN AND SOCIAL CHARACTERISTICS *

Characteristic	Mean parity at age :						Number (all ages)
	<20	20–24	25–29	30–34	35–39	40–44	
Residence and social status							
Rural							
Middle	0.63	1.92	3.89	5.57	6.34	7.03	1599
Low	0.64	2.11	4.30	5.17	6.71	6.90	440
Total	0.63	2.07	3.98	5.48	6.46	6.99	2039
Semi-urban							
Middle	0.59	2.10	3.24	4.49	5.03	5.43	1555
Low	(0.62)	(1.40)	(3.42)	(5.58)	(5.26)	(8.46)	81
Total	0.59	1.79	3.24	4.55	5.04	5.60	1636
Education of EW							
Rural							
Illiterate + no schooling	0.88	2.16	4.11	5.59	6.74	7.12	1317
Primary	0.51	1.83	3.51	5.25	6.07	6.64	703
Secondary	—	(0.77)	(2.00)	—	—	—	19
College + college graduate	—	—	—	—	—	—	0
Semi-urban							
Illiterate + no schooling	0.55	2.00	3.64	5.07	5.62	6.31	846
Primary	0.60	1.66	3.00	3.98	4.42	4.63	691
Secondary	(0.60)	(1.68)	(2.04)	(2.44)	(2.56)	(2.92)	95
College + college graduate	—	—	—	—	—	—	4
Education of EW's husband							
Rural							
Illiterate + no schooling	(0.87)	2.36	4.28	5.61	6.62	7.14	714
Primary	0.62	1.95	3.90	5.43	6.27	6.91	1237
Secondary	(0.38)	1.62	(3.36)	—	(6.62)	—	79
College + college graduate	—	—	—	—	—	—	9
Semi-urban							
Illiterate + no schooling	(0.50)	2.04	4.10	5.15	5.75	7.34	332
Primary	0.59	1.89	3.41	4.67	5.13	5.16	946
Secondary	0.60	1.68	2.26	3.62	4.19	3.96	284
College + college graduate	(0.00)	(1.33)	(2.05)	(3.04)	(2.13)	(3.45)	74

* Numbers in parentheses refer to fewer than 25 EW.

30 years, however, these higher status women caught up with and surpassed the low status women and continued to have higher mean parities until and including 44 years of age.

Excluding the college and graduate categories, in which there were very few eligible women, mean parity specific for age varied inversely with educational level in each residential group. In other words, the more education a woman had, the fewer births she was likely to experience. For women aged 40–44 in the rural area, those who were illiterate had an average parity of 7.12, compared with an average parity of 6.64 for women with primary education. Corresponding figures for urban women aged 40–44 were 6.31 and 4.63 (Fig. 2.E.1). A similar pattern was observed in regard to the husbands' education, small reductions in mean parity occurring as the educational level increased.

Both total mean parity and age-specific mean parity increased steadily with increasing duration of marriage for all social status and residential groups.

Family Size

Family size (the number of living children) is a function of parity and child loss. The figures for family size are therefore smaller than those for parity, depending on the magnitude and distribution of child loss. Apparently, rural women experienced slightly higher child loss than semi-urban women, as can be seen by comparing Table 2.E.3 with Table 2.E.4). At age 40–44, rural women had an average family size of 4.9, compared

TABLE 2.E.4. MEAN FAMILY SIZE BY AGE OF ELIGIBLE WOMEN
AND SOCIAL CHARACTERISTICS *

Characteristic	Mean family size at age :						Number (all ages)
	<20	20–24	25–29	30–34	35–39	40–44	
Residence and social status							
Rural							
Middle	0.53	1.58	3.00	4.21	4.83	5.10	1599
Low	0.51	1.69	3.42	3.90	5.17	4.87	440
Total	0.53	1.60	3.10	4.10	4.90	4.90	2039
Semi-urban							
Middle	0.56	1.55	2.68	3.64	3.94	4.14	1555
Low	(0.62)	(1.40)	(2.75)	(4.57)	(4.35)	(5.90)	81
Total	0.56	1.54	2.70	3.70	3.96	4.25	1636
Education of EW							
Rural							
Illiterate	0.72	1.70	3.15	4.30	4.90	5.10	938
No schooling	0.66	1.70	3.25	4.00	5.10	5.00	379
Primary	0.44	1.65	3.00	4.00	4.70	5.00	703
Secondary	—	(0.63)	(2.00)	—	—	—	19
College + college graduate	—	—	—	—	—	—	0
Semi-urban							
Illiterate	0.57	1.60	3.00	4.00	4.50	4.75	608
No schooling	(0.60)	1.80	2.80	3.90	3.80	4.75	238
Primary	0.56	1.50	2.50	3.40	3.60	3.50	691
Secondary	(0.60)	(1.50)	(1.90)	(2.40)	(2.35)	(2.65)	95
College + college graduate	—	—	—	—	—	—	4

* Numbers in parentheses refer to fewer than 25 EW.

with an average semi-urban family size of 4.3. These data mean, however, that an average rural woman aged 40–44 raised only about 0.7 children more than an average semi-urban woman (Fig. 2.E.1).

For each age group, except the under-20 group, rural women had higher mean family sizes than semi-urban women. No consistent pattern was found when the two social status groups of rural women were compared (Fig. 2.E.2).

As for parity, an inverse relationship was observed between family size and the educational level of the eligible women. In general, although fluctuations existed (Table 2.E.4), an increase in education meant a decrease in family size for each age group in both residential groups. For women aged 25 and over, a secondary education reduced the average family size by about one child as compared with women who had received primary or no education.

In all age groups, women who had married at an early age had more children than those who had married later in life (Table 2.E.5). Among women who had married at the same age, those living in the semi-urban areas had smaller families than those living in rural areas.

TABLE 2.E.5. MEAN FAMILY SIZE BY AGE OF ELIGIBLE WOMEN,
RESIDENCE, AND AGE AT MARRIAGE *

Residence and age at marriage	Mean family size at age :						Number (all ages)
	<20	20–24	25–29	30–34	35–39	40–44	
Rural							
<15	(0.67)	2.43	3.63	4.37	5.11	(4.61)	189
15–19	0.52	1.68	3.21	4.29	4.98	5.31	1548
20–24	0.0	0.80	2.14	3.43	4.65	5.00	285
25 and over	0.0	0.0	—	—	(2.83)	(4.25)	18
Semi-urban							
<15	(1.14)	(2.26)	3.66	4.16	4.47	(4.90)	156
15–19	0.53	1.65	2.76	3.91	4.32	4.50	1188
20–24	0.0	0.73	1.85	2.71	3.37	3.30	261
25 and over	0.0	0.0	—	(1.50)	(1.83)	(2.90)	29

* Numbers in parentheses refer to fewer than 25 EW.

Ideal Family Size

The average number of children considered ideal was 3.1 for rural women and 2.8 for semi-urban women (Table 2.E.5). Regardless of how many children they actually had, the majority of women (67% in rural areas and 79% in semi-urban areas) opted for 3 or fewer children. In the rural areas, there was very little variation in ideal family size by social status (middle status women and low status women preferred family sizes of 3.0

147

TABLE 2.E.6. MEAN IDEAL FAMILY SIZE BY POPULATION CHARACTERISTICS *

Population characteristics	Rural			Semi-urban		
	Middle	Low	Total	Middle	Low	Total
Mean ideal family size	3.04	3.12	3.05	2.80	2.78	2.80
Parity						
0	2.66	2.83	2.70	2.55	(2.10)	2.51
1	2.55	2.61	2.55	2.46	(2.60)	2.48
2	2.63	2.56	2.60	2.45	(2.07)	2.45
3	2.97	2.76	2.90	2.69	(3.40)	2.71
4	2.93	2.91	2.93	2.88	(3.00)	2.90
5	3.02	3.33	3.06	2.97	(2.83)	2.96
6 and over	3.43	3.42	3.43	3.15	3.19	3.15
Parity of EW's mother						
1	(3.04)	—	3.00	(2.90)	—	(2.91)
2	3.07	(3.37)	3.06	2.71	—	2.70
3	3.17	(3.00)	3.06	2.68	(2.33)	2.66
4	3.00	3.26	3.04	2.75	(3.11)	2.77
5	2.98	3.20	3.03	2.72	(2.16)	2.71
6	3.06	2.98	3.03	2.82	(3.20)	2.84
7	3.03	2.98	3.01	2.90	(2.69)	2.88
8	3.04	2.96	3.00	2.75	(3.10)	2.77
9	3.08	3.18	3.10	2.90	(2.78)	2.90
10 and over	3.20	3.32	3.21	2.94	(2.83)	2.93
Education of husband						
Illiterate + no schooling	3.23	3.22	3.22	3.07	2.85	3.03
Primary	2.99	2.94	2.98	2.80	(2.78)	2.79
Secondary	2.73	—	2.69	2.68	—	2.67
College + college graduate	(2.16)	—	(2.16)	2.37	—	2.37
Education of EW						
Illiterate + no schooling	3.50	3.19	3.14	3.00	2.79	2.98
Primary	2.92	2.89	2.91	2.64	(2.82)	2.64
Secondary	(2.38)	—	(2.36)	2.40	—	2.40
College + college graduate	—	—	—	—	—	—
Age of EW						
<20	2.57	2.80	2.61	2.63	(2.50)	2.62
20–24	2.71	2.70	2.71	2.55	(2.00)	2.53
25–29	2.95	3.10	2.98	2.66	(2.66)	2.66
30–34	3.26	3.16	3.24	2.82	(3.26)	2.84
35–39	3.24	3.48	3.29	3.04	(2.73)	3.02
40–44	3.30	3.09	3.25	3.10	(3.36)	3.11

* Numbers in parentheses refer to fewer than 25 EW.

and 3.1, respectively). Smaller families were more often preferred by younger than by older women, although the difference between the mean ideal family size of a woman under 20 years of age and that of a woman over 40 was only 0.7 children in the rural areas and 0.4 in the urban areas. There was also a small decline in ideal family size with increasing educational level of both the eligible woman and her husband. The parity of the woman's mother had little or no effect on her ideal family size, but a positive correlation existed between ideal family size and her own parity. However, the differences in ideal family size between women of different parities were very small.

In general, ideal family size rose with actual family size (Table 2.E.6). It is interesting to note, however, that very few women, regardless of actual family size, considered more than 4 children as being ideal.

TABLE 2.E.7. PERCENTAGE DISTRIBUTION OF IDEAL FAMILY SIZE BY ACTUAL FAMILY SIZE *

| Actual family size | Percentage of EW choosing ideal family size of: | | | | Number (all family sizes) |
	0–3	4	5	6 and over	
Rural					
0	76.9	20.4	—	—	147
1	66.9	27.0	(3.3)	(2.8)	724
2	80.6	17.9	—	0.0	196
3	66.4	28.4	(2.9)	(2.2)	451
4	63.1	30.7	(5.7)	—	176
5	71.2	26.9	—	(0.0)	104
6 and over	53.1	38.5	(3.7)	(4.6)	241
Total	67.1	27.6	3.1	2.1	2039
Semi-urban					
0	92.0	(4.4)	—	—	113
1	78.2	18.8	(1.8)	(1.2)	729
2	91.6	8.4	0.0	0.0	228
3	79.1	19.0	—	—	263
4	72.6	25.6	—	0.0	117
5	74.6	(23.8)	—	0.0	63
6 and over	57.7	34.1	(4.8)	—	123
Total	79.1	18.2	1.7	1.0	1636

* Numbers in parentheses refer to fewer than 25 EW.

149

Chapter Three

FAMILY FORMATION AND PREGNANCY OUTCOME

INTRODUCTION

M. R. Bone, C. C. Standley and A. R. Omran

The purpose of this chapter is to examine the relationships between pregnancy wastage on the one hand and family formation variables on the other. The family formation variables involved are : maternal age (age at termination of index pregnancy), pregnancy order, family size, and duration of the preceding pregnancy interval (the period between the end of the preceding pregnancy and the end of the index pregnancy).

In previous investigations, described in Part I, a J-shaped relationship has usually been found between pregnancy wastage and maternal age or pregnancy order. That is to say, wastage was lowest at intermediate ages and pregnancy orders and greatest for the latest ages and highest pregnancy orders. By contrast, the relationship between pregnancy wastage and the length of the preceding pregnancy interval has usually been shown to be a reverse J, i.e., wastage was greatest for the shortest intervals and lowest for those of intermediate length.

This chapter examines, first, whether the same relationships exist in the populations of the participating areas and, second, whether it is possible to indicate, in terms of the family formation variables, the most and least favourable conditions for conception to be followed by a successful pregnancy, i.e., one that results in a live-born child.

Information on pregnancy outcome was obtained by collecting from each eligible woman a detailed pregnancy history for the period between marriage and interview. Pregnancies resulting in either stillbirths or abortions were considered wasted. For the purposes of this study, stillbirths were defined as non-live births occurring 7 months or more after conception, and abortions as those occurring within 7 months of conception. Stillbirth rates, which are likely to be more reliable than abortion rates, are shown separately from the latter and in two of the analyses are based on total births rather than total pregnancies. This is done in order to ensure that consideration is given to the pregnancies that are still liable to end in stillbirth after abortions have reduced the original number of reported pregnancies.

The difficulties that arise in the analysis and interpretation of the data are as follows :

1. *Interrelationships amongst the family formation variables.* Many of the variables are interrelated, e.g., age, pregnancy interval, and pregnancy order. First and second pregnancies and short interpregnancy intervals are likely to be most frequent among the youngest women, while pregnancies of the highest orders and long interpregnancy intervals are more likely to be found among the oldest women of childbearing age. To examine the pure relationship between any two of the variables alone, it is necessary that the other variables should be held constant. In practice, it is seldom useful to control more than one extraneous variable, since many of the subgroups thus formed would be too small to exhibit trends.

2. *The nature of the sample.* The findings are based on retrospective evidence from samples of women, and not on current evidence from samples of pregnancies. The effects of this are :

(*a*) Pregnancies that occurred to non-eligible women (e.g., those now dead or too old for inclusion) in the same areas and during the same time period are disregarded.

(*b*) Women who have had many pregnancies make a larger contribution to the results than women with fewer pregnancies ; this may produce bias through differences in pregnancy outcome.

(*c*) The women's pregnancy histories cover varying periods up to some 30 years prior to the interview. During this time, the risks of pregnancy wastage may have changed and this could distort the relationships under study.

(*d*) It is unlikely that recall over periods of up to 30 years will be perfect, and there may be underreporting of pregnancies for other reasons in a single interview survey. In none of the areas, however, could any differences be found between fetal wastage rates for last pregnancies and those for all pregnancies, whether analysed by maternal age or by pregnancy order. This suggests that there was no underreporting of earlier pregnancies due to lack of recall. Nevertheless, the underreporting of pregnancy wastage seems to be a sizeable problem, especially in India. Preliminary results from a study in Gandhigram, where fetal wastage rates were low compared with all other areas, suggest that abortion in that area was some five times as frequent as reported and stillbirth rates about twice the reported figures. It seems highly improbable that underreporting in other areas reached this figure, since wastage in some was already considerable, the rates for all 5 areas varying from about 4% to 18% of reported pregnancies. A total fetal wastage of 15% or more is high compared with the findings of other surveys in both developed and developing countries, although considerably higher estimates have been made.[1]

3. *Interpretation of the relationships.* The relationships between pregnancy wastage and the family formation variables are not necessarily fortuitous. Firstly, a woman who wants a child and whose pregnancy ends in fetal death is likely to conceive again as soon as she can in the hope of producing a live child. If she is repeatedly unsuccessful, the statistics will show pregnancy loss following numerous, closely spaced pregnancies. The number and spacing of the pregnancies in such cases are the effects, not the causes, of pregnancy wastage. Secondly, induced abortion my be used intentionally as a method of birth control. An unsuccessful outcome of pregnancy then depends on deliberate choice by the woman, not on physiological factors. In 3 of the participating areas, there was suggestive evidence that the number of voluntary abortions was by no means negligible. For all these reasons, the findings on abortion reported in this chapter should, at the present stage, be interpreted with caution.

A. GANDHIGRAM

S. Gunasekaran and R. S. Kurup

Pregnancy Outcome

Of the 22 939 pregnancies reported by the 6541 women, 356 (1.6%) were stillbirths and 467 (2%) were abortions, giving a total wastage rate of 3.6% of all pregnancies. These rates are low compared with those obtained by the prospective study (which will be reported later) of the same population carried out over 2 years following the present survey.[2] Serious underreporting not only artificially depresses rates but also may distort the relationships under study, unless it is uniformly distributed among subgroups.

Wastage by Culture and Social Characteristics

Wastage per 100 pregnancies was, as shown in Table 3.A.1, lowest for Vellalas, for whom the rate was 1.7%, compared with around 4.0% for the other cultural groups (3.9% for Muslims, 4.0% for Scheduled Castes and 4.3% for Other Hindus).

Although the differences were relatively small, middle status women in each group (except the Vellalas) tended to report higher pregnancy wastage rates than the low status women. The reverse was observed for the Vellalas,

---

[1] *See:* POTTER, R. G. ET AL. Fetal wastage in seven Punjab villages. *Hum. Biol.*, **73**: 262–273 (1965). Other sources are quoted in this paper.

[2] Preliminary analysis suggests that the rates obtained prospectively were about four times those obtained from the retrospective history.

TABLE 3.A.1. PREGNANCY WASTAGE BY CULTURE AND SOCIAL STATUS

Culture and social status	No. of pregnancies	Stillbirths (%)	Abortions (%)
Muslim			
Middle	5413	2.2	1.8
Low	2268	2.0	1.6
Total	7681	2.2	1.7
Scheduled Castes			
Middle	1071	2.2	3.0
Low	2771	1.4	2.0
Total	3842	1.7	2.3
Other Hindus			
Middle	4530	1.5	3.1
Low	2413	1.1	2.7
Total	6943	1.4	2.9
Vellala			
Middle	2744	0.6	0.9
Low	1729	0.8	1.2
Total	4473	0.7	1.0

and their wastage rates for each social status were also lower than those of the corresponding social status groups of other cultures. This was not expected in view of the findings of another study conducted by our institute, which indicated that Vellalas resorted to induced abortion more frequently than other groups. It is possible, therefore, that Vellalas may have suppressed some of the induced abortion cases. Their lower stillbirth rates may, however, be more reliable and may reflect their better health and lower fertility.

Pregnancy Outcome and Maternal Age

Starting at a relatively high rate at ages under 20 or 25 years, pregnancy wastage rates for women of all 4 cultural groups first declined with age and then rose to a level higher than the initial rate to form a J-shaped curve (Table 3.A.2 and Fig. 3.A.1). At all maternal ages Vellalas reported lower wastage rates than the other 3 groups, which had similar rates to one another. Again, for every culture except Vellalas, the middle status women tended to have slightly higher wastage rates than low status women (Fig. 3.A.2).

The maternal age associated with minimal risks of wastage was 25–29 for Muslims (where the rate of wastage was 3.1% in this age group) and 20–24 for Other Hindus and Scheduled Castes (whose wastage rates were

154

TABLE 3.A.2. PREGNANCY OUTCOME BY CULTURE, SOCIAL STATUS, AND MATERNAL AGE *

Culture and social status	Maternal age	Total preg- nancies	Pregnancy outcome as percentage of all pregnancies			
			Live births	Still- births	Abor- tions	Pregnancy wastage
Muslim						
Middle	<20	1834	96.0	2.2	1.9	4.1
	20–24	1760	95.3	2.6	2.1	4.7
	25–29	1091	97.1	1.8	1.1	2.9
	30–34	533	96.6	1.9	1.5	3.4
	35–39	172	96.5	1.7	1.7	3.4
	40–44	23	87.0	8.7	4.3	13.0
Low	<20	767	95.8	2.3	1.8	4.1
	20–24	746	96.9	2.0	1.1	3.1
	25–29	472	96.4	2.1	1.5	3.6
	30–34	221	96.4	1.4	2.3	3.7
	35–39	60	96.7	0.0	3.3	3.3
	40–44	2	(2)	(0)	(0)	(0)
Total	<20	2601	95.9	2.2	1.8	4.0
	20–24	2506	95.8	2.4	1.8	4.2
	25–29	1563	96.9	1.9	1.2	3.1
	30–34	754	96.6	1.7	1.7	3.4
	35–39	232	96.6	1.3	2.2	3.5
	40–44	25	88.0	8.0	4.0	12.0
Scheduled Castes						
Middle	<20	419	93.8	1.7	4.5	6.2
	20–24	345	96.2	2.3	1.4	3.7
	25–29	190	95.8	2.1	2.1	4.2
	30–34	87	93.1	4.6	2.3	6.9
	35–39	23	91.3	4.3	4.3	8.6
	40–44	7	(6)	(0)	(1)	(1)
Low	<20	1063	96.5	1.7	1.8	3.5
	20–24	925	97.0	1.0	2.1	3.1
	25–29	529	96.0	1.9	2.1	4.0
	30–34	214	95.8	1.4	2.8	4.2
	35–39	38	97.4	0.0	2.6	2.6
	40–44	2	(2)	(0)	(0)	(0)
Total	<20	1482	95.7	1.7	2.6	4.3
	20–24	1270	96.8	1.3	1.9	3.2
	25–29	719	96.0	1.9	2.1	4.0
	30–34	301	95.0	2.3	2.7	5.0
	35–39	61	95.1	1.6	3.3	4.9
	40–44	9	(8)	(0)	(1)	(1)
Other Hindus						
Middle	<20	1339	95.4	2.2	2.5	4.7
	20–24	1559	96.1	1.3	2.6	3.9
	25–29	993	95.6	1.3	3.1	4.4
	30–34	498	95.0	0.8	4.2	5.0
	35–39	126	88.9	1.6	9.5	11.1
	40–44	15	86.7	0.0	13.3	13.3
Low	<20	775	95.7	1.9	2.3	4.2
	20–24	826	97.1	1.0	1.9	2.9
	25–29	508	97.2	0.2	2.6	2.8
	30–34	223	93.7	0.9	5.4	6.3
	35–39	75	92.0	1.3	6.7	8.0
	40–44	6	(6)	(0)	(0)	(0)
Total	<20	2114	95.5	2.1	2.4	4.5
	20–24	2385	96.4	1.2	2.3	3.5
	25–29	1501	96.1	0.9	2.9	3.8
	30–34	721	94.6	0.8	4.6	5.4
	35–39	201	90.0	1.5	8.5	10.0
	40–44	21	90.5	0.0	9.5	9.5
Vellala						
Middle	<20	739	98.8	0.4	0.8	1.2
	20–24	1194	98.2	0.8	1.1	1.9
	25–29	586	98.6	0.7	0.7	1.4
	30–34	186	98.4	0.5	1.1	1.6
	35–39	37	100.0	0.0	0.0	0.0
	40–44	2	(2)	(0)	(0)	(0)

155

TABLE 3.A.2 * (continued)

Culture and social status	Maternal age	Total pregnancies	Pregnancy outcome as percentage of all pregnancies			
			Live births	Still-births	Abortions	Pregnancy wastage
Vellala (*contd*)						
Low	<20	486	97.3	1.6	1.0	2.6
	20–24	693	98.8	0.1	1.0	1.1
	25–29	402	98.0	0.5	1.5	2.0
	30–34	113	98.2	0.0	1.8	1.8
	35–39	34	94.1	5.9	0.0	5.9
	40–44	1	(1)	(0)	(0)	(0)
Total	<20	1225	98.2	0.9	0.9	1.8
	20–24	1887	98.4	0.5	1.1	1.6
	25–29	988	98.4	0.6	1.0	1.6
	30–34	299	98.3	0.3	1.3	1.6
	35–39	71	97.2	2.8	0.0	2.8
	40–44	3	(3)	(0)	(0)	(0)

* Percentages in parentheses refer to fewer than 25 EW.

3.5% and 3.2%, respectively, in this age group). For Vellalas, all women under age 35 experienced approximately equal risks of pregnancy wastage (between 1.6% and 1.8%). The Vellala rate was lower than the rates for each of the other religious groups for each maternal age group. The differences among the 3 other groups were small. An almost similar pattern was found for abortion and stillbirth taken separately.

Except among the Other Hindus, stillbirth rates closely followed abortion rates throughout most of the age range (Fig. 3.A.1). Stillbirths as a percentage of total births are shown in Table 3.A.3 and Fig. 3.A.3. The relationship of the stillbirth rate to age follows a different pattern for each of the cultural groups. Although generally stillbirths decreased at first with age and then rose, the age group producing the lowest rate varied from the 20–24 year group among Scheduled Castes to the 30–34 year group among Vellalas and Other Hindus and the 35–39 year group among Muslims.

To examine the possibility of selective underreporting or memory lapse, the outcome of the last (and most easily remembered) pregnancy was analysed separately. As shown in Fig. 3.A.4, the pattern of pregnancy outcome for total pregnancies plotted against maternal age compares fairly well with that for the last pregnancy. This suggests that underreporting was more or less uniform and that the pattern of association of pregnancy wastage with family formation may not have been unduly distorted. It is unlikely, for example, that an older woman or a woman with many pregnancies would remember her losses more vividly than a younger woman or a woman with few pregnancies. It may also be added that underreporting seems to have affected abortion more than stillbirth, stillbirth being usually more reliably reported than abortion. In both cases, the pattern rather than the position of the curves should be considered.

156

FIG. 3.A.1. PREGNANCY WASTAGE BY MATERNAL AGE AND CULTURE

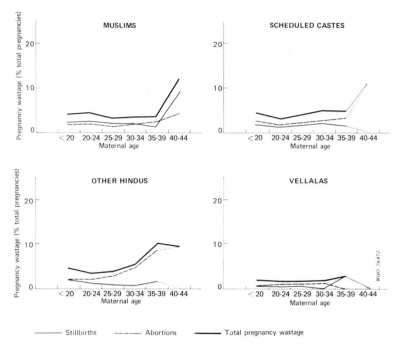

Stillbirths ———— Abortions ———— Total pregnancy wastage

Pregnancy Outcome and Pregnancy Order

Pregnancy wastage remained more or less constant up to the fifth, sixth or seventh pregnancy order and then increased, sharply in the case of the Scheduled Castes and Other Hindus, and less markedly among Muslims and Vellalas (Table 3.A.4). In the former two cases, abortions followed the same pattern, but for Muslims and Vellalas the abortion rate fell for the highest pregnancy orders (Fig. 3.A.5). Stillbirths more clearly described a J-shaped relationship with pregnancy order, but this was least evident for the Scheduled Castes. For the other 3 cultural groups, the fewest stillbirths occurred at the fourth, fifth, and sixth pregnancies, but for Scheduled Castes the third pregnancy was the most favourable (excluding the ninth because only 38 pregnancies of this order were reported).

Again, the outcome of the last pregnancy was analysed separately. As with maternal age, the pattern of pregnancy outcome in relation to birth order for total pregnancies compared fairly well with that for the last pregnancy (Fig. 3.A.4).

Wastage by both Pregnancy Order and Maternal Age

The pooled data presented in Fig. 3.A.6 and Table 3.A.5 permit a further assessment of the "relative effects" of pregnancy order and of maternal age on pregnancy wastage. When pregnancy order was controlled

157

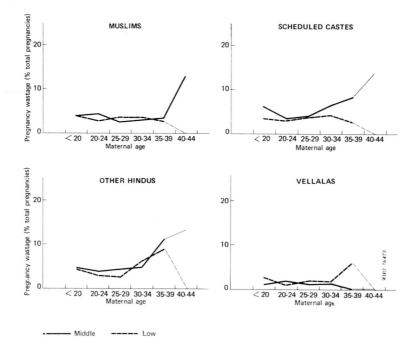

FIG. 3.A.2. PREGNANCY WASTAGE BY MATERNAL AGE,
SOCIAL STATUS, AND CULTURE

TABLE 3.A.3. STILLBIRTHS AS A PERCENTAGE OF TOTAL BIRTHS
BY CULTURE AND MATERNAL AGE *

Maternal age	Muslim		Scheduled Castes		Other Hindus		Vellala	
	Total births	Still-births (%)	Total births	Still-births (%)	Total births	Still-births (%)	Total births	Still-births (%)
<20	2553	2.3	1444	1.7	2063	2.1	1214	0.9
20–24	2461	2.4	1246	1.4	2329	1.2	1867	0.5
25–29	1544	1.9	704	2.0	1457	1.0	978	0.6
30–34	741	1.8	293	2.4	688	0.9	295	0.3
35–39	227	1.3	59	1.7	184	1.6	71	2.8
40–44	24	(8.3)	8	(0.0)	19	(0.0)	3	(0.0)

* Figures in parentheses refer to fewer than 25 EW.

for, wastage for the first, second and fifth pregnancy orders showed no
consistent relationship with maternal age. Pregnancy wastage tended to
describe a reversed J-shape curve, however, with maternal age for the
remaining pregnancy orders.

158

Control for age revealed some fluctuation between pregnancy wastage and pregnancy order. For each age group, the maximum risk occurred at pregnancy order 6 and over, while minimum risks occurred at pregnancy order 1 for women aged 30–34, at pregnancy order 2 for women aged 20–24 and 35–44, and at pregnancy order 5 for women aged under 20 and 25–29.

Pregnancy Wastage by Preceding Pregnancy Interval

Preceding pregnancy interval is defined as the period between the end of the preceding pregnancy and the end of the index pregnancy. Obviously then, the first pregnancy must be excluded from the analysis. The risk of poor pregnancy outcome (as shown in Table 3.A.6 and Fig. 3.A.7) was highest when the interval was less than one year, dropped steeply for intervals of one or under two years, and then remained more or less stable for intervals of 2–6 years or longer, when it increased slightly.

A high proportion of pregnancies terminated as abortions when the interval was less than one year. This interval was necessarily shorter than it otherwise would have been since the index pregnancy ended before term. With intervals of 2–5 years the percentage of abortions remained more or

FIG. 3.A.3. STILLBIRTHS AS A PERCENTAGE OF TOTAL BIRTHS, BY CULTURE AND MATERNAL AGE

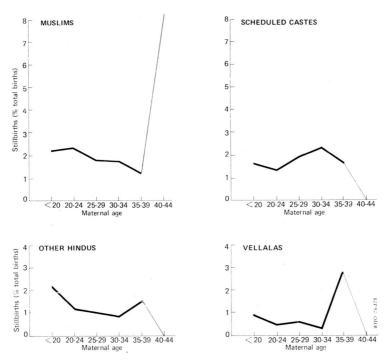

159

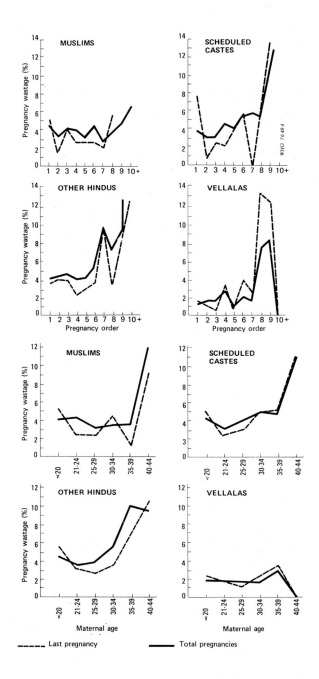

160

TABLE 3.A.4. PREGNANCY OUTCOME BY CULTURE AND PREGNANCY ORDER

Culture	Pregnancy order	Total preg-nancies	Pregnancy outcome as percentage of total pregnancies			
			Live births	Still-births	Abor-tions	Pregnancy wastage
Muslim	1	1745	95.5	2.8	1.7	4.5
	2	1512	96.8	2.0	1.3	3.3
	3	1265	95.9	1.8	2.3	4.1
	4	1007	96.2	1.8	2.0	3.8
	5	776	96.8	1.8	1.4	3.2
	6	552	95.7	2.0	2.4	4.4
	7	358	97.5	2.0	0.6	2.6
	8	215	96.3	2.3	1.4	3.7
	9	125	95.2	2.4	2.4	4.8
	10 and over	126	93.7	5.6	0.8	6.4
Scheduled Castes	1	917	96.2	1.6	2.2	3.8
	2	803	97.0	1.4	1.6	3.0
	3	664	97.0	1.2	1.8	3.0
	4	533	95.7	1.7	2.6	4.3
	5	394	96.2	1.5	2.3	3.8
	6	252	94.8	2.8	2.4	5.2
	7	143	94.4	3.5	2.6	5.6
	8	77	94.8	1.3	3.9	5.2
	9	38	89.5	0.0	10.5	10.5
	10 and over	21	71.4	9.5	19.0	28.5
Other Hindus	1	1760	96.4	1.9	1.8	3.7
	2	1508	96.2	1.4	2.5	3.9
	3	1198	95.9	1.2	2.9	4.1
	4	903	96.3	1.0	2.7	3.7
	5	656	96.3	1.1	2.6	3.7
	6	428	95.1	0.9	4.0	4.9
	7	242	90.9	1.2	7.9	9.1
	8	130	93.1	1.5	5.4	6.9
	9	68	91.2	1.5	7.4	8.9
	10 and over	50	74.0	4.0	22.0	26.0
Vellala	1	1393	98.7	0.9	0.4	1.3
	2	1162	98.3	0.3	1.4	1.7
	3	835	98.4	0.6	1.0	1.6
	4	529	97.4	0.8	1.9	2.7
	5	302	99.0	0.3	0.7	1.0
	6	145	97.9	0.0	2.1	2.1
	7	63	98.4	1.6	0.0	1.6
	8	27	92.6	7.4	0.0	7.4
	9	12	91.7	8.3	0.0	8.3
	10 and over	5	(5) [a]	0.0	0·0	0.0

[a] Refers to fewer than 25 EW.

less the same, while for intervals of more than 5 years the percentage showed an upward trend. In case of stillbirths, when shortening of the interval due to the length of the index pregnancy was minimal, the rates described almost the same pattern, the highest risks occurring for intervals less than one or two years.

FIG. 3.A.5. PREGNANCY WASTAGE BY CULTURE AND PREGNANCY ORDER

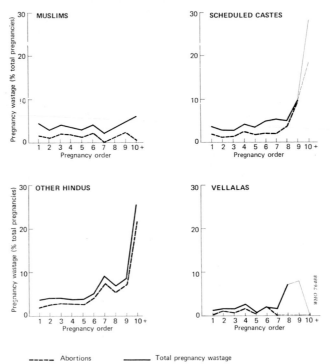

----- Abortions   —— Total pregnancy wastage

FIG. 3.A.6. PREGNANCY WASTAGE BY MATERNAL AGE AND PREGNANCY ORDER
FOR ALL AREAS COMBINED

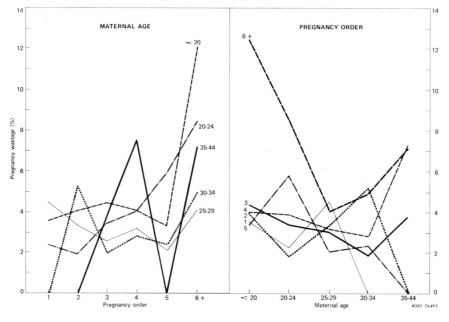

TABLE 3.A.5. PREGNANCY WASTAGE BY PREGNANCY ORDER AND MATERNAL AGE
FOR ALL CULTURES COMBINED

Maternal age	Pregnancy wastage (%) for pregnancy order :					
	1	2	3	4	5	6 and over
<20	3.6	4.1	4.5	4.1	3.4	12.5
20–24	2.4	1.9	3.4	4.0	5.9	8.6
25–29	4.7	3.5	2.7	3.3	2.2	4.2
30–34	0.0	5.4	2.0	2.9	2.5	5.1
35–44	—	0.0	4.0	7.7	0.0	7.5

TABLE 3.A.6. PREGNANCY WASTAGE BY DURATION OF PRECEDING
PREGNANCY INTERVAL FOR ALL CULTURES COMBINED

Preceding pregnancy interval (years)	Total pregnancies other than first	Pregnancy outcome as percentage of total pregnancies		
		Stillbirths	Abortions	Total fetal wastage
<1	305	6.9	21.6	28.5
1–2	4667	2.3	2.8	5.1
2–3	6929	1.0	1.5	2.5
3–4	3261	1.0	1.5	2.5
4–5	959	1.3	1.3	2.6
5–6	514	0.2	1.9	2.1
6 and over	489	1.2	1.8	3.0

FIG. 3.A.7. PREGNANCY WASTAGE BY DURATION OF PRECEDING PREGNANCY
INTERVAL FOR ALL CULTURES COMBINED

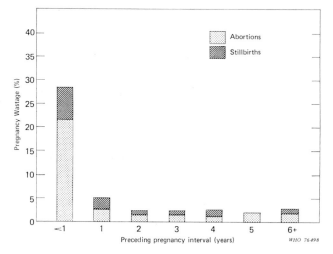

B. TEHERAN

B. D. Navidi-Kasmaii and V. Nahapetian

Pregnancy Wastage and Social Characteristics

Out of the 16 707 pregnancies reported by the 4209 women in the study, 243 (1.5%) resulted in stillbirths and 1834 (11%) in abortions. In other words, for the eligible women as a whole, more than 12 out of every 100 pregnancies were wasted.

Overall wastage was higher for Armenians than for Muslims (13.4% compared with 11.5%), and within each culture wastage was higher for those of middle social status than for those of low status. Abortion rates followed the same pattern as total wastage rates; stillbirth rates, on the other hand, were higher among low status than middle status Muslims, with almost no difference by social status among Armenians (Table 3.B.1).

The positive association between pregnancy wastage and social status was not in accordance with expectations and probably suggests that induced abortions were more often used as a method of birth control by middle status women, or perhaps that there was relative underreporting of pregnancy outcome by low status women. The figures for abortion represent both those occurring spontaneously and those induced deliberately. This issue will be discussed further below.

Pregnancy Wastage and Maternal Age

There was a marked relationship between pregnancy wastage and maternal age. Pregnancy wastage rose with the age of the pregnant women and the rise became increasingly steep as they approached the end of the childbearing period (Table 3.B.2 and Fig. 3.B.1). This pattern was evident for pregnancies occurring to women of both cultures, but pregnancy wastage was higher among Armenians than among Muslims for all maternal age groups, except those under 25.

Abortions accounted for the greater part of pregnancy wastage and abortion rates increased directly with maternal age. The curve for stillbirths in relation to maternal age described more or less a J-shape. That is, they were highest for the oldest women and lowest for those in their twenties (Fig. 3.B.2). This pattern is clearest when stillbirths are taken as a percentage of all births rather than of total pregnancies (Table 3.B.3 and Fig. 3.B.3). No matter what base was used for calculating the stillbirth rates, however, they were lowest in the 20–29 age range, while abortion rates were lowest for women whose pregnancies ended before they were 20 years old.

TABLE 3.B.1. PREGNANCY WASTAGE BY CULTURE AND SOCIAL STATUS

Culture and social status	No. of pregnancies	Stillbirths (%)	Abortions (%)
Muslim			
Middle	2992	0.8	13.4
Low	5661	1.5	8.7
Total	8653	1.2	10.3
Armenian			
Middle	3240	1.8	14.7
Low	4809	1.6	9.6
Total	8049	1.7	11.7

TABLE 3.B.2. PREGNANCY OUTCOME BY CULTURE, SOCIAL STATUS, AND MATERNAL AGE *

Culture and social status	Maternal age	Total preg-nancies	Pregnancy outcome as percentage of all pregnancies			
			Live births	Still-births	Abor-tions	Pregnancy wastage
Muslim						
Middle	<20	1089	89.3	1.1	9.6	10.7
	20–24	1032	88.5	0.7	10.9	11.6
	25–29	543	85.3	0.4	14.4	14.8
	30–34	239	69.9	0.8	29.3	30.1
	35–39	78	62.8	0.0	37.2	37.2
	40–44	11	(27.3)	(0.0)	(72.7)	(72.7)
Low	<20	1845	91.3	1.6	7.1	8.7
	20–24	1915	90.7	1.1	8.1	9.2
	25–29	1131	90.0	1.6	8.4	10.0
	30–34	565	85.1	1.6	13.3	14.9
	35–39	179	79.3	2.8	17.9	20.7
	40–44	26	76.9	3.8	19.2	23.0
Total	<20	2934	90.6	1.4	8.0	9.4
	20–24	2947	88.9	1.0	9.1	10.1
	25–29	1674	88.5	1.2	10.3	11.5
	30–34	804	80.6	1.4	18.0	19.4
	35–39	257	74.3	1.9	23.7	25.7
	40–44	37	62.2	2.7	35.1	37.8
Armenian						
Middle	<20	771	89.9	2.2	7.9	10.1
	20–24	1382	86.7	1.6	11.7	13.3
	25–29	700	78.4	1.3	20.3	21.6
	30–34	305	72.5	2.6	24.9	27.5
	35–39	70	57.1	2.9	40.0	42.9
	40–44	12	(33.3)	(0.0)	(66.7)	(66.7)
Low	<20	893	94.1	1.7	4.3	6.0
	20–24	1746	93.0	1.7	5.3	7.0
	25–29	1299	87.1	1.7	11.2	12.9
	30–34	675	80.0	1.3	18.7	20.0
	35–39	181	67.4	1.7	30.9	32.6
	40–44	15	(73.3)	(0.0)	(26.7)	(26.7)
Total	<20	1664	92.1	1.9	5.9	7.8
	20–24	3128	90.2	1.7	8.1	9.8
	25–29	1999	84.0	1.6	14.4	16.0
	30–34	980	77.7	1.7	20.6	22.3
	35–39	251	64.5	2.0	33.5	35.5
	40–44	27	55.6	0.0	44.4	44.4

* Percentages in parentheses refer to fewer than 25 EW.

FIG. 3.B.1. TOTAL PREGNANCY WASTAGE BY MATERNAL AGE, CULTURE, AND SOCIAL STATUS

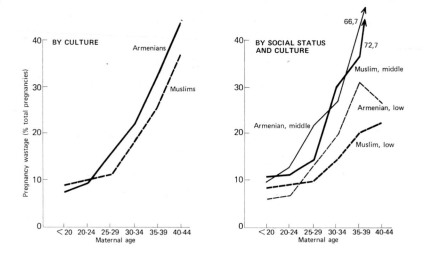

FIG. 3.B.2. ABORTIONS AND STILLBIRTHS BY CULTURE AND MATERNAL AGE

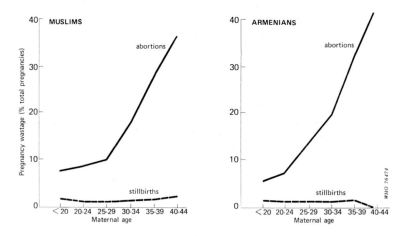

Maternal age	Muslims		Armenians	
	Total births	Stillbirths %	Total births	Stillbirths %
<20	2699	1.5	1565	2.0
20–24	2679	1.5	2874	1.8
25–29	1501	1.3	1711	1.8
30–34	659	1.7	778	2.2
35–39	196	2.6	167	3.0
40–44	24	(4.2)	15	(0.0)

* Percentages in parentheses refer to fewer than 25 EW.

In both cultural groups, pregnancy wastage was considerably less for women of low social status than for those of middle status in each maternal age range. This again suggests either greater selective underreporting by low status women or more probably, greater use of induced abortion by middle status women.

To examine the possibility that there may have been selective under-reporting or memory lapse, the outcome of the last (and most easily remembered) pregnancy was analysed separately. As shown in Fig. 3.B.4, the pattern of wastage for the last pregnancy conforms fairly closely with that of all pregnancies by maternal age. This suggests that underreporting was more or less uniform and that the pattern of association of pregnancy wastage with family formation may not have been unduly distorted.

Pregnancy Wastage and Pregnancy Order

After the second pregnancy, pregnancy wastage in both cultural groups rose steeply with pregnancy order, but the rise was steeper for Armenians than for Muslims, among whom the rate rose from 7.9% of the second pregnancies to 28.8% of the tenth and later pregnancies. For Armenians the corresponding rates were 7.4% and 39.8% (Table 3.B.4 and Fig. 3.B.5). For both Muslims and Armenians, abortion rates, which accounted for most of the difference, rose directly with pregnancy order, and stillbirth rates described a shallow J-shape, with the lowest rates occurring at preg-nancy order 3. Again, the relationship was most marked when stillbirths were taken as a percentage of births at each pregnancy order.

Because of the unexpected direction of the relationship between social status and age-specific pregnancy wastage, it seemed worth while to examine differences between the effects of pregnancy order on pregnancy wastage in the two cultural groups. In both of them, and for every pregnancy order except the first, the pregnancies of middle status women were more often lost than those of low status women. Moreover, the slight decline between

FIG. 3.B.3. STILLBIRTHS AS A PERCENTAGE OF TOTAL BIRTHS,
BY MATERNAL AGE AND BY CULTURE AND SOCIAL STATUS

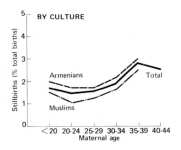

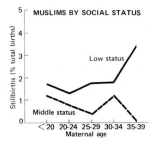

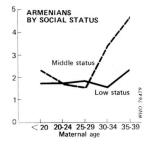

FIG. 3.B.4. PREGNANCY WASTAGE BY CULTURE, MATERNAL AGE, AND
PREGNANCY ORDER, FOR TOTAL PREGNANCIES AND FOR LAST PREGNANCY

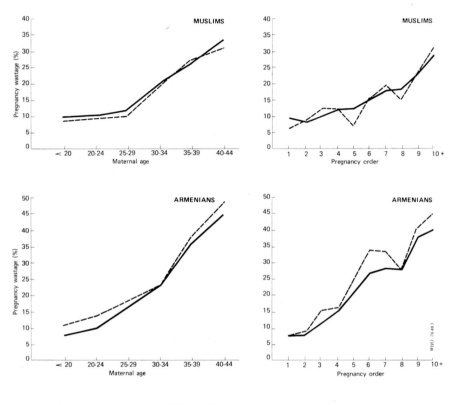

----- Last pregnancy   ——— Total pregnancies

TABLE 3.B.4. PREGNANCY OUTCOME BY CULTURE AND PREGNANCY ORDER

Culture	Pregnancy order	Total preg-nancies	Pregnancy outcome as percentage of total pregnancies			
			Live births	Still-births	Abor-tions	Pregnancy wastage
Muslim	1	1934	91.3	1.9	6.8	8.7
	2	1700	92.2	0.8	7.1	7.9
	3	1385	89.9	0.7	9.4	10.1
	4	1079	88.1	0.9	10.9	11.8
	5	821	87.8	1.0	11.2	12.2
	6	597	84.6	1.5	13.9	14.4
	7	416	82.5	1.9	15.6	17.5
	8	287	81.5	1.0	17.4	18.4
	9	180	76.7	2.8	20.6	23.4
	10 or more	254	71.3	2.0	26.8	28.8
Armenian	1	1940	92.9	2.1	5.0	7.1
	2	1687	92.6	1.6	5.8	7.4
	3	1386	89.4	1.2	9.5	10.7
	4	1056	84.9	1.4	13.6	15.0
	5	782	79.2	1.4	19.4	20.8
	6	513	73.9	2.3	23.8	26.1
	7	307	72.0	2.6	25.4	28.0
	8	186	72.6	2.7	24.7	27.4
	9	99	62.6	2.0	35.4	37.4
	10 or more	93	60.2	1.1	38.7	39.8

the first and second pregnancy was entirely confined to the low status group ; for the middle status group wastage soared with pregnancy order, almost without interruption (Fig. 3.B.5, lower half). This again suggests either more underreporting by low status women or a greater use of induced abortion by middle status women.

Again, the last pregnancy was analysed separately, and it was found that, as with maternal age, the relationship between the last pregnancy and pregnancy order was similar to that between all pregnancies and pregnancy order (Fig. 3.B.4).

Wastage by both Pregnancy Order and Maternal Age

Pregnancy wastage by both pregnancy order and maternal age is given in Table 3.B.5 and Fig. 3.B.6. The data refer to both Muslims and Armenians together because of the small numbers of pregnancies. Although there were fluctuations in both the youngest (<20) and the oldest (35–44) age groups, control for age showed that for a given age group wastage tended to rise with each pregnancy order.

Controlling for pregnancy order, the curve for pregnancy wastage rates plotted against maternal age tended to be J-shaped or U-shape for all pregnancy orders, the lowest risks occurring at ages 20–29. For younger mothers, especially those under 20, any pregnancy beyond the third

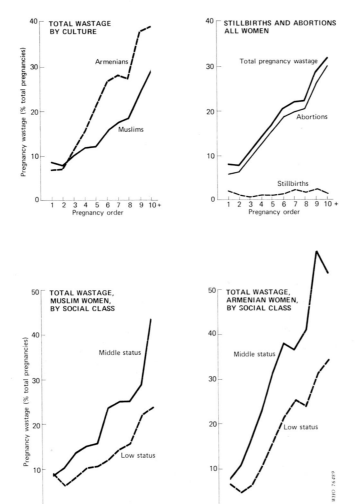

171

TABLE 3.B.5. PREGNANCY WASTAGE BY PREGNANCY ORDER AND MATERNAL AGE
FOR BOTH CULTURES COMBINED *

Maternal age	Pregnancy wastage (%) for pregnancy order:					
	1	2	3	4	5	6 and over
<20	8.2	8.8	9.2	22.9	(13.0)	(33.3)
20–24	6.4	6.4	10.8	12.5	16.7	19.9
25–29	10.8	7.2	9.1	12.9	15.0	18.9
30–34	(18.2)	17.1	14.9	15.5	17.9	23.5
35–44	(—)	(22.2)	(11.1)	(20.0)	30.2	33.0

* Figures in parentheses refer to fewer than 25 EW.

was more likely to end in an abortion or a stillbirth, as were pregnancies of all orders (except the third) when the mothers were aged 30 or older. The sixth or later pregnancy carried a high risk at all ages, the risks increasing steeply when pregnancies occurred too early or too late in the reproductive span.

Pregnancy Wastage by Preceding Pregnancy Interval

Preceding pregnancy interval is defined as the period between the end of the preceding pregnancy and the end of the index pregnancy. The first pregnancy must consequently be excluded from the analysis. The risk of poor pregnancy outcome plotted against preceding birth intervals formed a reversed J-shape (Fig. 3.B.7). Wastage was highest for intervals of less than one year (66%), fell steeply for the interval between 1 and 2 years (22.7%) and between 2 and 3 years (9.4%), and then declined more gradually to a rate of 6.3% for the interval between 3 and 4 years. Thereafter, the trend increased to 8.9%, 13.5%, and 21.2% for intervals of 4, 5, and 6 or more years, respectively (Table 3.B.6).

TABLE 3.B.6. PREGNANCY OUTCOME BY DURATION OF PRECEDING
PREGNANCY INTERVAL FOR BOTH CULTURES COMBINED

Duration of interval (years)	Total pregnancies	Pregnancy outcome as percentage of total pregnancies			
		Live births	Stillbirths	Abortions	Pregnancy wastage
<1	206	34.0	0.0	66.0	66.0
1–2	3605	77.3	2.2	20.5	22.7
2–3	4505	90.6	0.9	8.4	9.4
3–4	2445	93.7	0.5	5.4	6.3
4–5	1107	91.1	2.1	8.4	8.9
5–6	484	86.6	0.6	11.4	13.5
6 and over	480	84.2	1.3	15.2	15.8

172

FIG. 3.B.6. PREGNANCY WASTAGE BY MATERNAL AGE AND PREGNANCY ORDER
FOR BOTH CULTURES COMBINED

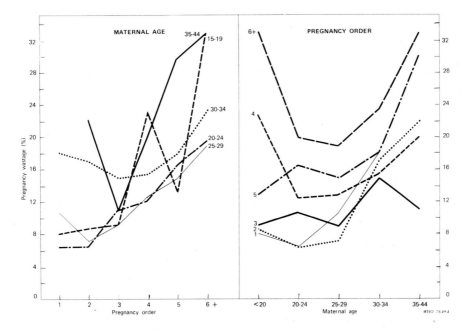

FIG. 3.B.7. PREGNANCY WASTAGE BY DURATION OF PRECEDING
PREGNANCY INTERVAL FOR BOTH CULTURES COMBINED

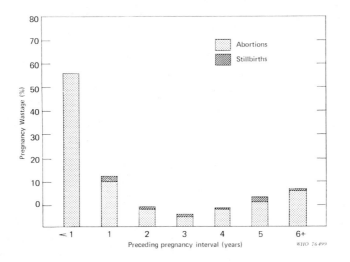

173

The J-shaped relationship is entirely accounted for by abortions. Still-births were highest for the interval between 1 and 2 years (2.2%) and the interval between 5 and 6 years (2.1%).

Some association between short intervals and wastage necessarily follows from the definition of preceding pregnancy interval. This interval is shorter than it would otherwise have been if the index pregnancy ended before term. At the other extreme, the increase in wastage with longer intervals may be due to a direct relationship between interval length and maternal age.

C. BEIRUT

C. Churchill, I. Lorfing, H. Zurayk and J. Azar

Pregnancy Outcome

Of the 14 955 pregnancies reported by the 3004 women in the study, 176 (1.2%) were stillbirths and 2511 (16.8%) were abortions. That is, for the eligible women as a whole, 18 out of every 100 pregnancies were wasted.

Pregnancy Wastage and Social Characteristics

Wastage was lower for Shiites than for Maronites (15.7% compared with 20.7%). The difference was almost entirely due to abortions, which terminated 19.6% of pregnancies in Maronite women and 14.5% in Shiite women (Table 3.C.1).

TABLE 3.C.1. PREGNANCY WASTAGE BY CULTURE AND SOCIAL STATUS

Culture and social status	No. of pregnancies	Stillbirths (%)	Abortions (%)
Shiite			
Middle	3654	1.3	15.8
Low	4661	1.2	13.5
Total	8315	1.2	14.5
Maronite			
Middle	3710	0.9	20.7
Low	2930	1.4	18.3
Total	6640	1.1	19.6

There was little difference in stillbirth rates between middle status and low status Shiites (1.3% and 1.2%, respectively), but among Maronites, middle status women experienced a lower stillbirth rate (0.9%) than that of low status women (1.4%).

174

TABLE 3.C.2. PREGNANCY OUTCOME BY CULTURE, SOCIAL STATUS,
AND MATERNAL AGE *

Culture and social status	Maternal age	Total preg- nancies	Pregnancy outcome as percentage of total pregnancies			
			Live births	Still- births	Abor- tions	Pregnancy wastage
Shiite Middle	<20	658	83.1	1.8	15.0	16.8
	20–24	1250	86.1	1.0	13.0	14.0
	25–29	911	85.1	1.1	13.8	14.9
	30–34	566	81.1	1.4	17.5	18.9
	35–39	225	67.1	1.8	31.1	32.9
	40–44	44	47.7	0.0	52.3	52.3
Low	<20	863	87.6	1.4	11.0	12.4
	20–24	1650	86.7	1.0	12.3	13.3
	25–29	1199	84.9	1.0	14.1	15.1
	30–34	656	84.6	1.5	13.9	15.4
	35–39	257	75.1	1.9	23.0	24.9
	40–44	36	61.1	5.6	33.3	38.9
Total	<20	1521	85.7	1.6	12.8	14.4
	20–24	2900	86.4	1.0	12.6	13.6
	25–29	2110	85.0	1.0	14.0	15.0
	30–34	1222	83.0	1.5	15.5	17.0
	35–39	482	71.4	1.9	26.8	28.7
	40–44	80	53.7	2.5	43.8	46.3
Maronite Middle	<20	441	80.7	0.5	18.8	19.3
	20–24	1241	85.3	0.6	14.1	14.7
	25–29	1139	80.3	0.9	18.8	19.7
	30–34	629	69.3	1.3	29.4	30.7
	35–39	236	58.1	1.7	40.3	42.0
	40–44	24	(37.5)	(0.0)	(62.5)	(62.5)
Low	<20	352	86.6	1.4	11.9	13.3
	20–24	944	84.7	0.5	14.7	15.2
	25–29	921	78.9	1.7	19.3	21.0
	30–34	535	75.3	2.2	22.4	24.6
	35–39	165	67.9	1.8	30.3	32.1
	40–44	13	(46.2)	(0.0)	(53.8)	(53.8)
Total	<20	793	83.4	0.9	15.8	16.7
	20–24	2185	85.0	0.6	14.4	15.0
	25–29	2060	79.7	1.3	19.0	20.3
	30–34	1164	72.1	1.7	26.2	27.9
	35–39	401	62.1	1.7	36.2	37.0
	40–44	37	40.5	0.0	59.5	59.5

* Percentages in parentheses refer to fewer than 25 EW.

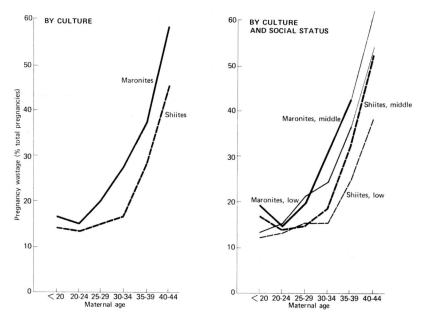

Pregnancy Wastage and Maternal Age

Pregnancy wastage rates described a J-shaped curve when plotted against maternal age at the time the pregnancy terminated. After a small initial decline for women in the early twenties, wastage rose increasingly steeply, reaching about 50% of all pregnancies at age 40–44 (Table 3.C.2). This same pattern was evident for both Shiite and Maronite women, but at each maternal age, wastage was greater for Maronites than for Shiites (Fig. 3.C.1). The maternal age associated with the lowest risks of wastage was 20–24 for both Shiite and Maronite women, whose wastage rates at this age were 13.6% and 15.0%, respectively.

By far the greater part of pregnancy wastage was accounted for by abortions. Abortion rates showed a J-shaped relationship to maternal age in both cultural groups, with Maronite rates being higher than Shiite rates at each age range. In each cultural group, stillbirth rates varied little with maternal age; in addition, there was little difference in rates between Shiite women and Maronite women (Fig. 3.C.2).

For most age groups and in both cultures, women of middle social status reported more wastage than those of low status. The difference, again, was almost entirely due to abortions in both cultures. Stillbirth rates for Shiites differed little for the two social status groups, while among Maronites, although the differences were small, low status women reported a higher proportion of stillbirths than middle status women at most ages.

FIG. 3.C.2. ABORTIONS AND STILLBIRTHS BY CULTURE AND MATERNAL AGE

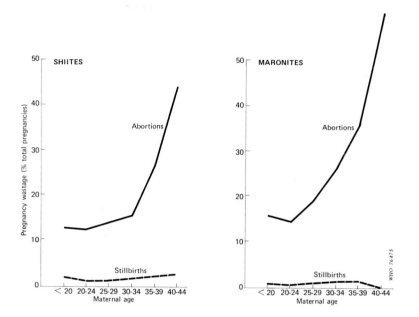

Stillbirths as a percentage of total births are shown in Table 3.C.3 and Fig. 3.C.3. Stillbirth rates showed a J-shaped relationship to maternal age, with the lowest rate occurring at the maternal age range 20–24 years for both Shiite and Maronite women.

The figures for abortion referred to both spontaneous and induced abortions. The positive association with social status suggests that low status women selectively underreported their abortions and/or, perhaps, that middle status women used induced abortion more frequently than low status women as a birth control method. It will be remembered that

TABLE 3.C.3. STILLBIRTHS AS A PERCENTAGE OF TOTAL BIRTHS, BY CULTURE AND MATERNAL AGE

Maternal age	Shiites		Maronites	
	Total births	Stillbirths (%)	Total births	Stillbirths (%)
<20	1327	1.8	668	1.0
20–24	2535	1.1	1871	0.7
25–29	1815	1.2	1668	1.6
30–34	1032	1.7	859	2.3
35–39	353	2.5	256	2.7
40–44	45	4.4	15	(0.0) [a]

[a] Refers to fewer than 25 EW.

177

voluntary abortion is a well established custom in Lebanon. Women discuss the subject freely among themselves, indicating its social acceptability, and although the practice is illegal, abortions are readily available. However, pregnancy wastage and maternal age exhibit a J-shaped relationship in all age groups and this cannot be explained by differences in induced abortion rates. It is highly unlikely that older women would resort to induced abortion more frequently than women in the younger age groups, at least not to the extent shown in Table 3.C.2 and Fig. 3.C.2. Thus, at least some of the rise in wastage with age must have been due to increases in spontaneous abortion rates, in addition to the relative increase in stillbirth rates.

To examine the possibility that there may have been selective under-reporting or memory lapse, the outcome of the last (and most easily remembered) pregnancy was analysed separately. As shown in Fig. 3.C.4, the pattern for total pregnancies in relation to maternal age compares fairly well with that for the last pregnancy. This suggests that underreporting was more or less uniform and that the pattern of association of pregnancy wastage with family formation may not have been unduly distorted.

Pregnancy Wastage and Pregnancy Order

On the whole, pregnancy wastage increased with pregnancy order, although there was a small decline in the wastage rates among Shiites

FIG. 3.C.3. STILLBIRTHS AS A PERCENTAGE OF TOTAL BIRTHS, BY CULTURE, SOCIAL STATUS, AND MATERNAL AGE

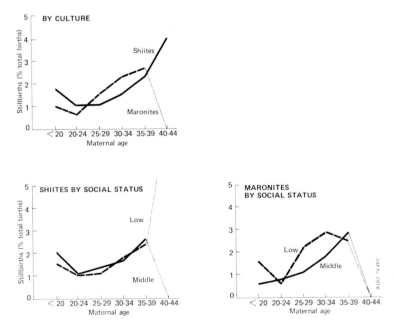

178

between the first and second, and between the second and third pregnancies. The general increase was considerably greater for Maronite than for Shiite women, although rates for the first and second pregnancies were very similar in the two groups (Table 3.C.4 and Fig. 3.C.5).

Most of the rise in wastage with increasing pregnancy order was due to abortion. Stillbirth rates remained low and fluctuated with pregnancy order, although they clearly rose for pregnancy orders of 10 or higher in both cultural groups.

Again, the outcome of the last pregnancy was analysed separately, and, as was the case with maternal age, the results in each cultural group were similar to those for all pregnancies (Fig. 3.C.4).

FIG. 3.C.4. PREGNANCY WASTAGE BY CULTURE, MATERNAL AGE, AND
PREGNANCY ORDER, FOR TOTAL PREGNANCIES AND FOR LAST PREGNANCY

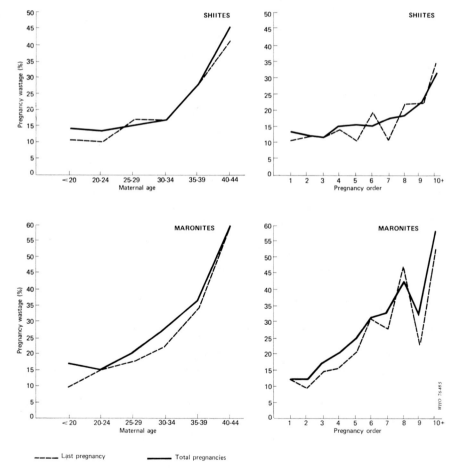

TABLE 3.C.4. PREGNANCY OUTCOME BY CULTURE AND PREGNANCY ORDER

Culture	Pregnancy order	Total pregnancies	Pregnancy outcome as percentage of total pregnancies			
			Live births	Still-births	Abor-tions	Pregnancy wastage
Shiite	1	1434	86.8	1.6	11.6	13.2
	2	1298	87.6	1.4	11.0	12.4
	3	1165	87.9	0.7	11.4	12.1
	4	995	85.0	0.9	14.1	15.0
	5	854	84.7	1.2	14.2	15.4
	6	679	84.7	0.6	14.7	15.3
	7	529	82.8	1.3	15.9	17.2
	8	410	81.0	1.5	17.6	19.1
	9	302	77.5	1.7	20.9	22.6
	10 and over	649	69.3	2.0	28.7	30.7
Maronite	1	1364	87.8	1.3	10.9	12.2
	2	1245	87.9	0.7	11.4	12.1
	3	1079	82.9	1.0	16.0	17.0
	4	877	79.7	0.6	19.7	20.3
	5	699	75.6	1.5	22.9	24.4
	6	472	68.6	1.1	30.3	31.4
	7	332	67.2	1.5	31.3	32.8
	8	225	57.3	1.3	41.3	42.6
	9	144	68.8	0.0	31.3	31.3
	10 and over	233	41.6	3.0	55.4	58.4

Wastage by Both Pregnancy Order and Maternal Age

Data for pregnancy wastage by both birth order and maternal age are given in Table 3.C.5 and Fig. 3.C.6 (because of the small numbers, the data for Shiite and for Maronite women have been combined).

Controlling for maternal age, age groups 20–24 and 25–29 had higher wastage rates for later order pregnancies than for earlier pregnancies. However, for the under 20, 30–34, and 35–44 age groups, there was no definite trend.

For most pregnancy orders, wastage was greatest at the extremes of the age range and therefore least at intermediate ages.

Wastage by Preceding Pregnancy Interval

Preceding pregnancy interval is defined as the period between the end of the preceding pregnancy and the end of the index pregnancy. Thus, the first pregnancy has to be excluded from the analysis. The curve for wastage by preceding pregnancy interval formed a reverse J-shape, starting with a wastage rate of 49.1% for intervals of less than one year, decreasing to a low rate of 8.7% for 3-year intervals, and then rising to 18% for intervals of 6 or more years (Table 3.C.6 and Fig. 3.C.7).

FIG. 3.C.5. PREGNANCY WASTAGE BY PREGNANCY ORDER AND CULTURE

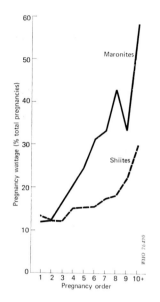

TABLE 3.C.5. PREGNANCY WASTAGE BY PREGNANCY ORDER AND MATERNAL AGE FOR BOTH CULTURES COMBINED

Maternal age	Pregnancy wastage (%) for pregnancy order :					
	1	2	3	4	5	6 and over
<20	13.5	14.2	17.0	36.7	21.1	37.5
20–24	11.2	10.8	13.6	15.9	21.3	25.5
25–29	13.3	10.9	13.2	16.1	17.3	24.3
30–34	17.9	21.0	18.5	19.7	17.2	24.6
35–44	25.0	35.3	34.8	16.3	34.8	36.0

A higher proportion of pregnancies terminated as abortions when the interval was less than 1 year. It should be noted, however, that a preceding interval was, by definition, shorter after an abortion than it otherwise would have been if the index pregnancy had been carried to term. For intervals between 2 and 6 years, the percentage of abortions remained more or less the same, while for intervals of 6 or more years, the abortion rates showed an upward trend. The stillbirth rates showed more fluctuation ; the rates remained stable for intervals of less than 1 year and for 1 year, decreased to 0.9% and 0.4% for 2-year and 3-year intervals respectively, rose to 0.8% and 1.1% for 5-year and 6-year intervals respectively, and dropped to 0.6% for intervals of 6 or more years.

181

FIG. 3.C.6. PREGNANCY WASTAGE BY MATERNAL AGE AND PREGNANCY ORDER FOR BOTH CULTURES COMBINED

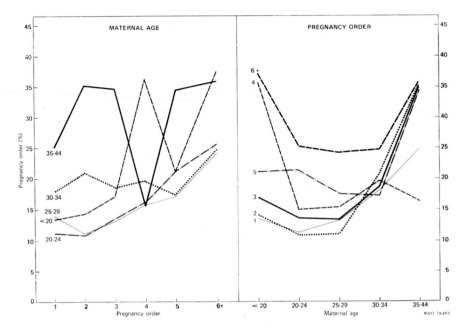

TABLE 3.C.6. PREGNANCY OUTCOME BY DURATION OF PRECEDING PREGNANCY INTERVAL FOR BOTH CULTURES COMBINED

Duration of interval (years)	Total pregnancies	Pregnancy outcome as percentage of total pregnancies			
		Live births	Stillbirths	Abortions	Pregnancy wastage
<1	957	51.0	1.3	47.8	49.1
1–2	5258	77.9	1.4	20.7	22.1
2–3	3944	88.9	0.9	10.2	11.1
3–4	1209	91.3	0.4	8.3	8.7
4–5	374	89.3	0.8	9.9	10.7
5–6	174	88.5	1.1	10.3	11.4
6 and over	1721	82.0	0.6	17.4	18.0

182

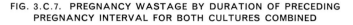

FIG. 3.C.7. PREGNANCY WASTAGE BY DURATION OF PRECEDING
PREGNANCY INTERVAL FOR BOTH CULTURES COMBINED

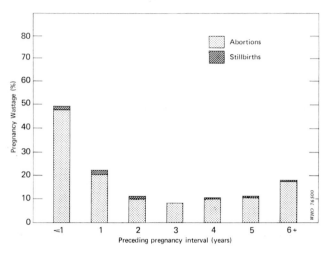

D. MANILA

V. Balderrama-Guzman, G. B. Roman and S. Ignacio-Morelos

Pregnancy Wastage and Social Status

Of the 16 017 pregnancies reported by the 3998 women in the study, 154 (1.0%) resulted in stillbirths and 1258 (7.9%) in abortion. That is, for the eligible women as a whole, almost 9 out of every 100 pregnancies were wasted.

Wastage was somewhat higher for the urban women (9.2%) than for the rural women (8.5%). Within each residential group, slightly more of the middle status women's pregnancies were wasted than were those of the low status group (in rural areas, 8.5% and 8.1%, respectively ; in urban areas, 9.4% and 8.9%, respectively ; see Table 3.D.1).

These groups may have differed in the timing and duration of their exposure to risk, and it will be shown later that while the difference between urban and rural women was consistently maintained when other variables were controlled, the social status difference was not.

Pregnancy Outcome and Maternal Age

There was a clear and J-shaped relationship between pregnancy wastage rates and maternal age in both the rural and urban areas. Pregnancy wastage decreased for women in the early twenties, remained more or less stable until the end of their third decade, and then rose increasingly steeply

183

as they approached the end of the childbearing period (Table 3.D.2 and Fig. 3.D.1).

The J-shaped relationship was most evident for abortions, which comprised the greater part of pregnancy wastage. In the rural area, stillbirth

TABLE 3.D.1. PREGNANCY OUTCOME BY RESIDENCE AND SOCIAL STATUS

Residence and social status	No. of pregnancies	Stillbirths (%)	Abortions (%)
Rural			
Middle	6692	1.0	7.5
Low	1869	0.9	7.2
Total	8561	1.0	7.5
Urban			
Middle	6411	0.9	8.5
Low	1045	1.4	7.5
Total	7456	0.9	8.3

FIG. 3.D.1. PREGNANCY WASTAGE BY MATERNAL AGE, RESIDENCE, AND SOCIAL STATUS

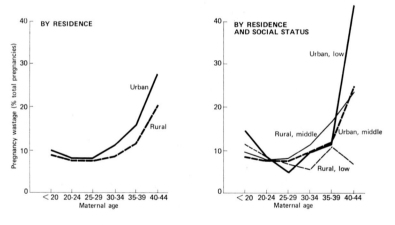

FIG. 3.D.2. ABORTIONS AND STILLBIRTHS BY RESIDENCE AND MATERNAL AGE

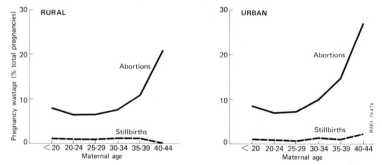

TABLE 3.D.2. PREGNANCY OUTCOME BY RESIDENCE, SOCIAL STATUS,
AND MATERNAL AGE *

Residence, social status and maternal age	Total pregnancies	Pregnancy outcome as percentage of total pregnancies			
		Live births	Stillbirths	Abortions	Pregnancy wastage
RURAL					
Middle					
<20	726	91.3	1.4	7.3	8.7
20–24	2269	92.6	0.8	6.7	7.5
25–29	2052	92.3	0.9	6.8	7.7
30–34	1139	90.5	1.3	8.2	9.5
35–39	439	87.7	1.1	11.2	12.3
40–44	67	74.6	0.0	25.4	25.4
Total	6692	91.5	1.0	7.5	8.5
Low					
<20	258	88.4	1.2	10.5	11.7
20–24	622	91.8	1.1	7.1	8.2
25–29	518	93.1	1.0	6.0	7.0
30–34	323	94.1	0.3	5.6	5.9
35–39	133	88.7	0.8	10.5	11.3
40–44	15	(93.3)	(0.0)	(6.7)	(6.7)
Total	1869	91.9	0.9	7.2	8.1
All rural					
<20	984	90.5	1.3	8.1	9.4
20–24	2891	92.4	0.9	6.7	7.6
25–29	2570	92.4	0.9	6.7	7.6
30–34	1462	91.3	1.1	7.6	8.7
35–39	572	87.9	1.0	11.0	12.0
40–44	82	78.0	0.0	22.0	22.0
Total	8561	91.6	1.0	7.5	8.5
URBAN					
Middle					
<20	991	90.8	1.0	8.2	9.2
20–24	2283	92.2	0.7	7.1	7.8
25–29	1793	91.7	0.4	7.8	8.2
30–34	969	88.3	1.4	10.2	11.6
35–39	338	83.1	1.5	15.4	16.9
40–44	37	75.7	2.7	21.6	24.3
Total	6411	90.7	0.9	8.5	9.4
Low					
<20	135	85.9	1.5	12.6	14.1
20–24	375	91.7	2.1	6.1	8.2
25–29	302	94.7	1.0	4.3	5.3
30–34	169	90.5	1.2	8.3	9.5
35–39	53	88.7	0.0	11.3	11.3
40–44	11	(54.5)	(0.0)	(45.5)	(45.5)
Total	1045	91.1	1.4	7.5	8.9
All urban					
<20	1126	90.2	1.1	8.7	9.8
20–24	2658	92.1	0.9	7.0	7.9
25–29	2095	92.2	0.5	7.3	7.8
30–34	1138	88.7	1.4	9.9	11.3
35–39	391	83.9	1.3	14.8	16.1
40–44	48	70.8	2.1	27.1	29.2
Total	7456	90.7	0.9	8.3	9.2

* Percentages in parentheses refer to fewer than 25 EW.

rates declined slightly between the ages of less than 20 and 20–24 years, then remained fairly stable until 40–44 years, in which age group the rate decreased to 0.0. In the urban area, however, the highest stillbirth rates occurred among women who were 40 or older at the time of the birth (2.1%), and the lowest rate was found among those who were 25–29 (0.5%: Fig. 3.D.2). When stillbirths are calculated as a percentage of total births, urban rates show a J-shaped relationship to maternal age, while the curve for rural rates has a reversed J-shape (until age 40–44, when the rate drops to 0.0%; see Table 3.D.3 and Fig. 3.D.3). The trends for the middle social status group were approximately the same in the two residential areas, while for the low status group no definite trends were evident.

TABLE 3.D.3. STILLBIRTHS AS A PERCENTAGE OF TOTAL BIRTHS BY RESIDENCE AND MATERNAL AGE

Maternal age	Rural		Urban		Total	
	Total births	Still-births (%)	Total births	Still-births (%)	Total births	Still-births (%)
<20	904	1.4	1028	1.2	1932	1.3
20–24	2696	0.9	2473	1.0	5169	1.0
25–29	2399	1.0	1942	0.6	4341	0.8
30–34	1351	1.2	1025	1.6	2376	1.3
35–39	509	1.2	333	1.5	842	1.3
40–44	64	0.0	35	2.9	99	1.0

Pregnancy wastage was higher in the urban than in the rural area, especially from the age of 30 upwards. Thus urban women aged 40–44 at termination reported having lost 29.2% of their pregnancies, compared with a loss of 22.0% recalled by rural women of the same maternal age (Table 3.D.2).

In the rural area, middle status women over 25 years of age at the time of birth reported higher wastage rates than did low status women of the same maternal age. The same relationship held in the urban area, with the exception of the 40–44 year age group, for which the wastage rate was higher among low status than among middle status women. It should be noted, however, that only 11 pregnancies occurred in this low status group.

To examine the possibility of selective underreporting or memory lapses, the outcome of the last (and more easily remembered) pregnancy was analysed separately. As shown in Fig. 3.D.4, the patterns for pregnancy wastage by maternal age were similar for the last pregnancy to those for total pregnancies. This suggests that the pattern of association of pregnancy wastage with family formation may not have been unduly distorted.

186

FIG. 3.D.3. STILLBIRTHS AS A PERCENTAGE OF TOTAL BIRTHS BY RESIDENCE, SOCIAL STATUS, AND MATERNAL AGE

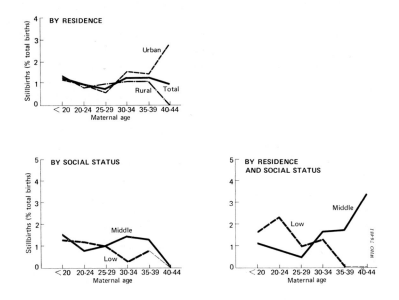

FIG. 3.D.4. PREGNANCY WASTAGE BY RESIDENCE, MATERNAL AGE, AND PREGNANCY ORDER, FOR TOTAL PREGNANCIES AND FOR LAST PREGNANCY

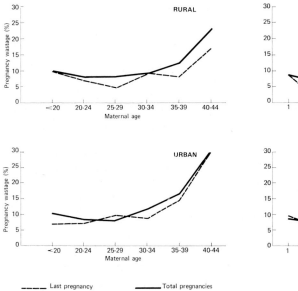

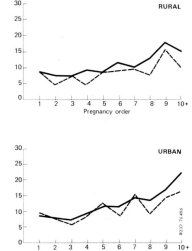

------ Last pregnancy　　　——— Total pregnancies

Pregnancy Outcome and Pregnancy Order

Although there were fluctuations, the curve relating pregnancy wastage to pregnancy order forms a flattened J-shape in both rural and urban areas. This pattern was again due entirely to the abortion figures, as stillbirth rates were fairly constant for all pregnancy orders (Table 3.D.4 and Fig. 3.D.5).

No consistent difference of any importance between the urban and rural areas was found, although the urban rate tended to be slightly above the rural rate. The basic similarity in the relationship for both areas seemed to justify amalgamating the two sets of figures.

Again the last pregnancy was analysed separately and, as with maternal age, the pattern of the relationship between birth order and outcome of the last pregnancy was similar to that between birth order and outcome of total pregnancies (Fig. 3.D.4).

TABLE 3.D.4. PREGNANCY OUTCOME BY RESIDENCE AND PREGNANCY ORDER

Residence	Pregnancy order	Total pregnancies	Pregnancy outcome as percentage of total pregnancies			
			Live births	Still-births	Abortions	Pregnancy wastage
Rural	1	1861	92.2	1.2	6.6	7.8
	2	1645	92.8	0.9	6.3	7.2
	3	1387	93.0	0.5	6.5	7.0
	4	1103	91.7	1.0	7.3	8.3
	5	854	92.0	1.2	6.8	8.0
	6	613	89.2	1.3	9.5	10.8
	7	421	90.5	1.4	8.1	9.5
	8	277	87.7	0.0	12.3	12.3
	9	178	83.1	2.2	14.6	16.8
	10 and over	222	85.6	0.5	14.0	14.5
Urban	1	1867	91.6	0.9	7.5	8.4
	2	1551	92.5	0.8	6.7	7.5
	3	1214	92.8	0.7	6.5	7.2
	4	893	91.3	1.3	7.4	8.7
	5	646	88.9	0.8	10.4	11.2
	6	451	89.1	1.1	9.8	10.9
	7	312	86.2	0.6	13.1	13.7
	8	214	87.4	1.4	11.2	12.6
	9	125	84.0	0.0	16.0	16.0
	10 and over	183	78.7	2.2	19.1	21.3

Pregnancy Wastage, Maternal Age, and Pregnancy Order

Because of the small numbers, the data for urban and rural areas were pooled (Table 3.D.5 and Fig. 3.D.6). The rates for most birth orders exhibited a U-shaped or reversed J-shaped relationship with maternal age ;

in addition, the risks increased after the second and third pregnancies, both for younger and for older mothers.

Control for age generally showed a rise in wastage rates with increasing pregnancy orders. This trend was more manifest for women under 25 years or over 35 years of age.

FIG. 3.D.5. PREGNANCY WASTAGE BY PREGNANCY ORDER AND RESIDENCE

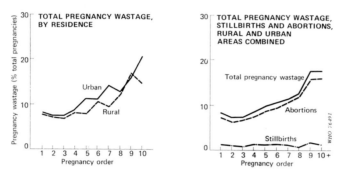

TABLE 3.D.5. PREGNANCY WASTAGE BY PREGNANCY ORDER AND MATERNAL AGE FOR URBAN AND RURAL AREAS COMBINED

Maternal age	Pregnancy wastage (%) for pregnancy order:					
	1	2	3	4	5	6 and over
<20	9.1	9.9	12.2	20.0	12.5	—
20–24	7.0	6.8	7.1	9.4	14.0	22.7
25–29	9.4	6.4	5.6	6.9	7.4	11.7
30–34	7.1	9.0	8.9	9.0	9.5	10.7
35–44	—	9.4	14.6	17.2	14.1	15.5

Wastage by Preceding Pregnancy Interval

Preceding pregnancy interval is defined as the period between the end of the preceding pregnancy and the end of the index pregnancy; consequently, the first pregnancy has to be excluded from the analysis. There was a U-shaped relationship between pregnancy wastage and preceding pregnancy interval (Fig. 3.D.7). The risk of poor pregnancy outcome was highest when the interval was less than 1 year (18.8%), decreased to rates of 6.9%, 4.9%, and 4.8% for intervals of 1, 2, and 3 years, respectively, and then increased for intervals of 4, 5, and 6 or more years to rates of 6.2%, 9.1%, and 13.9%, respectively (Table 3.D.6).

A higher proportion of pregnancies terminated as abortions when the interval was less than 1 year. It should be noted, however, that a preceding interval was, by definition, shorter after an abortion than it otherwise would

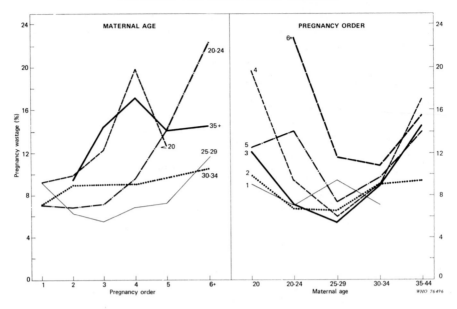

have been if the index pregnancy had been carried to term. For intervals between 2 and 5 years, the percentage of abortions remained more or less the same, while for intervals of more than 5 years, the percentages showed an upward trend. A similar pattern was observed for stillbirths. It is of some interest to note that the increase of wastage with longer pregnancy intervals may have been due in part to the older age of the mother.

FIG. 3.D.7. PREGNANCY WASTAGE BY PRECEDING PREGNANCY INTERVAL

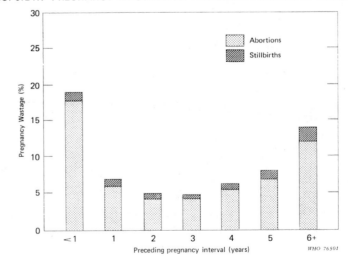

190

TABLE 3.D.6. PREGNANCY WASTAGE BY DURATION OF PRECEDING
PREGNANCY INTERVAL FOR URBAN AND RURAL AREAS COMBINED

Preceding pregnancy interval (years)	Total pregnancies other than the first	Pregnancy outcome as percentage of total pregnancies		
		Stillbirths	Abortions	Total pregnancy wastage
<1	1153	1.2	17.6	18.8
1–2	5789	1.0	5.9	6.9
2–3	3618	0.9	4.0	4.9
3–4	1058	0.5	4.3	4.7
4–5	370	0.5	5.7	6.2
5–6	143	1.2	6.9	8.1
6 and over	157	2.2	11.7	13.9

E. ANKARA

K. Sümbüloglu, M. Bertan and N. H. Fişek

Pregnancy Outcome

Out of the 18 026 pregnancies reported by the 3675 women in the study, 252 (1.4%) ended in stillbirths and 2470 (13.7%) in abortions. For the total study population, about 15% of all pregnancies were wasted.

Pregnancy Wastage and Social Characteristics

Wastage was lower for rural than for semi-urban women (13% against 18.3%). The difference was almost entirely due to abortions, which terminated 11.6% of the pregnancies of rural women and 16.7% of those of semi-urban women (Table 3.E.1).

There was no difference between stillbirth rates of middle compared to low status rural women (both 1.4%). However, among semi-urban women, middle status women experienced a lower stillbirth rate (1.5%) than did low status women (2.2%).

Pregnancy Wastage and Maternal Age

Total pregnancy wastage generally increased directly with maternal age at the time the pregnancies terminated. For semi-urban women in their teens, wastage was 13%, but for those aged 40–44 the rate had increased to 62.1%. Corresponding rates for rural women were 9.6% and 20.5% (Table 3.E.2 and Fig. 3.E.1). For each maternal age cohort, wastage was higher for semi-urban than for rural women.

191

TABLE 3.E.1. PREGNANCY WASTAGE BY RESIDENCE AND SOCIAL STATUS

Residence and social status	No. of pregnancies	Stillbirths (%)	Abortions (%)
Rural			
Middle	8200	1.4	12.0
Low	2420	1.4	10.3
Total	10620	1.4	11.6
Semi-urban			
Middle	6977	1.5	16.9
Low	420	2.2	13.7
Total	7397	1.6	16.7

TABLE 3.E.2. PREGNANCY OUTCOME BY RESIDENCE, SOCIAL STATUS,
AND MATERNAL AGE *

Residence and social status	Maternal age	Total pregnancies	Pregnancy outcome as percentage of total pregnancies			
			Live births	Still-births	Abor-tions	Pregnancy wastage
Semi-urban						
Middle	<20	1521	87.4	1.8	10.8	12.6
	20–24	2637	83.7	1.8	14.4	16.3
	25–29	1679	81.1	0.6	18.3	18.9
	30–34	854	71.2	1.8	27.0	28.8
	35–39	268	67.2	2.2	30.6	32.3
	40–44	24	(29.2)	(0.0)	(70.8)	(70.8)
Low	<20	98	80.6	7.1	12.2	19.4
	20–24	144	88.9	0.7	10.4	11.1
	25–29	95	84.2	0.0	15.8	15.8
	30–34	55	78.2	1.8	20.0	21.8
	35–39	18	(83.3)	(0.0)	16.7	16.7
	40–44	5	(80.0)	(0.0)	20.0	20.0
Total	<20	1619	87.0	2.1	10.9	13.0
	20–24	2781	84.0	1.8	14.2	16.0
	25–29	1774	81.3	0.6	18.2	18.7
	30–34	909	71.6	1.8	26.6	28.4
	35–39	286	68.2	2.1	29.7	31.8
	40–44	29	37.9	0.0	62.1	62.1
Rural						
Middle	<20	1701	90.8	1.4	7.9	9.2
	20–24	2977	88.8	1.4	9.8	11.2
	25–29	2079	86.0	1.0	13.0	14.0
	30–34	1080	80.9	1.5	17.6	19.1
	35–39	334	70.1	2.7	27.2	29.9
	40–44	30	73.3	3.3	23.3	26.7
Low	<20	475	88.8	1.7	9.5	11.2
	20–24	833	90.0	1.8	8.2	9.9
	25–29	626	89.6	1.2	9.3	10.4
	30–34	360	83.3	1.4	15.3	16.7
	35–39	123	81.3	0.0	18.7	18.7
	40–44	9	(100.0)	(0.0)	(0.0)	(0.0)
Total	<20	2176	90.4	1.4	8.2	9.6
	20–24	3810	89.1	1.5	9.4	10.9
	25–29	2705	86.8	1.0	12.2	13.2
	30–34	1440	81.5	1.5	17.0	18.5
	35–39	457	73.1	2.0	24.9	26.9
	40–44	39	79.5	2.6	18.0	20.5

* Percentages in parentheses refer to fewer than 25 EW.

192

FIG. 3.E.1. PREGNANCY WASTAGE BY MATERNAL AGE, RESIDENCE, AND SOCIAL STATUS

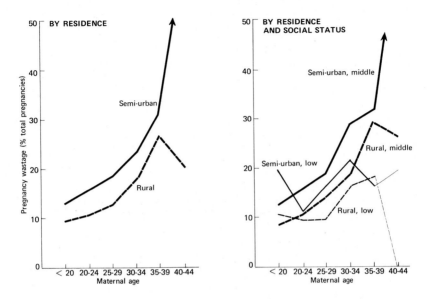

FIG. 3.E.2. ABORTIONS AND STILLBIRTHS BY RESIDENCE AND MATERNAL AGE

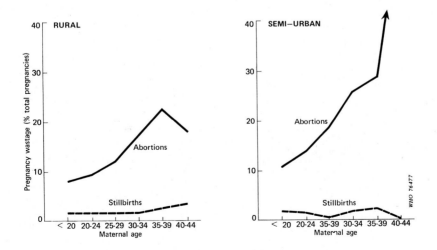

TABLE 3.E.3. STILLBIRTHS AS A PERCENTAGE OF TOTAL BIRTHS, BY CULTURE AND MATERNAL AGE

Maternal age	Rural		Semi-urban	
	Total births	Stillbirths (%)	Total births	Stillbirths (%)
<20	1973	1.6	1430	2.4
20–24	3452	1.7	2385	2.1
25–29	2380	1.2	1452	0.7
30–34	1196	1.8	667	2.4
35–39	343	2.6	201	3.0
40–44	32	3.1	11	0.0

FIG. 3.E.3. STILLBIRTHS AS A PERCENTAGE OF TOTAL BIRTHS, BY RESIDENCE, SOCIAL STATUS, AND MATERNAL AGE

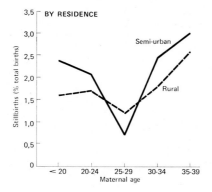

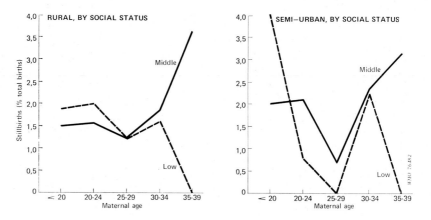

194

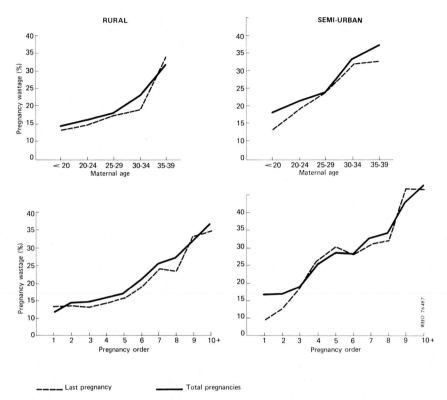

FIG. 3.E.4. PREGNANCY WASTAGE BY RESIDENCE, MATERNAL AGE, AND PREGNANCY ORDER, FOR TOTAL PREGNANCIES AND FOR LAST PREGNANCY

- - - - Last pregnancy   ——— Total pregnancies

By far the greater part of pregnancy wastage was accounted for by abortions. Abortion rates showed a direct relationship to maternal age, but there was no apparent trend in stillbirth rates (Fig. 3.E.2). There was little variation in the stillbirth rates by residence, but semi-urban women had somewhat higher rates of abortion than did rural women.

Except for women in their teens, all age groups of middle social status reported higher rates of wastage than did those of low social status, among both rural and semi-urban women. The difference was almost entirely due to abortions. Stillbirth rates among both rural and semi-urban women differed little by social status in most maternal age groups.

Stillbirths as a percentage of total births are shown in Table 3.E.3 and Fig. 3.E.3. In general, stillbirths were lowest in the 25–29-year age group in both residential areas and highest among women of low social status aged less than 20 years in the semi-urban area.

The figures for abortion represent both spontaneous and induced abortions. Thus, the positive association with social status suggests that low status women selectively underreported their abortions and/or that middle status women used induced abortion more frequently than did low

195

TABLE 3.E.4. PREGNANCY OUTCOME BY RESIDENCE AND PREGNANCY ORDER

Residence	Pregnancy order	Total pregnancies	Pregnancy outcome as percentage of total pregnancies			
			Live births	Still-births	Abortions	Pregnancy wastage
Semi-urban	1	1520	88.4	2.6	9.0	11.6
	2	1367	88.4	1.3	10.3	11.6
	3	1163	86.4	1.0	12.6	13.6
	4	942	79.7	1.1	19.2	20.3
	5	749	76.4	1.5	22.2	23.6
	6	565	77.2	1.4	21.4	22.8
	7	403	72.5	0.7	26.8	27.5
	8	277	71.1	2.2	26.7	28.9
	9	177	62.2	3.4	34.5	37.9
	10 and over	239	55.7	0.8	43.5	44.4
Rural	1	1896	92.9	1.6	5.5	7.1
	2	1725	90.5	1.4	8.1	9.5
	3	1548	90.3	1.2	8.5	9.7
	4	1371	89.1	1.0	9.9	10.9
	5	1160	87.8	1.8	10.4	12.2
	6	926	84.2	1.2	14.6	15.8
	7	704	79.7	1.6	18.7	20.3
	8	513	77.6	1.4	21.0	22.4
	9	325	72.6	2.2	25.2	27.4
	10 and over	455	68.4	1.1	30.6	31.6

status women as a birth control method. However, the association between abortion and maternal age remains unexplained. It is highly unlikely that older women would have resorted to induced abortion more frequently than younger women. Thus, at least some of the rise in wastage with maternal age could have been due to an increase in spontaneous abortion rates.

FIG. 3.E.5. PREGNANCY WASTAGE BY PREGNANCY ORDER AND RESIDENCE

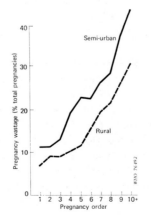

196

TABLE 3.E.5. PREGNANCY WASTAGE BY PREGNANCY ORDER AND MATERNAL AGE
FOR BOTH AREAS COMBINED

Maternal age	Pregnancy wastage (%) for pregnancy order :					
	1	2	3	4	5	6 and over
<20	9.2	11.4	17.3	26.4	26.3	—
20–24	9.8	10.0	11.2	16.5	19.8	25.4
25–29	4.7	9.8	8.5	9.9	15.0	22.3
30–34	—	9.7	8.2	20.3	14.7	24.5
35–39	—	25.0	28.6	30.8	18.5	29.3
40–44	—	—	—	50.0	66.6	36.2

FIG. 3.E.6. PREGNANCY WASTAGE BY MATERNAL AGE AND PREGNANCY ORDER
FOR BOTH AREAS COMBINED

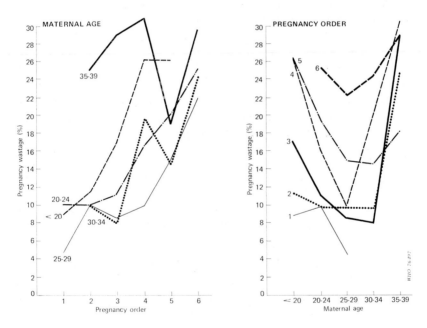

To examine the possibility of selective underreporting or memory lapse, the outcome of the last (and most easily remembered) pregnancy was analysed separately. As shown in Fig. 3.E.4, the patterns for pregnancy wastage by maternal age were similar for the last pregnancy to those for total pregnancies. This suggests that the pattern of association of pregnancy wastage with family formation may not have been unduly distorted.

197

Pregnancy Wastage and Pregnancy Order

On the whole, wastage increased with pregnancy order, but at each order it was higher for semi-urban than for rural women (Table 3.E.4 and Fig. 3.E.5).

Most of the rise in wastage rates with increasing pregnancy order was due to abortion. There was no clear relationship between stillbirth rates and pregnancy order.

Again, the outcome of the last pregnancy was analysed separately, and it was found that, as with maternal age, the relationship between the last pregnancy and pregnancy order was similar to that between all pregnancies and pregnancy order (Fig. 3.E.4).

Wastage by Both Pregnancy Order and Maternal Age

Pregnancy wastage by both pregnancy order and maternal age is shown in Table 3.E.5 and Fig. 3.E.6. Because of the small numbers, these show pooled data (rural and semi-urban pregnancies combined).

Controlling for maternal age shows that for almost all age groups, wastage rates tended to increase with pregnancy order. However, for the 35–39 and 40–44-year age groups there was no definite trend.

For most pregnancy orders, 25–34 years appeared to be the maternal age range at which pregnancy was most likely to have a favourable outcome. Relatively high risks of wastage occurred in fourth and fifth order pregnancies in women in their teens, and in pregnancies of all birth orders in older mothers (over 35 years).

Wastage by Preceding Pregnancy Interval

Preceding pregnancy interval is defined as the period between the end of the preceding pregnancy and the end of the index pregnancy. Thus, the first pregnancy is automatically excluded from the analysis. The curve for wastage by preceding pregnancy interval exhibited a reversed J-shape, starting with a wastage rate of 39.2% for intervals of less than 1 year, decreasing to a low rate of 6.2% for 3-year intervals, and then rising to 15.2% for intervals of 6 or more years (Table 3.E.6 and Fig. 3.E.7).

The highest proportion of pregnancies terminating in abortions (37.4%) occurred when the interval was less than 1 year. It should be noted, however, that a preceding interval was, by definition, shorter after an abortion than it otherwise would have been if the index pregnancy had been carried to term. Since abortions accounted for most of the pregnancy wastage, abortion rates by preceding pregnancy interval exhibited a trend almost identical with that for total pregnancy wastage (reversed J-shape). There were only small variations in stillbirth rates.

TABLE 3.E.6. PREGNANCY OUTCOME BY DURATION OF PRECEDING PREGNANCY INTERVAL FOR BOTH AREAS COMBINED

Duration of interval (years)	Total pregnancies	Pregnancy outcome as percentage of total pregnancies			
		Live births	Stillbirths	Abortions	Pregnancy wastage
<1	2177	60.8	1.8	37.4	39.2
1–2	6738	83.6	1.7	14.7	16.4
2–3	4951	91.0	1.3	7.7	9.0
3–4	2309	93.8	0.8	5.4	6.2
4–5	933	91.6	1.2	7.2	8.4
5–6	469	87.8	2.1	10.0	12.1
6 and over	448	88.8	1.3	9.8	11.2
Total	18015	84.8	1.4	13.7	15.2

FIG. 3.E.7. PREGNANCY WASTAGE BY DURATION OF PRECEDING PREGNANCY INTERVAL FOR BOTH AREAS COMBINED

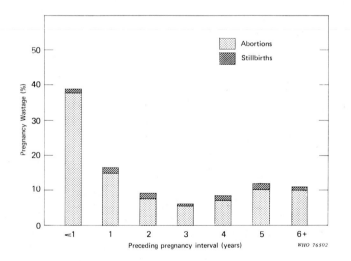

WHO 76502

199

Chapter Four

FAMILY FORMATION
AND CHILDHOOD MORTALITY

INTRODUCTION

M. R. Bone, C. C. Standley and A. R. Omran

In earlier investigations, reviewed in Part I, a J-shaped relationship has usually been found between neonatal mortality rates and maternal age or birth order : mortality rates for the first month of life decline at first as the mother's age rises or the birth order increases, but they rise again to a peak towards the end of the mother's childbearing years and for the highest birth orders.

Mortality rates for the first year and first 5 years of life, on the other hand, usually rise consistently with birth order, but describe a U-shaped pattern in relation to maternal age : they are lowest when the mother is of intermediate age and highest towards the beginning and end of the childbearing period.

Mortality rates for the first year of life have been found to decline as the interval between the index birth and the previous birth increases ; in some cases, they increase again if the intervals become unusually long.

In the present chapter the relationship between family formation variables and child mortality is examined for 5 periods of risk : the first month ; the second to the eleventh month ; the first year ; the first to the fifth year ; and the first 5 years of life, the object being to find out whether the relationships discovered elsewhere also held for the participating areas.

The family formation variables are those already referred to : maternal age, birth order, and preceding pregnancy interval. The data concerned were collected from each eligible woman at interview as an extension of the detailed pregnancy history mentioned in the Introduction to chapter 3. For each live birth, the informant was asked whether the child was still living, and, if not, how long after birth it had died.

The problems of analysis and interpretation are for the most part similar to those described for pregnancy outcome.

The difficulties created by the interrelationships amongst family formation variables need not be discussed again here. In addition, it has to be remembered that, as in all retrospective pregnancy history studies, the child mortality rates derived differ from those obtained in conventional demographic studies. In particular, infant mortality rates are usually based on the total live births occurring in a defined population during one calendar year. Those in the present enquiry are based, instead, on the number of children ever born to the eligible women. The study mortality rates differ from conventional rates in the following ways :

1. Live births to the eligible women exclude some births occurring in the area population during a given time period but include others : births to non-eligible women (e.g., those now dead or too old) that took place during the same period and in the same area are excluded ; conversely, births to eligible women who were living outside the area at the time are included.

2. During the period of some 30 years over which the births occurred, the risks may have changed. This not only complicates comparisons between the study rates and conventional mortality rates, but may also distort the relationships between mortality and the family formation variables. An attempt has been made to overcome this problem by considering only births that occurred in the last 10 years.

3. All births for each eligible woman are included, which means that the more fertile the women, the larger their contribution to the results. If the risks of a child's dying are related to the mother's fertility, then death rates based on all births that have ever occurred in a population of women will differ from those that would have been derived from births occurring in a specific year (even if the risks did not change over time).

4. Another problem common to most child mortality studies is that mortality rates are shown for risk periods of 1 month, 1 year, and 5 years following birth. Whilst the great majority of births will have occurred more than one year before the interview and almost all more than one month previously, a considerable proportion will have taken place within the preceding 5 years. Children born less than 5 years before the interview will not have been exposed to the hazard of death for 5 full years ; if they are only 4 years old, for example, they may yet die before their 5th birthday. It is especially for the 1–4-year period that the rates may be artificially low.

5. The retrospective nature of the enquiry means that some underreporting of births—particularly those of children who died shortly after birth—is probable. However, this is likely to be less than in the case of pregnancies, and a comparison between mortality for recent births and that for all births did not suggest selective underreporting of earlier deaths. In most cases, as will be shown, there appeared to have been a decline in child mortality over the generations. Such a decline would not be detectable had there been gross underreporting of earlier deaths. Moreover, a prospective study being undertaken in Gandhigram supports the evidence of the present study.

202

The investigators were well aware from the outset of the above considerations and of the fact that they not only render comparisons with conventional mortality rates difficult but also complicate the relationships to be examined and qualify the comparisons made between subgroups. In the analyses in chapter 4 an attempt is made, wherever possible, to disentangle the relationships of interest by holding the confounding factors constant.

The difficulties are best illustrated in the case of preceding pregnancy interval. Generally, mortality rates decline as the preceding pregnancy interval lengthens. The question of interest is whether a short preceding interval depresses a child's chances of survival. For instance, the duration of interpregnancy intervals is related to maternal age, which is related, in turn, to child mortality ; it is the youngest mothers who are most likely to experience the shortest intervals, as was confirmed in the samples investigated. It is therefore necessary to hold maternal age constant if one wishes to discover the relationship between interval length and mortality. But interval length is also likely to be related to parity. Women who have many births are likely to have shorter interpregnancy intervals than those who have few. Hence, parity, or birth order, must also be controlled.

A third problem, which is particularly troublesome when carrying out retrospective studies, arises from the relationship of interval length to the age of the preceding child at death. If it died soon after birth, the next pregnancy is likely to occur earlier than it would have done if the preceding child had survived longer. This may in part be voluntary, as an attempt to replace the dead child, and in part physiological, since if breastfeeding (but not contraception) is commonly practised in the area, its curtailment in the case of a child who dies young will also curtail the period of postpartum sterility. This is relevant to the present problem if a child's chances of survival are related to the survival of preceding children born to the same woman. That is to say, some women may experience short intervals because their children die young and not vice versa, a question discussed in more detail in chapter 8. As shown in chapter 7, interpregnancy intervals following the birth of children who died within a month were indeed considerably more likely to be short (under 1 year or between 1 and 2 years) than those succeeding the birth of a child who survived until the date of interview. The problem in a retrospective study is complicated by the possibility that short intervals for women who frequently lose children unduly weight the total of short intervals : it may be the repeated experience of poor reproducers and not the short intervals that determines the pattern. In order to examine this possibility it would also be necessary to control the outcome of the preceding pregnancy.

A further difficulty arises entirely from the retrospective nature of the enquiry. Since, on average, the shortest interpregnancy intervals occur to the youngest mothers and many of the women were no longer young when interviewed, the information often related to pregnancies that had occurred years before. Because there is evidence in some areas that child mortality rates have declined over the years, a disproportionate number of these pregnancies, compared with those to older women having longer inter-pregnancy intervals, will have been subject to the higher risks of death prevailing at an earlier period. Consequently, the relationship found between child mortality and preceding pregnancy interval cannot be taken by itself as evidence that short preceding intervals hamper children's chances of survival.

One factor that may confound these relationships is possible changes in child mortality risks during the women's lifetime. In an attempt to mitigate the effects of such changes, analyses have also been made of data relating only to pregnancies occurring within the 10 years preceding interview. Since neither the date of birth nor the date of the interview were recorded, this 10-year period was situated approximately from the women's age at interview and the ages at which they had experienced their pregnancies. Thus, for a woman aged 30–34 at interview, pregnancies during the preceding 10 years were taken as those occurring while she was in the age groups 25–29 and 30–34.

Although this procedure reduces the distortion resulting from changes in mortality over time, it does increase that due to truncated risk periods. That is, the proportion of children born less than 1 month, 1 year, or 5 years before interview is greater amongst the births of the previous 10 years than amongst all births. The effect is to reduce death rates below what they will eventually be to a greater extent among children born in the last 10 years than in the case of all births. The artefactual reduction in mortality will be greatest for deaths under 5 years and least for those under 1 month.

At the beginning of each area report, the proportions of the women's children who had died within the specified risk periods are given for the area samples. These are of immediate interest, and where there are differences between groups the question arises whether these are due to differences in family formation patterns or are of cultural origin. The cultural differences may themselves be related to socioeconomic circumstances, as expressed by social status, for which mortality rates are also given.

If the differences between groups are entirely due to family formation variables, then, when these are controlled, there should be no difference between cultural groups. Other things being equal, mortality for each maternal age group, as well as the pattern of their relationship, should be identical. In fact, other things are not equal and, as already discussed, it is not possible to hold constant all the other variables concerned : if birth order, preceding birth interval, and time were all to be controlled, subgroups would dwindle to negligible numbers. We can therefore only begin to examine the question by finding out, for example, whether the differences between subgroups are maintained when child mortality rates are made specific for maternal age.

This consideration also applies to comparisons between the participating areas, and, of course, to any made between them and data from other investigations.

A. GANDHIGRAM

K. A. Pisharoti and S. Gunasekaran

Child Mortality by Culture and Social Status

The 6541 eligible women in the study reported a total of 22 116 live births over the years of marriage. Of these live-born children, 10.2% had died within a month of birth, 13.9% within a year, and 20.5% within 5 years. Approximately 1 child out of every 5 reported as a live birth died before the age of 5 years. The highest loss (24.3%) occurred in Scheduled Castes, and the lowest (18.4%) among Muslim children (Table 4.A.1 and Fig. 4.A.1). Mortality was slightly higher among the children of women of low social status than among those of middle status women in each cultural group except the Scheduled Castes. There were also other variations in the components of mortality by culture. Mortality under 1 month of age was highest among Vellalas and lowest among Muslims; 1–4-year mortality was highest among Scheduled Castes and lowest among Vellalas, while mortality at 1–11 months did not show great variations among the 4 cultural groups. These differences were maintained after controlling for social class.

Child Mortality and Maternal Age

Child mortality rates (mortality under 5 years of age) were negatively related to maternal age in each of the 4 cultural groups except the Vellalas. Among Vellalas child mortality rates declined initially with maternal age, until the age of 30–34, when they rose again. Neonatal mortality rates (under 1 month of age) described a U-shape or reversed J-shape in relation to maternal age among Muslims, Other Hindus, and Vellalas, while a rise in post-neonatal mortality (1–11 months) with increasing maternal age was observed only among Scheduled Castes. Mortality at 1–4 years generally declined with maternal age in each of the 4 cultural groups (Table 4.A.2 and Fig. 4.A.2).

Vellala women under 40 years of age experienced the highest mortality rates under 1 month, while among the Scheduled Castes the children of women under 35 at the time of birth had the highest 1–4-year mortality rates. No consistent relationship by culture was observed for mortality at 1–11 months.

One of the factors that may distort the relationship between maternal age and child mortality is changes in risk factors with time. To introduce an approximate control for this parameter, the women were divided into 3 cohorts: those aged under 25 years at interview, those between 25 and 34 inclusive, and those aged 35 and over. Table 4.A.3 shows the child mortality rates corresponding to the maternal age groups for these 3 cohorts. It can be seen that, on the whole, reported mortality declined over time for

TABLE 4.A.1. CHILD MORTALITY BY CULTURE AND SOCIAL STATUS

Culture and social status	Deaths per 100 reported live births at :					Total reported live births
	<1 month	1–11 months	<1 year	1–4 years	<5 years	
Muslim						
Middle	7.6	3.9	11.5	6.3	17.8	5198
Low	7.5	4.3	11.8	8.0	19.8	2186
Total	7.6	4.0	11.6	6.8	18.4	7384
Scheduled Castes						
Middle	9.8	4.7	14.5	10.7	25.2	1015
Low	10.4	4.1	14.5	9.8	24.3	2675
Total	10.2	4.2	14.5	9.9	24.3	3690
Other Hindus						
Middle	11.4	3.1	14.5	6.0	20.5	4322
Low	10.9	4.1	15.0	7.1	22.1	2322
Total	11.2	3.5	14.7	7.1	21.8	6644
Vellala						
Middle	12.4	3.5	15.9	2.9	18.8	2702
Low	13.9	2.8	16.7	5.1	21.8	1696
Total	12.9	3.2	16.1	3.7	19.8	4398

FIG. 4.A.1. CHILD MORTALITY BY CULTURE AND SOCIAL STATUS

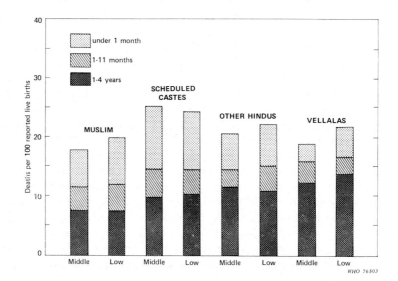

WHO 76503

206

each maternal age group representing more than one generation: for example, in the cohort of Muslim women aged 35 or more at interview, 8.6% of the children born to them before they were 25 years old died within 1 month of birth, whereas Muslim women aged under 25 at the interview lost only 5.3% of their children within the first month. For deaths under 5 years, however, the decline may be exaggerated by the shortening of the period of exposure to risk for the children of women in the younger cohorts.

In Table 4.A.3, the rows giving total mortality rates show the relationship between maternal age and child mortality for each cultural group, and correspond to the curves shown in Fig. 4.A.2. The figures above the diagonal lines show mortality rates for children born recently to women in each cohort and it can be seen that the patterns of the relationship between maternal age and child mortality differ somewhat from those obtained when births from all periods are included. Table 4.A.4 gives percentages of deaths among children born during the 10 years preceding the interview. Deaths under 1 month for women giving birth during this period showed a reversed J-shaped relation to maternal age among Other Hindus, a V-shaped relation among Vellalas, and a negative relation among Scheduled Castes. Mortality rates for ages 1–11 months were inconsistent in the different cultural groups, while 1–4-year mortality rates either varied little or declined (Fig. 4.A.2).

Child Mortality and Birth Order

In each cultural group, child mortality rates under 5 years of age were highest at birth order 1 and generally decreased, with some fluctuation, as birth order increased. Mortality rates under 1 month exhibited an approximately U-shaped relationship to birth order among Muslim women, while the relationship among the other 3 cultural groups was negative (with fluctuations at birth order 3 for Other Hindus and at birth order 4 for Scheduled Castes and Vellalas). Mortality rates for ages 1–11 months were highest at intermediate birth orders (4, 5, and 6 or more) among women of the Scheduled Castes, but varied little by birth order among Other Hindu and Vellala women. Mortality at 1–4 years showed no consistent relationship with birth order in any of the cultural groups (Table 4.A.5 and Fig. 4.A.3).

As with maternal age, it is appropriate when considering birth order to calculate rates for recent births only, in order to minimize possible distortions due to changes in mortality rates over time. Table 4.A.6 and Fig. 4.A.3 show the relationship of child mortality to birth order when considering births during the 10 years preceding interview only. Although there were fluctuations in each cultural group at intermediate birth orders, in general mortality rates under 1 month described a U-shape or reversed J-shape in relation to birth order. Mortality rates for ages 1–11 months generally declined with birth order among Scheduled Castes but showed no consistent relationship to birth order among Muslims, Other Hindus, or Vellalas.

TABLE 4.A.2. CHILD MORTALITY BY CULTURE AND MATERNAL AGE
(TOTAL EXPERIENCE) *

Culture and maternal age	Reported live births	Deaths per 100 reported live births at :				
		<1 month	1–11 months	<1 year	1–4 years	<5 years
Muslim						
<20	2495	9.7	4.3	14.0	8.2	22.2
20–24	2401	6.7	4.8	11.5	6.1	17.6
25–29	1514	6.1	2.8	8.9	6.6	15.5
30–34	728	6.2	3.2	9.4	5.6	15.0
35–39	224	7.6	3.1	10.7	4.4	15.1
40–44	22	(0.0)	(9.0)	(9.0)	(4.5)	(13.5)
Total	7384	7.6	4.0	11.6	6.8	18.4
Scheduled Castes						
<20	1419	14.5	4.7	19.2	11.3	30.5
20–24	1229	9.5	4.3	13.8	9.6	23.4
25–29	690	4.8	2.9	7.7	9.6	17.3
30–34	286	5.9	4.1	10.0	6.5	16.5
35–39	58	3.4	6.8	10.2	3.4	13.6
40–44	8	(12.5)	(0.0)	(12.5)	(0.0)	(12.5)
Total	3690	10.2	4.2	14.4	9.9	24.3
Other Hindus						
<20	2019	16.2	3.7	19.9	7.7	27.6
20–24	2300	10.2	3.5	13.7	6.3	20.0
25–29	1443	8.5	3.3	11.8	5.3	17.1
30–34	682	6.9	3.4	10.3	5.5	15.8
35–39	181	8.3	2.3	10.6	3.4	14.0
40–44	19	(0.0)	(5.3)	(5.3)	(5.3)	(10.6)
Total	6644	11.2	3.5	14.7	6.4	21.1
Vellala						
<20	1203	17.6	3.2	20.8	3.6	24.4
20–24	1857	12.8	3.5	16.3	3.2	19.5
25–29	972	8.5	3.2	11.7	4.7	16.4
30–34	294	9.2	1.4	10.6	4.1	14.7
35–39	69	14.5	1.4	15.9	1.4	17.3
40–44	3	(0.0)	(0.0)	(0.0)	(0.0)	(0.0)
Total	4398	12.9	3.2	16.1	3.8	19.9

* Figures in parentheses refer to fewer than 25 EW.

TABLE 4.A.3. CHILD MORTALITY BY MATERNAL AGE, CULTURE, AND AGE AT INTERVIEW

Age of child at death	Age of mother at interview	Deaths as percentages of live births at maternal age:			Deaths as percentages of live births at maternal age:		
		<25	25–34	35–44	<25	25–34	35–44
		Muslim			Other Hindus		
under 1 month	<25	5.3	—	—	13.1	—	—
	25–34	9.4	4.8	—	12.8	6.5	—
	35–44	8.6	7.2	6.9	13.4	9.2	7.5
	Total	8.3	6.1	6.9	13.0	8.0	7.5
1–11 months	<25	3.6	—	—	3.2	—	—
	25–34	4.5	2.2	—	3.7	2.4	—
	35–44	5.3	3.6	3.6	3.6	4.1	2.5
	Total	4.5	2.9	3.6	3.6	3.3	2.5
under 1 year	<25	8.9	—	—	16.3	—	—
	25–34	13.9	7.0	—	16.5	8.9	—
	35–44	13.9	10.8	10.5	17.0	13.3	10.0
	Total	12.8	9.0	10.5	16.6	11.3	10.0
1–4 years	<25	4.4	—	—	3.7	—	—
	25–34	7.6	4.5	—	7.7	3.8	—
	35–44	8.7	8.0	4.4	8.1	6.7	3.5
	Total	7.1	6.4	4.4	7.0	5.4	3.5
under 5 years	<25	13.3	—	—	20.0	—	—
	25–34	21.5	11.5	—	24.2	12.7	—
	35–44	22.6	18.8	14.9	25.1	20.0	13.5
	Total	19.9	15.4	14.9	23.6	16.7	13.5
		Scheduled Castes			Vellala		
under 1 month	<25	10.5	—	—	14.3	—	—
	25–34	12.2	5.0	—	14.4	7.5	—
	35–44	14.4	5.3	4.5	15.6	9.8	13.9
	Total	12.2	5.1	4.5	14.7	8.7	13.9
1–11 months	<25	4.9	—	—	2.2	—	—
	25–34	4.2	2.9	—	3.3	2.7	—
	35–44	4.9	3.7	6.0	4.6	2.8	1.4
	Total	4.5	3.3	6.0	3.4	2.7	1.4
under 1 year	<25	15.4	—	—	16.5	—	—
	25–34	16.4	7.9	—	17.7	10.2	—
	35–44	19.3	9.0	10.5	20.2	12.6	15.3
	Total	16.7	8.4	10.5	18.1	11.4	15.3
1–4 years	<25	4.7	—	—	1.2	—	—
	25–34	12.0	5.2	—	4.0	5.8	—
	35–44	14.2	13.3	3.0	3.8	3.4	1.4
	Total	10.5	8.8	3.0	3.4	4.5	1.4
under 5 years	<25	20.1	—	—	17.7	—	—
	25–34	28.4	13.1	—	21.7	16.0	—
	35–44	33.5	22.3	13.5	24.0	16.0	16.7
	Total	27.2	17.2	13.5	21.5	15.9	16.7

TABLE 4.A.4. CHILD MORTALITY DURING THE 10 YEARS PRECEDING INTERVIEW,
BY CULTURE AND MATERNAL AGE *

Culture and maternal age	Reported live births	Deaths per 100 reported live births at :				
		<1 month	1–11 months	<1 year	1–4 years	<5 years
Muslim						
<20	730	6.0	4.0	10.0	5.6	15.6
20–24	1047	5.9	4.3	10.2	4.5	14.7
25–29	830	5.1	1.8	6.9	4.7	11.6
30–34	533	6.0	3.0	9.0	4.5	13.5
35–39	224	7.6	3.1	10.7	4.5	15.2
40–44	22	(0.0)	(9.1)	(9.1)	(4.5)	(13.6)
Total	3386	5.8	3.4	9.2	4.8	14.0
Scheduled Castes						
<20	499	11.6	5.4	17.0	5.4	22.4
20–24	625	8.6	4.6	13.3	8.5	21.8
25–29	446	5.6	3.1	8.7	6.1	14.8
30–34	238	5.0	2.9	8.0	5.5	13.4
35–39	58	3.4	6.9	10.3	3.4	13.8
40–44	8	(12.5)	(0.0)	(12.5)	(0.0)	(12.5)
Total	1874	8.1	4.3	12.4	6.5	18.9
Other Hindus						
<20	561	15.9	3.9	19.8	4.1	23.9
20–24	1008	8.2	3.9	12.1	4.4	16.5
25–29	781	6.5	2.8	9.3	4.4	13.7
30–34	470	6.0	3.6	9.6	3.4	13.0
35–39	181	8.3	2.2	10.5	3.3	13.8
40–44	19	(0.0)	(5.3)	(5.3)	(5.3)	(10.5)
Total	3020	8.8	3.5	12.3	4.1	16.4
Vellala						
<20	345	16.2	1.7	18.0	1.2	19.1
20–24	815	12.0	3.3	15.3	1.8	17.2
25–29	548	7.3	2.9	10.2	5.8	16.1
30–34	201	10.4	1.0	11.4	2.0	13.4
35–39	69	14.5	1.4	15.9	1.4	17.4
40–44	3	(0.0)	(0.0)	(0.0)	(0.0)	(0.0)
Total	1981	11.4	2.6	14.0	2.8	16.8

* Figures in parentheses refer to fewer than 25 EW.

FIG. 4.A.2. CHILD MORTALITY BY CULTURE AND MATERNAL AGE: TOTAL AND DURING PRECEDING 10 YEARS

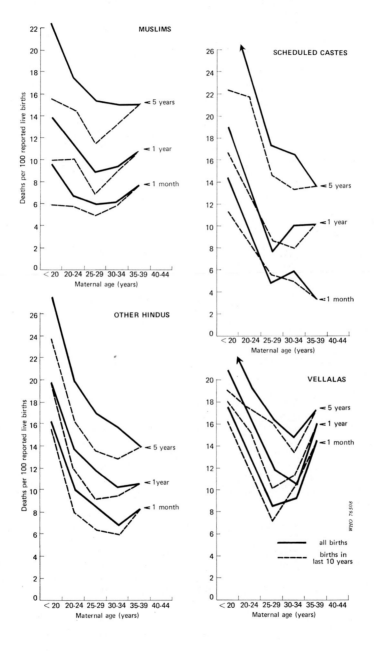

TABLE 4.A.5. CHILD MORTALITY BY BIRTH ORDER AND CULTURE (TOTAL EXPERIENCE)

Culture and birth order	Reported live births	Deaths per 100 reported live births at :				
		<1 month	1–11 months	<1 year	1–4 years	<5 years
Muslim						
1	1730	9.6	3.5	13.1	6.8	19.9
2	1495	6.7	3.9	10.6	6.8	17.4
3	1228	7.2	4.6	11.8	7.3	19.1
4	966	6.4	4.8	11.2	6.8	18.0
5	735	6.5	4.3	10.8	7.2	18.0
6 and over	1230	7.6	3.4	11.0	6.2	17.2
Total	7384	7.6	4.0	11.6	6.8	18.4
Scheduled Castes						
1	909	15.1	4.4	19.5	9.8	29.3
2	794	10.3	5.1	15.4	11.8	27.2
3	648	8.0	4.1	12.1	9.0	21.1
4	510	9.8	3.0	12.8	10.4	23.2
5	369	6.5	3.8	10.3	10.9	21.2
6 and over	460	6.7	3.9	10.7	7.2	17.8
Total	3690	10.2	4.2	14.4	9.9	24.3
Other Hindus						
1	1746	15.3	3.6	18.9	6.7	25.6
2	1486	10.3	3.3	13.6	5.8	19.4
3	1164	10.7	3.1	13.8	7.6	21.4
4	865	9.8	3.2	13.0	6.9	19.9
5	606	8.6	3.5	12.1	5.2	17.3
6 and over	777	8.5	4.1	12.6	5.3	17.9
Total	6644	11.2	3.5	14.7	6.4	21.1
Vellala						
1	1390	15.8	2.8	18.6	2.8	21.4
2	1152	12.8	3.3	16.1	3.4	19.5
3	823	10.7	3.4	14.1	4.7	18.8
4	513	12.5	3.7	16.2	4.7	20.9
5	287	10.1	3.5	13.6	5.9	19.5
6 and over	233	9.4	2.6	12.0	2.6	14.6
Total	4398	12.9	3.2	16.1	3.7	19.8

TABLE 4.A.6. CHILD MORTALITY DURING LAST 10 YEARS PRECEDING INTERVIEW, BY BIRTH ORDER AND CULTURE

Culture and birth order	Reported live births	Deaths per 100 reported live births at:				
		<1 month	1–11 months	<1 year	1–4 years	<5 years
Muslim						
1	600	7.0	3.8	10.8	5.0	15.8
2	567	5.1	3.5	8.6	5.1	13.8
3	514	5.5	2.9	8.4	4.1	12.5
4	472	5.5	4.0	9.5	4.4	14.0
5	418	4.5	3.8	8.4	5.0	13.4
6 and over	815	6.5	2.6	9.1	4.9	14.0
Total	3386	5.8	3.4	9.2	4.8	14.0
Scheduled Castes						
1	333	13.5	5.7	19.2	5.4	24.6
2	326	7.7	4.9	12.6	6.7	19.3
3	322	7.1	4.7	11.8	4.0	15.8
4	295	8.5	3.4	11.9	9.2	21.0
5	245	4.5	4.1	8.6	9.4	18.0
6 and over	353	6.5	3.1	9.6	5.4	15.0
Total	1874	8.1	4.3	12.4	6.5	18.9
Other Hindus						
1	585	13.3	4.3	17.6	3.8	21.4
2	585	7.2	3.4	10.6	3.1	13.7
3	524	9.0	2.5	11.5	4.6	16.0
4	429	7.2	3.3	10.5	5.1	15.6
5	361	7.5	2.8	10.2	3.3	13.6
6 and over	536	7.6	4.3	11.9	4.9	16.8
Total	3020	8.8	3.5	12.3	4.1	16.4
Vellala						
1	494	13.4	2.2	15.6	1.0	16.6
2	486	11.9	2.5	14.4	2.5	6.9
3	395	10.1	2.3	12.4	3.0	15.4
4	283	10.6	3.5	14.1	4.2	18.4
5	163	9.2	4.3	13.5	6.1	19.6
6 and over	160	10.0	1.9	11.9	3.1	15.0
Total	1981	11.4	2.6	14.0	2.8	16.8

213

FIG. 4.A.3. CHILD MORTALITY BY CULTURE AND BIRTH ORDER:
TOTAL AND DURING PRECEDING 10 YEARS

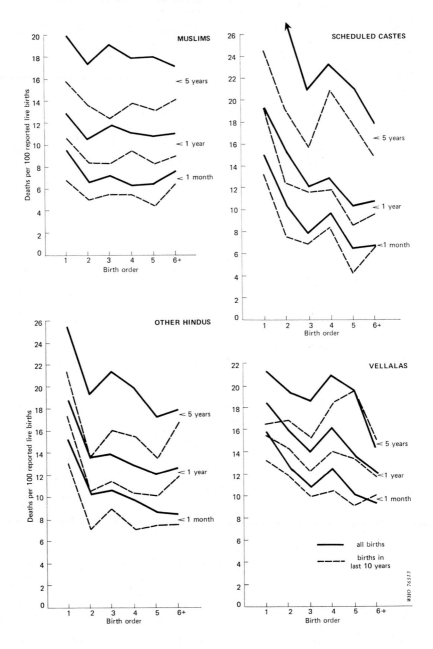

Mortality at 1–4 years generally increased with birth order among Vellalas, but showed no consistent relationship to birth order among women in the other 3 cultural groups.

Child Mortality, Birth Order, and Maternal Age

When maternal age was controlled, the percentage of deaths within 1 year of birth at first declined with birth order and then increased, so that the lowest rates occurred for intermediate orders (Table 4.A.7).

TABLE 4.A.7. DEATHS UNDER 1 YEAR OF AGE, BY MATERNAL AGE AND BIRTH ORDER: WEIGHTED AVERAGES FOR THE FOUR CULTURES *

Maternal age	Deaths per 100 reported live births at birth order:					
	1	2	3	4	5	6
<25	16.71	12.62	11.67	15.44	15.15	—
25–34	9.91	7.16	7.27	8.60	9.19	8.16
35–44	—	7.41	4.88	13.16	6.94	11.76

* Weighting was done by the method given by Cochran, W. E., for estimating totals and means over sub-populations in: *Sampling techniques*, 2nd ed., New York, Wiley, 1963, pp. 33, 146, & 147.

Child Mortality and Preceding Pregnancy Intervals

The relationship of child mortality to preceding pregnancy intervals (excluding first births) exhibited a reversed J-shape for all the components of child mortality except 1–4 years. That is, mortality risks under 5 years were extremely high (25.8% for pooled data, or one out of every 4 live births) for pregnancy intervals of 1 year or less. The risks remained high (19%) for intervals of 2 years, then declined for longer intervals or more spaced births. This pattern was sustained for each cultural group (Table 4.A.8 and Fig. 4.A.4). The lowest risks were associated with intervals of 4 years for Muslims and Vellalas, and with 5 or more years for Scheduled Castes and Other Hindus.

215

TABLE 4.A.8. CHILD MORTALITY DURING 10 YEARS PRECEDING INTERVIEW, BY CULTURE AND DURATION OF PRECEDING PREGNANCY INTERVAL *

Culture	Duration of preceding pregnancy interval (years)	Deaths per 100 reported live births in 10 years preceding interview, at :					Total live births in past 10 years
		<1 month	1–11 months	<1 year	1–4 years	<5 years	
Muslim	<1	14.3	7.1	21.4	0.0	21.4	28
	1	6.8	3.8	10.6	6.3	16.9	710
	2	4.8	3.0	7.8	4.8	12.6	1204
	3	5.5	3.1	8.6	3.2	11.8	549
	4	4.6	3.3	7.9	3.3	11.2	152
	5 and over	6.7	2.4	9.1	3.6	12.7	165
Scheduled Castes	<1	(5.6)	(0.0)	(5.6)	(0.0)	(5.6)	18
	1	11.2	5.5	16.7	7.8	24.5	412
	2	6.2	3.3	9.5	8.2	17.7	639
	3	4.6	4.3	8.9	5.0	13.9	303
	4	5.6	4.5	10.1	2.3	12.4	89
	5 and over	4.4	2.3	6.7	3.3	10.0	90
Other Hindus	<1	14.9	12.8	27.7	(0.0)	27.7	47
	1	12.5	3.8	16.3	4.3	20.6	606
	2	6.9	3.6	10.5	4.2	14.7	925
	3	5.5	2.5	8.0	3.7	11.7	512
	4	4.7	0.6	5.3	5.9	11.2	169
	5 and over	3.1	2.6	5.7	4.1	9.8	193
Vellala	<1	(7.7)	(0.0)	(7.7)	(7.7)	(15.4)	13
	1	15.5	2.0	17.5	3.2	20.7	348
	2	10.3	3.6	13.9	3.5	17.4	591
	3	8.1	2.4	10.5	4.7	15.2	295
	4	6.4	3.7	10.1	2.7	12.8	109
	5 and over	8.8	1.4	10.2	0.7	10.9	137

* Figures in parentheses refer to fewer than 25 EW.

FIG. 4.A.4. CHILD MORTALITY DURING 10 YEARS PRECEDING INTERVIEW,
BY DURATION OF PRECEDING PREGNANCY INTERVAL

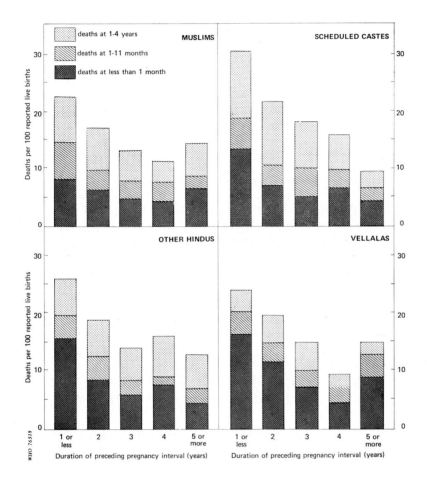

B. TEHERAN

V. Nahapetian and B. D. Navidi-Kasmaii

Child Mortality by Culture and Social Status

Of the 14 602 live births reported by the eligible women, 3.7% resulted in deaths within the first month of life, 9.6% within the first year, and 13.3% within the first 5 years. Muslims reported a higher overall percentage of child deaths than Armenians (Table 4.B.1 and Fig. 4.B.1). Mortality under 1 month for Muslims was almost twice that for Armenians (4.8% compared with 2.5%), while among children aged 1–4 years the mortality rate for Muslims was more than double that for Armenians. Within each culture, mortality was higher among the children born to women of low social status than among those of middle status women.

Child Mortality and Maternal Age

Among Muslims, child mortality rates (per 100 reported live births) at different risk periods (under 1 month, 1–11 months, 1–4 years, and under 5 years) declined with maternal age, except in the 1–4-year group (Table 4.B.2 and Fig. 4.B.2). Among Armenians child mortality was much lower than among Muslims at almost all maternal ages and risk periods, and it declined with maternal age.

One of the factors that may distort the relationship between child mortality and maternal age is changes in risk factors with time. In order to introduce an approximate control for such changes, the women were divided into 3 age cohorts: those aged under 25 at interview, those between 25 and 34, and those aged 35 and over.

Table 4.B.3 compares child mortality for these 3 groups according to their corresponding age groups at childbirth. It is evident that the reported

TABLE 4.B.1. CHILD MORTALITY BY CULTURE AND SOCIAL STATUS

Culture and social status	Deaths per 100 reported live births at:					Total reported live births
	<1 month	1–11 months	<1 year	1–4 years	<5 years	
Muslim						
Middle	4.7	5.5	10.2	3.7	13.9	2568
Low	4.8	7.0	11.8	5.5	17.3	5083
Total	4.8	6.5	11.3	4.9	16.2	7651
Armenian						
Middle	2.1	4.0	6.1	1.6	7.7	2683
Low	2.7	6.0	8.7	2.5	11.2	4268
Total	2.5	5.2	7.7	2.1	9.8	6951

FIG. 4.B.1. CHILD MORTALITY BY CULTURE AND SOCIAL STATUS

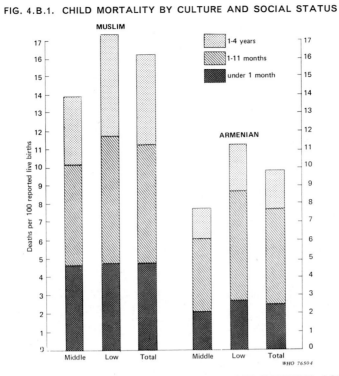

WHO 76504

TABLE 4.B.2. CHILD MORTALITY BY CULTURE AND MATERNAL AGE *

Culture and maternal age	Reported live births	Deaths per 100 reported live births at :				
		<1 month	1–11 months	<1 year	1–4 years	<5 years
Muslim						
<20	2658	6.3	8.5	14.8	6.3	21.1
20–24	2650	4.3	5.7	10.0	5.3	15.3
25–29	1481	3.8	5.5	9.3	3.6	12.9
30–34	648	3.1	3.9	7.0	2.1	9.1
35–39	191	3.1	8.4	11.5	1.5	13.0
40–44	23	(4.3)	(0.0)	(4.3)	(4.3)	(8.6)
Total	7651	4.8	6.5	11.3	5.0	16.3
Armenian						
<20	1526	3.1	9.0	12.1	2.8	14.9
20–24	2818	2.9	4.8	7.7	2.1	9.8
25–29	1677	1.3	3.8	5.1	1.8	6.9
30–34	756	2.5	3.1	5.6	1.2	6.8
35–39	161	0.0	2.4	2.4	1.2	3.6
40–44	13	(7.7)	(0.0)	(7.7)	(0.0)	(7.7)
Total	6951	2.5	5.2	7.7	2.1	9.8

* Figures in parentheses refer to fewer than 25 EW.

219

FIG. 4.B.2. CHILD MORTALITY BY CULTURE AND MATERNAL AGE: TOTAL AND DURING PRECEDING 10 YEARS

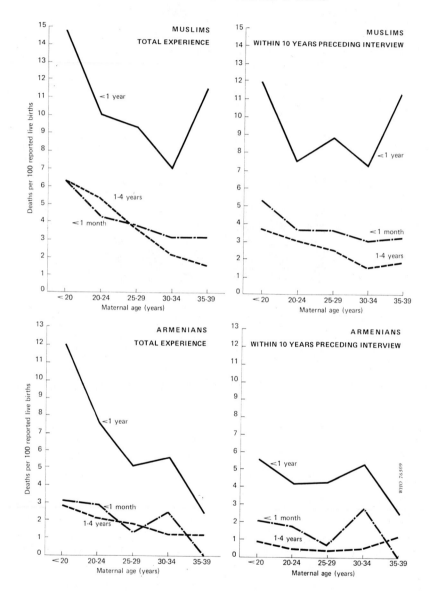

percentages of deaths of children born to women aged under 25 years at the time of giving birth have declined over the last 10 years ; for example, Muslim women over 35 at interview had lost, within one month of birth, 6.4% of the children born to them when they were under 25, while those women aged under 25 at interview had lost only 4.3% of their children within the first month. Although the decline, particularly for deaths under 5 years, may be exaggerated by the shortening of the period of exposure to risk, the fact that women aged 25–34 at interview reported an intermediate rate of child mortality does indicate a downward trend. A decline in mortality over successive generations, in the case of children born to mothers aged 25–34, is evident only for Armenians.

Under these circumstances, the effect of pooling the experience of different generations is to exaggerate or even reverse the direction of the relationship between child mortality and maternal age. This can be seen in Table 4.B.3 by comparing the trends shown by the figures above the diagonal lines (i.e., mortality among recent births to women of each cohort) with those shown in the rows giving total mortality rates (all cohorts pooled).

Mortality among children born during the 10 years preceding the interview was evidently lower than that when births occurring over the total pregnancy history period were considered. This was true for both Muslims and Armenians and for all risk periods (Table 4.B.4 and Fig. 4.B.2).

Among Muslim children, mortality rates were highest when the mothers were under 20 years of age at the time of birth, the rates declining thereafter with maternal age. At older ages (35–39) [1] the risks of mortality increased among children aged 1–11 months, an increase that was also reflected in the under 1-year and under 5-year periods.

For Armenians, whose child mortality rates were lower, children born to young mothers (under 20) also exhibited a high mortality ; for older mothers the rates fluctuated around a low level.

Child Mortality and Birth Order

As with maternal age, the relationship between the proportion of children dying and birth order was found to be distorted by the effects of changes in mortality over time. Table 4.B.5 and Fig. 4.B.3 show, according to birth order, total child mortality rates and deaths among children born during the 10 years preceding the interview. The latter figures (which provide a more reliable guide than the former) show a shallow U-shaped relationship to birth order. The highest risks were experienced by first order children and by those of sixth and higher birth orders, and the lowest risks at intermediate birth orders. The exception was mortality at 1–4 years, which did not conform to this pattern.

---

[1] The number of births to women aged 40–44 were too small to be included in the analysis.

221

Culture	Age of child at death	Age of mother at interview	Deaths as percentages of live births at maternal age :		
			<25	25–34	35–44
Muslim	under 1 month	<25	4.3	—	—
		25–34	5.4	3.8	—
		35–44	6.4	3.4	3.3
		Total	5.3	3.6	3.3
	1–11 months	<25	5.4	—	—
		25–34	6.9	5.2	—
		35–44	8.3	4.8	7.5
		Total	7.1	4.9	7.5
	under 1 year	<25	9.7	—	—
		25–34	12.3	9.0	—
		35–44	15.7	8.2	10.8
		Total	12.4	8.5	10.8
	1–4 years	<25	2.8	—	—
		25–34	5.5	1.9	—
		35–44	3.9	4.3	1.9
		Total	5.7	3.2	1.9
	under 5 years	<25	12.5	—	—
		25–34	17.8	10.9	—
		35–44	19.6	12.5	12.7
		Total	18.1	11.7	12.7
Armenian	under 1 month	<25	1.5	—	—
		25–34	2.1	1.2	—
		35–44	4.7	1.9	0.6
		Total	3.0	1.7	0.6
	1–11 months	<25	2.5	—	—
		25–34	5.4	3.3	—
		35–44	8.9	3.6	2.2
		Total	6.3	3.5	2.2
	under 1 year	<25	4.0	—	—
		25–34	7.5	4.5	—
		35–44	13.6	5.5	2.8
		Total	9.3	5.2	2.8
	1–4 years	<25	0.4	—	—
		25–34	1.6	0.3	—
		35–44	4.1	2.5	1.2
		Total	2.4	1.7	1.2
	under 5 years	<25	4.4	—	—
		25–34	9.1	4.8	—
		35–44	17.7	8.0	4.0
		Total	11.7	6.9	4.0

TABLE 4.B.4. CHILD MORTALITY DURING THE 10 YEARS PRECEDING INTERVIEW,
BY CULTURE AND MATERNAL AGE *

Culture and maternal age	Reported live births	Deaths per 100 reported live births at:				
		<1 month	1–11 months	<1 year	1–4 years	<5 years
Muslim						
<20	979	5.3	6.7	12.0	3.3	15.3
20–24	1208	3.6	3.9	7.5	2.8	10.3
25–29	825	3.6	5.2	8.8	2.3	11.1
30–34	428	3.0	4.2	7.2	1.4	8.6
35–39	191	3.1	8.4	11.5	1.6	13.1
40–44	23	(4.3)	(0.0)	(4.3)	(4.3)	(8.7)
Total	3654	4.0	5.2	9.2	2.6	11.8
Armenian						
<20	338	2.1	3.5	5.6	0.9	6.5
20–24	960	1.8	2.4	4.2	0.5	4.7
25–29	730	0.7	3.6	4.3	0.4	4.7
30–34	418	2.9	2.4	5.3	0.5	5.8
35–39	161	0.0	2.5	2.5	1.2	3.7
40–44	13	(7.7)	(0.0)	(7.7)	(0.0)	(7.7)
Total	2626	1.6	2.8	4.4	0.6	5.0

* Figures in parentheses refer to fewer than 25 EW.

Child Mortality, Birth Order, and Maternal Age

With increasing birth order there was an overall rise in the percentage of deaths under one year among children born to women in most age groups (Table 4.B.6). The rise was, however, frequently preceded by an initial decline, so that the lowest proportion of deaths occurred at intermediate birth orders, resulting in a U-shaped or V-shaped pattern.

Child Mortality and Preceding Pregnancy Intervals

The relationship between child mortality and the preceding pregnancy intervals (excluding first births) was a negative one for all the components of child mortality (Table 4.B.7 and Fig. 4.B.4). Thus, the mortality risks for those children under 5 years were high for pregnancy intervals of 2 years or less (18.8% for Muslim and 11.3% for Armenian children) and declined for longer pregnancy intervals. This pattern was sustained for both cultures.

TABLE 4.B.5. CHILD MORTALITY BY BIRTH ORDER AND CULTURE
(TOTAL EXPERIENCE AND WITHIN 10 YEARS PRECEDING INTERVIEW)

Culture and birth order	Reported live births	Deaths per 100 reported live births at :				
		<1 month	1–11 months	<1 year	1–4 years	<5 years
Muslim						
Total experience						
1	1922	6.3	7.7	14.0	4.8	18.8
2	1643	4.6	6.2	10.8	6.6	17.4
3	1282	4.1	5.7	9.8	5.8	15.6
4	960	3.6	6.8	10.4	4.1	14.5
5	703	3.7	5.8	9.5	3.9	13.4
6 and over	1141	4.9	6.1	11.0	3.2	14.2
Total	7651	4.8	6.5	11.3	5.0	16.3
Within 10 years preceding interview						
1	815	5.3	6.2	11.5	2.2	13.7
2	720	3.6	4.3	7.9	3.5	11.4
3	584	3.9	3.9	7.9	3.1	11.0
4	456	2.2	5.5	7.7	2.4	10.1
5	374	2.9	5.3	8.3	2.4	10.7
6 and over	705	4.7	5.7	10.4	2.0	12.3
Total	3654	4.0	5.2	9.2	2.6	11.8
Armenian						
Total experience						
1	1920	2.8	6.2	9.0	2.0	11.0
2	1653	2.5	5.5	8.0	2.4	10.4
3	1273	2.4	4.7	7.1	2.2	9.3
4	897	2.1	5.2	7.3	1.6	8.9
5	558	2.0	3.2	5.2	1.2	6.4
6 and over	650	2.6	4.2	6.8	1.8	8.6
Total	6951	2.5	5.2	7.7	2.1	9.8
Within 10 years preceding interview						
1	631	2.1	2.8	4.9	0.6	5.5
2	615	1.0	1.9	2.9	0.5	3.4
3	490	1.8	3.7	5.5	0.8	6.3
4	347	1.7	3.5	5.2	0.3	5.5
5	229	1.3	1.8	3.1	0.4	3.5
6 and over	314	1.6	3.5	5.1	0.6	5.7
Total	2626	1.6	2.8	4.4	0.6	5.0

FIG. 4.B.3. CHILD MORTALITY BY BIRTH ORDER AND CULTURE:
TOTAL AND DURING PRECEDING 10 YEARS

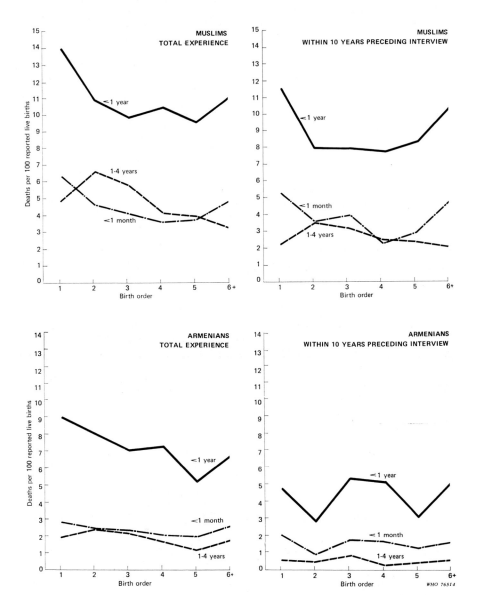

TABLE 4.B.6. DEATHS UNDER 1 YEAR DURING 10 YEARS PRECEDING INTERVIEW, BY BIRTH ORDER, CULTURE, AND MATERNAL AGE *

Culture	Maternal age	Deaths per 100 reported live births at birth order:					
		1	2	3	4	5	6 and over
Muslim	<20	13.1	9.8	12.3	(0.0)	(50.0)	(0.0)
	20–24	6.6	7.4	7.9	7.4	5.3	17.8
	25–29	(0.0)	3.5	5.7	8.6	9.3	12.3
	30–34	(20.0)	(0.0)	(0.0)	7.5	7.2	7.8
	35–39	(25.0)	(0.0)	(7.7)	(0.0)	(11.8)	8.4
	40–44	—	—	(0.0)	(0.0)	(0.0)	(5.9)
Armenian	<20	5.2	6.2	(20.0)	(0.0)	—	—
	20–24	4.1	2.5	5.2	13.4	(0.0)	—
	25–29	10.5	2.3	4.7	4.2	1.1	8.3
	30–34	(0.0)	(5.6)	8.8	3.1	5.2	5.7
	35–39	(0.0)	(0.0)	(0.0)	(0.0)	3.7	2.6
	40–44	—	(0.0)	(0.0)	(0.0)	(0.0)	(10.0)

* Figures in parentheses refer to fewer than 25 EW.

TABLE 4.B.7. CHILD MORTALITY DURING 10 YEARS PRECEDING INTERVIEW, BY CULTURE AND DURATION OF PRECEDING PREGNANCY INTERVAL *

Culture	Duration of preceding pregnancy interval (years)	Deaths per 100 live births in 10 years preceding interview, at:					Total live births in past 10 years
		<1 month	1–11 months	<1 year	1–4 years	<5 years	
Muslim	<1	(0.0)	(5.0)	(5.0)	(0.0)	(5.0)	20
	1	6.4	8.5	14.9	3.9	18.8	698
	2	3.2	5.0	8.2	3.2	11.4	1026
	3	2.9	2.5	5.4	1.8	7.2	663
	4	1.7	2.7	4.4	1.7	6.1	294
	5 and over	1.4	3.2	4.6	0.9	5.5	218
Armenian	<1	(0.0)	(0.0)	(0.0)	(0.0)	(0.0)	8
	1	3.7	6.1	9.8	1.5	11.3	327
	2	1.2	3.3	4.5	0.4	4.9	671
	3	1.3	2.6	3.9	0.2	4.1	463
	4	0.8	1.1	1.9	0.4	2.3	263
	5 and over	1.0	0.4	1.4	0.3	1.7	293

* Figures in parentheses refer to fewer than 25 EW.

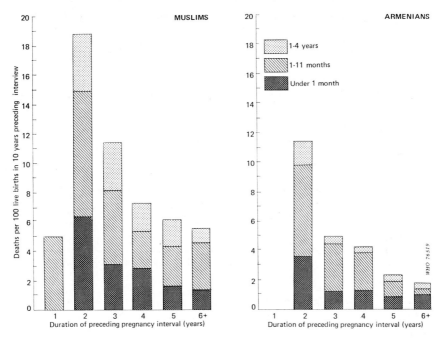

FIG. 4.B.4. CHILD MORTALITY DURING 10 YEARS PRECEDING INTERVIEW, BY CULTURE AND DURATION OF PRECEDING PREGNANCY INTERVAL

C. BEIRUT

C. Churchill, I. Lorfing, H. Zurayk and J. Azar

Child Mortality by Culture and Social Status

Of the 12 268 live births reported by the eligible women, 5.1% did not survive their fifth birthday, 1.8% died during the first month of life, and 3.9% died sometime in the first year. These rates are low compared to those of other developing countries.

Shiite women reported higher mortality rates for their children under 5 years of age than did Maronite women (Table 4.C.1 and Fig. 4.C.1). Among the Maronites, the rates for mortality under 1 month were higher for lower status women, while the death rates at 1–11 months and at 1–4 years were higher for women of the middle social status. The mortality rates for the Shiite children were consistently higher in the low status than in the middle status group.

Child Mortality and Maternal Age

Child mortality rates at first declined with increasing maternal age and then rose again for all risk groups except 1–11 months and 1–4 years. This

227

general pattern applied to the children of both Shiite and Maronite women. A U-shaped relationship with maternal age was noticeable for deaths under 1 month and under 1 year, more especially among Shiites. Among Maronites, although there was a decline in child mortality for women giving birth at over 40, this information could not be considered reliable owing to the small number of births occurring to Maronite women of this age (Table 4.C.2 and Fig. 4.C.2).

The extent of the initial decline and the final rise varied according to the risk period concerned, and it was only for deaths occurring under 1 month of age that the rates for both cultural groups were higher towards the end of the childbearing period than at the beginning.

TABLE 4.C.1. CHILD MORTALITY BY CULTURE AND SOCIAL STATUS

Culture and social status	Deaths per 100 reported live births at :					Total reported live births
	<1 month	1–11 months	<1 year	1–4 years	<5 years	
Shiite						
Middle	1.3	2.3	3.6	1.6	5.2	3029
Low	2.3	2.7	5.0	1.7	6.7	3975
Total	1.9	2.6	4.5	1.5	6.0	7004
Maronite						
Middle	1.9	1.4	3.3	0.8	4.1	2911
Low	1.5	1.5	3.0	1.2	4.2	2353
Total	1.7	1.4	3.1	0.9	4.1	5264

FIG. 4.C.1. CHILD MORTALITY BY CULTURE AND SOCIAL STATUS

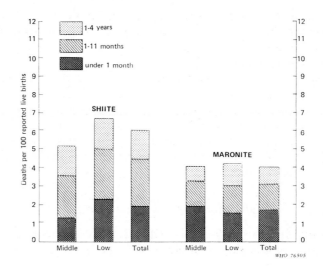

WHO 76505

TABLE 4.C.2. CHILD MORTALITY BY CULTURE AND MATERNAL AGE *

Culture and maternal age	Reported live births	Deaths per 100 reported live births at :				
		<1 month	1–11 months	<1 year	1–4 years	<5 years
Shiite						
<20	1303	2.1	3.4	5.5	1.8	7.3
20–24	2507	1.7	3.0	4.7	1.4	6.1
25–29	1793	1.4	1.6	3.0	1.6	4.6
30–34	1014	2.2	2.2	4.4	1.5	5.9
35–39	344	2.9	1.7	4.6	1.2	5.8
40–44	43	7.0	0.0	7.0	0.0	7.0
Total	7004	1.9	2.6	4.5	1.5	6.0
Maronite						
<20	661	1.8	1.6	3.4	1.9	5.3
20–24	1858	1.2	1.8	3.0	1.2	4.2
25–29	1642	1.7	1.4	3.1	0.9	4.0
30–34	839	2.1	1.2	3.3	0.2	3.5
35–39	249	3.2	0.8	4.0	0.8	4.8
40–44	15	(0.0)	(0.0)	(0.0)	(0.0)	(0.0)
Total	5264	1.7	1.4	3.1	0.9	4.0

* Figures in parentheses refer to fewer than 25 EW.

Some of the births to women who delivered when they were under 20 will have occurred up to 30 years before the interview ; whereas all of the births reported by women who gave birth at age 40 and over will have taken place within the preceding 5 years. If child mortality risk factors have changed over the period, this could distort the relationship between mortality and maternal age. Table 4.C.3 shows child mortality rates according to maternal age and the age of the mother at interview. In this way a rough control is introduced for changes in risk factors.

It can be seen that, with one exception, women aged 35 and over at interview had lost, within each risk period, a higher percentage of the children born to them before they were 25 than had the women still aged under 25. For example, Shiite women aged 35 and over at interview had lost within a month of birth 2.2% of the children born to them before they were 25 years old ; while those still aged under 25 years at interview had lost only 1.7%. This suggests a decline in child mortality over the 30 years recalled by the eligible women.

The exception concerns Maronite children who died in the first month of life ; the mortality rates in this case appear to have increased over the years from 1.0% to 2.1% of all live-born children of women aged under 25 at the time. It is possible that the apparent change is due to disproportionate underreporting of deaths by the older women.

229

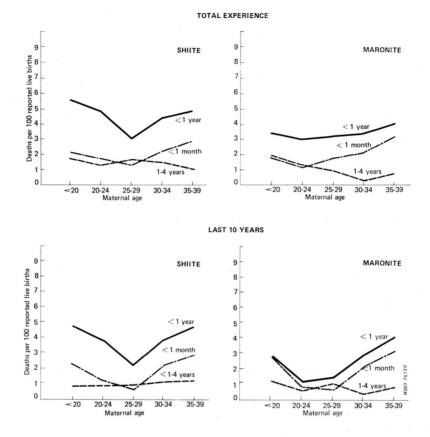

The decline in mortality rates that has been shown to have occurred may be exaggerated by the shortening of the actual periods of exposure to risk, particularly in the case of deaths occurring before the fifth birthday ; thus, some of the recent births will have occurred less than 5 years prior to interview. If, nevertheless, the trends are real, the relationship between mortality and maternal age should assume more of a J-shape than is shown in Table 4.C.2 and Fig. 4.C.2. This can be seen in Table 4.C.3, in which the figures in the total rows represent the relationship of child mortality to maternal age for all age cohorts of women pooled (the pattern shown in Table 4.C.2), while the figures above the diagonal lines show only recent births to women of each age cohort. For recent births it is the oldest mothers who show the highest child mortality rates in every case, and the decline at intermediate ages is more marked than when all cohorts are pooled.

The relationship between maternal age and percentages of deaths of children born within 10 years preceding interview is shown in more detail

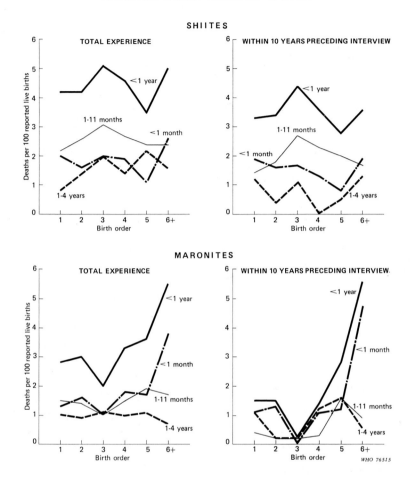

FIG. 4.C.3. CHILD MORTALITY BY CULTURE AND BIRTH ORDER:
TOTAL AND DURING PRECEDING 10 YEARS

in Table 4.C.4 and Fig. 4.C.2. For women of both cultures, this relationship describes a U-shaped curve, both for deaths under 1 year and for deaths under 1 month. The other risk periods show no familiar pattern for either culture.

Child Mortality and Birth Order

Changes in mortality rates over time distort not only the relationship between maternal age and death rates, but also that between death rates and birth order. The following analyses therefore present births during

Culture	Age of child at death	Age of mother at interview	Deaths as percentages of live births at maternal age :		
			<25	25–34	35–44
Shiites	under 1 month	<25	1.7	—	—
		25–34	1.7	0.8	—
		35–44	2.2	2.3	3.4
		Total	1.8	1.7	3.4
	1–11 months	<25	2.4	—	—
		25–34	2.8	1.5	—
		35–44	4.5	2.1	1.6
		Total	3.2	1.8	1.6
	under 1 year	<25	4.1	—	—
		25–34	4.5	2.3	—
		35–44	6.7	4.4	5.0
		Total	5.0	3.5	5.0
	1–4 years	<25	0.5	—	—
		25–34	1.3	0.7	—
		35–44	2.8	2.3	1.1
		Total	1.5	1.5	1.1
	under 5 years	<25	4.6	—	—
		25–34	5.8	3.0	—
		35–44	9.5	6.7	6.1
		Total	6.5	5.0	6.1
Maronites	under 1 month	<25	2.1	—	—
		25–34	1.5	1.0	—
		35–44	1.0	2.3	3.0
		Total	1.4	1.9	3.0
	1–11 months	<25	0.3	—	—
		25–34	0.6	0.7	—
		35–44	3.4	1.6	0.8
		Total	1.6	1.3	0.8
	under 1 year	<25	2.4	—	—
		25–34	2.1	1.7	—
		35–44	4.4	3.9	3.8
		Total	3.0	3.2	3.8
	1–4 years	<25	0.6	—	—
		25–34	0.8	0.7	—
		35–44	2.1	0.6	0.8
		Total	1.3	0.7	0.8
	under 5 years	<25	3.0	—	—
		25–34	2.9	2.4	—
		35–44	6.5	4.5	4.6
		Total	4.3	3.9	4.6

the 10 years before interview, as well as the patterns displayed by all births for the purpose of comparison (Table 4.C.5 and Fig. 4.C.3).

For the children of Maronite women, death rates under 1 month and under 1 year varied with birth order, giving a curve with a definite J-shape. The mortality rates for other age periods did not follow any well-defined pattern, while for the children of Shiite women no discernible pattern emerged for any of the risk periods.

Child Mortality, Birth Order, and Maternal Age

When child mortality rates are analysed by birth order and maternal age simultaneously, the rates for deaths under 1 month and for 1–11 months become too small for valid conclusions to be drawn. For this reason, the rate for deaths under 1 year has been used in the analysis, as shown in Table 4.C.6.

TABLE 4.C.4. CHILD MORTALITY DURING 10 YEARS PRECEDING INTERVIEW, BY CULTURE AND MATERNAL AGE *

Culture and maternal age	Reported live births	Deaths per 100 reported live births at:				
		<1 month	1–11 months	<1 year	1–4 years	<5 years
Shiite						
<20	426	2.3	2.4	4.7	0.7	5.4
20–24	1182	1.3	2.4	3.7	0.8	4.5
25–29	948	0.6	1.5	2.1	0.8	2.9
30–34	644	2.2	1.7	3.9	1.1	5.0
35–39	344	2.9	1.7	4.6	1.2	5.8
40 and over	43	7.0	0.0	7.0	0.0	7.0
Total	3587	1.6	1.9	3.5	0.9	4.4
Maronite						
<20	153	2.6	0.0	2.6	1.3	3.9
20–24	656	0.9	0.2	1.1	0.6	1.7
25–29	709	0.7	0.7	1.4	1.0	2.4
30–34	509	2.1	0.8	2.9	0.4	3.3
35–39	249	3.2	0.8	4.0	0.8	4.8
40 and over	15	(0.0)	(0.0)	(0.0)	(0.0)	(0.0)
Total	2291	1.5	0.5	2.0	0.7	2.7

* Figures in parentheses refer to fewer than 5 EW.

TABLE 4.C.5. CHILD MORTALITY BY CULTURE AND BIRTH ORDER
(TOTAL EXPERIENCE AND BIRTHS WITHIN 10 YEARS PRECEDING INTERVIEW)

Culture and birth order	Reported live births	Deaths per 100 reported live births at:				
		<1 month	1–11 months	<1 year	1–4 years	<5 years
Shiite						
Total experience						
1	1412	2.0	2.2	4.2	0.8	5.0
2	1268	1.6	2.6	4.2	1.4	5.6
3	1093	2.0	3.1	5.1	2.0	7.1
4	888	1.9	2.7	4.6	1.4	6.0
5	720	1.1	2.4	3.5	2.2	5.7
6 and over	1623	2.6	2.4	5.0	1.6	6.6
Total	7004	1.9	2.6	4.5	1.5	6.0
Within 10 years preceding interview						
1	574	1.9	1.4	3.3	1.2	4.5
2	554	1.6	1.8	3.4	0.4	3.8
3	524	1.7	2.7	4.4	1.1	5.5
4	443	1.3	2.3	3.6	0.0	3.6
5	398	0.8	2.0	2.8	0.5	3.3
6 and over	1094	1.9	1.7	3.6	1.3	4.9
Total	3587	1.6	1.9	3.5	0.9	4.4
Maronite						
Total experience						
1	1350	1.3	1.5	2.8	1.0	3.8
2	1195	1.6	1.4	3.0	0.9	3.9
3	980	1.0	1.0	2.0	1.1	3.1
4	721	1.8	1.5	3.3	1.0	4.3
5	469	1.7	1.9	3.6	1.1	4.7
6 and over	549	3.8	1.7	5.5	0.7	6.2
Total	5264	1.7	1.4	3.1	0.9	4.0
Within 10 years preceding interview						
1	455	1.1	0.4	1.5	1.1	2.6
2	468	1.3	0.2	1.5	0.2	1.7
3	430	0.0	0.2	0.2	0.2	0.5
4	349	1.1	0.3	1.4	1.2	2.6
5	249	1.2	1.6	2.8	1.6	4.4
6 and over	340	4.7	0.9	5.6	0.6	6.2
Total	2291	1.5	0.5	2.0	0.7	2.7

234

TABLE 4.C.6. DEATHS UNDER 1 YEAR DURING 10 YEARS PRECEDING INTERVIEW, BY BIRTH ORDER, CULTURE, AND MATERNAL AGE *

Culture	Maternal age	Deaths per 100 reported live births at birth order:					
		1	2	3	4	5	6 and over
Shiite	<20	3.7	5.7	8.3	(0.0)	—	—
	20–24	3.1	2.6	4.1	4.9	4.4	6.5
	25–29	1.6	1.1	1.5	1.7	2.4	2.9
	30–34	(9.1)	(8.7)	11.1	6.4	2.6	2.8
	35–39	(0.0)	(20.0)	(10.0)	(0.0)	(0.0)	4.7
	40–44	—	—	—	(0.0)	(0.0)	7.3
Maronite	<20	1.8	5.6	(0.0)	—	(0.0)	—
	20–24	0.9	1.8	0.0	1.6	(0.0)	(0.0)
	25–29	3.0	0.0	0.6	0.7	2.3	5.8
	30–34	0.0	2.0	0.0	1.0	3.8	6.4
	35–39	(0.0)	(0.0)	(0.0)	5.4	2.5	5.3
	40–44	(0.0)	(0.0)	—	(0.0)	(0.0)	(0.0)

* Figures in parentheses refer to fewer than 25 EW.

Within the first year of life and for most maternal age groups death rates at first declined and then rose with birth order, reaching a maximum at the highest birth orders. There were two exceptions : firstly, death rates under 1 year for children of women giving birth under 20 years rose uninterruptedly for the short range of birth orders available ; secondly, for Shiite women between 30 and 34, death rates under 1 year decreased with rising birth order.

TABLE 4.C.7. CHILD MORTALITY DURING 10 YEARS PRECEDING INTERVIEW, BY CULTURE AND DURATION OF PRECEDING PREGNANCY INTERVAL

Culture	Duration of preceding pregnancy interval (years)	Deaths per 100 live births in 10 years preceding interview, at:					Total live births in past 10 years
		<1 month	1–11 months	<1 year	1–4 years	<5 years	
Shiite	<1	5.2	3.9	9.1	0.0	9.1	154
	1	2.0	2.7	4.7	0.9	5.6	1356
	2	1.2	1.3	2.5	1.2	3.7	1101
	3	0.0	0.6	0.6	0.0	0.6	319
	4	0.0	1.2	1.2	1.1	2.3	87
	5 and over	2.9	1.4	4.3	0.0	4.3	70
Maronite	<1	4.2	3.2	7.4	1.0	8.4	95
	1	1.7	0.8	2.5	0.6	3.1	646
	2	1.2	0.4	1.6	0.7	2.3	643
	3	0.7	0.0	0.7	0.7	1.4	286
	4	2.0	0.0	2.0	0.9	2.9	102
	5 and over	1.7	0.0	1.7	0.0	1.7	119

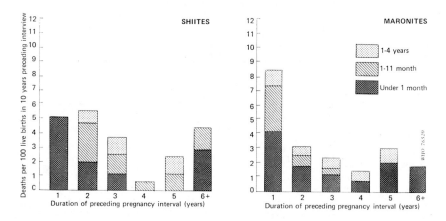

Child Mortality and Preceding Pregnancy Intervals

The relationship between child mortality rates and preceding pregnancy intervals (excluding first births) described a reversed J-shaped curve for all the components of child mortality. That is, mortality risks under 5 years were high (9.1% and 8.4% for Shiite and Maronite children respectively) for pregnancy intervals of 1 year or less and declined for longer pregnancy intervals. The pattern was sustained for both cultures, with the lowest risks for a preceding pregnancy interval of 4 years (Table 4.C.7 and Fig. 4.C.4).

D. MANILA

V. Balderrama-Guzman, G. B. Roman and A. R. Omran

Child Mortality by Residence and Social Status

The women in the study reported 14 605 live births over their years of marriage. Of these children, 2.8% had died during the first month of life, 5.0% during the first year, and 7.5% within the first 5 years. For all social

236

TABLE 4.D.1. CHILD MORTALITY BY RESIDENCE AND SOCIAL STATUS

Residence and social status	Deaths per 100 reported live births at:					Total reported live births
	<1 month	1–11 months	<1 year	1–4 years	<5 years	
Rural						
Middle	2.6	1.9	4.5	1.8	6.3	6122
Low	3.3	2.8	6.1	3.3	9.4	1717
Total	2.7	2.1	4.8	2.1	6.9	7839
Urban						
Middle	2.9	2.2	5.1	2.5	7.6	5814
Low	3.5	3.6	7.1	7.8	14.9	952
Total	3.0	2.4	5.4	3.0	8.4	6766

status groups and all risk periods, urban mortality was higher than rural (Table 4.D.1 and Fig. 4.D.1). For both urban and rural groups, children from low status families had a higher rate of mortality than those from middle status families.

FIG. 4.D.1. CHILD MORTALITY BY RESIDENCE AND SOCIAL STATUS

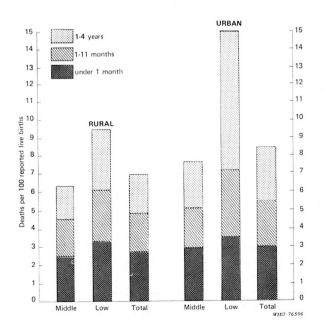

WHO 76506

237

Child Mortality and Maternal Age

Among rural women child mortality generally declined with maternal age, although the decline was not consistent throughout the age range (Table 4.D.2 and Fig. 4.D.2).

TABLE 4.D.2. CHILD MORTALITY BY RESIDENCE AND MATERNAL AGE

Residence and maternal age	Reported live births	Deaths per 100 reported live births at:				
		<1 month	1–11 months	<1 year	1–4 years	<5 years
Rural						
<20	891	3.8	2.7	6.5	2.3	8.8
20–24	2671	3.3	1.8	5.1	2.1	7.2
25–29	2375	2.1	2.3	4.4	1.8	6.2
30–34	1335	2.1	2.0	4.1	2.4	6.5
35–39	503	2.4	2.2	4.6	1.6	6.2
40–44	64	1.6	0.0	1.6	3.2	4.8
Total	7839	2.7	2.1	4.8	2.1	6.9
Urban						
<20	1016	3.7	2.8	6.5	2.8	9.3
20–24	2448	3.1	2.0	5.1	3.1	8.2
25–29	1931	2.5	2.5	5.0	3.1	8.1
30–34	1009	2.4	2.6	5.0	3.0	8.0
35–39	328	3.0	3.3	6.3	2.1	8.4
40–44	34	8.8	0.0	8.8	0.0	8.8
Total	6766	2.9	2.4	5.3	3.0	8.3

Mortality rates for the children of urban women, on the other hand, described more of a J-shaped pattern in relation to age, in first month of life as well as in the risk periods under 1 year and under 5 years. The rates for the risk periods 1–11 months and 1–4 years declined with maternal age, especially among children of women in the age group 40–44 years, where the numbers were small.

At most maternal ages, mortality among the children of urban women was higher than among those of rural women, and the difference was greatest for deaths under 5 years.

One of the factors that may distort the relationship between child mortality and maternal age is changes in risk factors with time. Births in

FIG. 4.D.2. CHILD MORTALITY BY RESIDENCE AND MATERNAL AGE: TOTAL AND DURING PRECEDING 10 YEARS

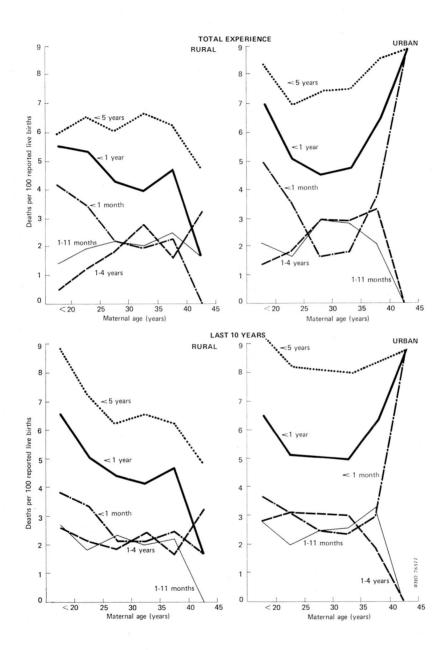

TABLE 4.D.3. CHILD MORTALITY BY MATERNAL AGE, RESIDENCE, AND AGE AT INTERVIEW

Residence	Age of child at death	Age of mother at interview	Deaths as percentages of live births at maternal age :		
			<25	25–34	35–44
Rural	under 1 month	<25	3.4	—	—
		25–34	3.3	2.0	—
		35–44	3.6	2.2	2.3
		Total	3.4	2.1	2.3
	1–11 months	<25	1.5	—	—
		25–34	2.0	2.2	—
		35–44	2.4	2.3	1.9
		Total	2.0	2.3	1.9
	under 1 year	<25	4.9	—	—
		25–34	5.3	4.2	—
		35–44	6.0	4.5	4.2
		Total	5.4	4.4	4.2
	1–4 years	<25	0.5	—	—
		25–34	2.3	1.7	—
		35–44	3.2	2.3	1.8
		Total	2.2	2.0	1.8
	under 5 years	<25	5.4	—	—
		25–34	7.6	5.9	—
		35–44	9.2	6.8	6.0
		Total	7.6	6.4	6.0
Urban	under 1 month	<25	4.5	—	—
		25–34	2.8	1.6	—
		35–44	2.6	3.2	3.6
		Total	3.3	2.4	3.6
	1–11 months	<25	1.8	—	—
		25–34	1.8	2.4	—
		35–44	3.6	2.7	3.1
		Total	2.0	3.4	3.1
	under 1 year	<25	6.3	—	—
		25–34	4.6	4.0	—
		35–44	6.2	5.9	6.7
		Total	5.5	5.0	6.7
	1–4 years	<25	1.2	—	—
		25–34	2.6	2.6	—
		35–44	4.3	3.4	2.0
		Total	2.9	3.0	2.0
	under 5 years	<25	7.5	—	—
		25–34	8.2	6.6	—
		35–44	10.5	9.3	8.7
		Total	8.4	8.0	8.7

TABLE 4.D.4. CHILD MORTALITY DURING 10 YEARS PRECEDING INTERVIEW,
BY RESIDENCE AND MATERNAL AGE

Residence and maternal age	Reported live births	Deaths per 100 reported live births at:				
		<1 month	1–11 months	<1 year	1–4 years	<5 years
Rural						
<20	289	4.1	1.4	5.5	0.4	5.9
20–24	1133	3.4	1.9	5.3	1.2	6.5
25–29	1310	2.1	2.1	4.2	1.8	6.0
30–34	934	2.0	1.9	3.9	2.7	6.6
35–39	503	2.4	2.2	4.6	1.6	6.2
40–44	64	1.6	0.0	1.6	3.1	4.7
Total	4233	2.6	1.9	4.5	1.8	6.3
Urban						
<20	473	4.9	2.1	7.0	1.3	8.3
20–24	1297	3.5	1.6	5.1	1.8	6.9
25–29	1165	1.6	2.9	4.5	2.9	7.4
30–34	751	1.8	2.9	4.7	2.8	7.5
35–39	328	3.1	3.3	6.4	2.1	8.5
40–44	34	8.8	0.0	8.8	0.0	8.8
Total	4048	2.8	2.4	5.2	2.2	7.4

the study population occurred over a time-span of 30 years preceding the interview.

To introduce an approximate control for changes in mortality risks over this period the women were divided into 3 age cohorts: those aged under 25 years at interview, those from 25 to 34 inclusive, and those aged 35 and over. Table 4.D.3 compares child mortality for these 3 groups according to the mother's age at childbirth. Among children born to rural women aged under 25 at the time of birth, death rates during the first month of life have shown only a slight and inconsistent decline in successive cohorts. The decline was slightly more marked for deaths under 1 year and deaths under 5 years.

For urban children who were born when their mothers were under 25, death rates for the first month and the first year increased somewhat; however, mortality under 5 years decreased.

If attention is confined to the relationship between maternal age and mortality among the most recent births occurring to each cohort (shown by the figures above the diagonal lines in Table 4.D.3), the patterns are somewhat different. The mortality experience among children born during the 10 years preceding the interview is shown in Table 4.D.4 and Fig. 4.D.3.

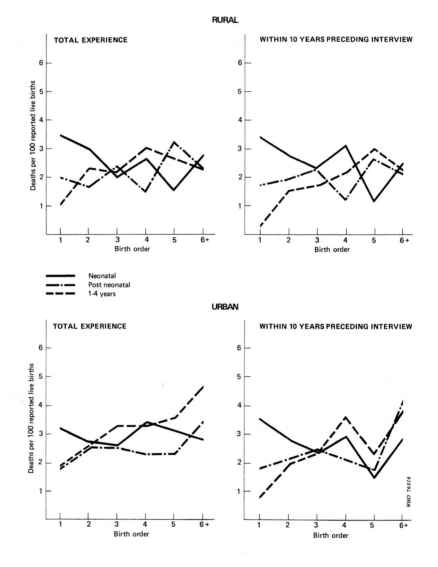

FIG. 4.D.3. CHILD MORTALITY BY RESIDENCE AND BIRTH ORDER:
TOTAL AND DURING PRECEDING 10 YEARS

TABLE 4.D.5. CHILD MORTALITY BY RESIDENCE AND BIRTH ORDER (TOTAL EXPERIENCE AND BIRTHS WITHIN 10 YEARS PRECEDING INTERVIEW)

Residence and birth order	Reported live births	Deaths per 100 reported live births at :				
		<1 month	1–11 months	<1 year	1–4 years	<5 years
Rural						
Total experience						
1	1840	3.4	2.0	5.4	1.0	6.4
2	1608	3.0	1.7	4.7	2.3	7.0
3	1321	2.0	2.4	4.4	2.2	6.6
4	1032	2.6	1.5	4.1	3.0	7.1
5	748	1.5	3.2	4.7	2.7	7.4
6 and over	1290	2.7	2.3	5.0	2.3	7.3
Total	7839	2.7	2.1	4.8	2.1	6.9
Within 10 years preceding interview						
1	785	3.4	1.7	5.1	0.3	5.4
2	741	2.8	1.9	4.7	1.5	6.2
3	666	2.3	2.3	4.5	1.7	6.2
4	581	3.1	1.2	4.3	2.2	6.5
5	467	1.1	2.6	3.6	3.0	6.6
6 and over	993	2.4	2.1	4.5	2.3	6.8
Total	4233	2.6	1.9	4.5	1.7	6.3
Urban						
Total experience						
1	1827	3.2	1.8	5.0	1.8	6.8
2	1495	2.7	2.5	5.2	2.5	7.7
3	1126	2.6	2.5	5.1	3.3	8.4
4	800	3.4	2.3	5.7	3.3	9.0
5	553	3.1	2.3	5.4	3.6	9.0
6 and over	965	2.8	3.4	6.2	4.7	10.9
Total	6766	2.9	2.4	5.3	3.0	8.3
Within 10 years preceding interview						
1	991	3.5	1.8	5.4	0.8	6.2
2	858	2.8	2.1	4.9	1.9	6.8
3	664	2.3	2.4	4.7	2.3	6.9
4	478	2.9	2.1	5.0	3.6	8.6
5	346	1.5	1.7	3.2	2.3	5.5
6 and over	771	2.8	4.1	6.9	3.8	10.7
Total	4048	2.8	2.4	5.2	2.3	7.4

Among urban children, death rates under 1 month, and to a lesser extent under 1 year and under 5 years, described a J-shape in relation to maternal age. The rates for 1–11 months and 1–4 years tended to decline with increasing maternal age. The high mortality rates among children born to rural mothers under 20 years of age was evident only for the risk periods under 1 month and under 1 year. Both rates thereafter declined with maternal age. Mortality in the period 1–11 months increased almost steadily with age. The pattern in the other risk periods was not consistent.

Child Mortality and Birth Order

Mortality experience for total births and for births occurring in the 10 years preceding the interview is shown in Table 4.D.5 and Fig. 4.D.3. Because of possible risk changes with time, the latter period is more reliable.

For children in rural areas, death rates under 1 month and under 1 year both gave a reverse J-shaped curve when plotted against birth order; the highest risks were experienced by first-born children; death rates then declined at first but from birth order 6 onwards there was a relative rise in mortality risks. The rates at both 1–11 months and 1–4 years tended to increase with birth order. Mortality under 5 followed a similar pattern.

In the urban area, deaths under 1 month and under 1 year showed a reversed J-shaped or U-shaped relationship to birth order. Mortality rates at 1–11 months and at 1–4 years increased with birth order. A similar increase with birth order was also observed for mortality under 5 years.

Child Mortality, Birth Order, and Maternal Age

When child mortality rates are analysed by birth order and maternal age simultaneously, the rates for deaths under 1 month and for 1–11 months become too small for valid conclusions to be drawn. For this reason, the rate for deaths under 1 year has been given in Table 4.D.6.

With increasing birth order, mortality during the first year of life tended to increase among the children of women in some age groups; for other age groups, the relationship was U-shaped, and for still others, the pattern was not clear.

Child Mortality and Duration of Preceding Pregnancy Intervals

In both the urban and rural areas, child mortality declined as the interval since the preceding birth increased, although the relationship was rather more erratic than that found by other collaborating centres (Table 4.D.7 and Fig. 4.D.4).

TABLE 4.D.6. DEATHS UNDER 1 YEAR DURING THE 10 YEARS PRECEDING INTERVIEW,
BY RESIDENCE, BIRTH ORDER, AND MATERNAL AGE *

Residence	Maternal age	Deaths per 100 live births at birth order :					
		1	2	3	4	5	6 and over
Rural	<20	5.2	7.7	(0.0)	(0.0)	(0.0)	(0.0)
	20–24	7.0	3.6	4.3	7.7	(4.8)	(14.3)
	25–29	2.0	4.3	5.7	3.0	3.5	3.9
	30–34	0.0	1.8	3.1	4.6	2.3	5.4
	35–39	(0.0)	(7.1)	(0.0)	6.9	6.5	4.1
	40–44	—	—	(0.0)	(0.0)	(0.0)	1.8
Urban	<20	4.9	10.8	(18.8)	(50.0)	—	—
	20–24	5.8	4.5	4.5	7.0	(0.0)	(0.0)
	25–29	4.8	2.3	3.9	4.8	3.6	9.2
	30–34	4.8	4.7	6.2	3.7	2.3	5.6
	35–39	(9.1)	(12.5)	(0.0)	(0.0)	7.4	7.0
	40–44	—	(0.0)	(0.0)	(0.0)	(0.0)	12.0

* Figures in parentheses refer to fewer than 25 EW.

TABLE 4.D.7. CHILD MORTALITY DURING THE 10 YEARS PRECEDING INTERVIEW,
BY RESIDENCE AND DURATION OF PRECEDING PREGNANCY INTERVAL

Residence	Duration of preceding pregnancy interval (years)	Deaths per 100 live births in 10 years preceding interview, at :					Total live births in past 10 years
		<1 month	1–11 months	<1 year	1–4 years	<5 years	
Rural	<1	6.6	9.1	15.7	2.1	17.8	197
	1	2.3	1.8	4.1	2.2	6.3	1507
	2	2.0	1.6	3.6	2.3	5.9	1162
	3	2.8	0.3	3.1	0.8	3.9	386
	4	2.0	2.0	4.0	1.9	5.9	152
	5 and over	0.0	1.9	1.9	2.0	3.9	103
Urban	<1	4.1	3.8	7.9	5.6	13.5	266
	1	2.8	2.6	5.4	2.3	7.7	1618
	2	1.8	2.3	4.1	2.7	6.8	812
	3	3.3	2.5	5.8	2.0	7.8	243
	4	1.0	5.1	6.1	3.0	9.1	99
	5 and over	1.1	0.0	1.1	1.1	2.2	91

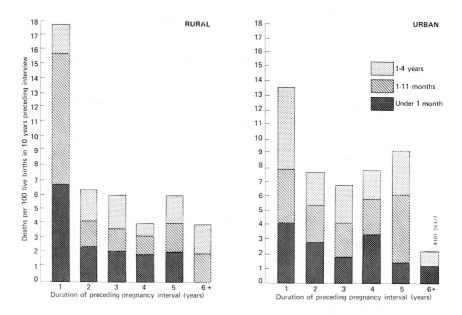

ANKARA

M. Bertan, K. Sümbüloglu and N. H. Fişek

Child Mortality by Residence and Social Status

Of the 15 289 children born to the women in the study, 3.8% had died within a month of birth, 13.2% within a year, and 17.5% within 5 years. For each social status group at all risk periods, semi-urban mortality was lower than rural (Table 4.E.1 and Fig. 4.E.1). With the exception of mortality during the first month, the rate of child mortality in the rural area was higher in the low status than in the middle status group, while with the exception of mortality at 1–11 months, the rate in the semi-urban area was higher in the middle status.

Child Mortality and Maternal Age

In the semi-urban area, child mortality declined with increasing maternal age at all risk periods. Among the children from the rural area, deaths declined with maternal age until the mother was 40–44 years old, when the

246

rate rose slightly. However, deaths under 1 month and at 1–11 months in the rural area showed a U-shaped relationship to maternal age. The rates initially declined and then rose again, reaching their initial level towards the end of the mother's child-bearing years (Table 4.E.2 and Fig. 4.E.2). Rural infant mortality rates, on the other hand, exhibited a reversed J-shaped relationship to maternal age.

For almost all risk periods and for every maternal age group, the percentages of deaths among children of rural women were higher than those among the semi-urban women's children.

TABLE 4.E.1. CHILD MORTALITY BY RESIDENCE AND SOCIAL STATUS

Residence and social status	Deaths per 100 reported live births at :					Total reported live births
	<1 month	1–11 months	<1 year	1–4 years	<5 years	
Rural						
Middle	4.0	10.2	14.2	3.7	18.9	7104
Low	3.6	11.2	14.8	5.3	20.1	2145
Total	3.9	10.4	14.3	4.8	19.1	9249
Semi-urban						
Middle	3.6	7.8	11.4	3.6	15.0	5695
Low	2.6	8.6	11.2	1.7	12.9	349
Total	3.6	7.8	11.4	3.5	14.9	6044

In an attempt to examine changes in risk factors with time, the women were divided into 3 age cohorts : those under 25 at interview, those from 25 to 34 inclusive, and those from 35 to 45. The percentages of their children dying at the corresponding maternal age groups are shown in Table 4.E.3.

It can be seen that the percentages of children dying have declined over time, a trend that appears most markedly in the urban area. For example, semi-urban women still aged under 25 at interview reported that 2.5% of their children had died within a month of birth (those aged 35 at interview said that 7.1% of the children born to them before they were 25 had died within a month of birth). It is possible that some of the reduction in mortality was due to the shortening of the periods of exposure to risk for women still under 25 ; that is, some of their children may have been born less than 1 month prior to interview and many of the women will have further children (who may die) before they are 25. However, the lower percentage of deaths under 1 month among children of women aged between 25 and 34 compared with children of older women, if only those births occurring when each age group was under 25 are considered, indicates that the reduction in mortality is genuine.

247

FIG. 4.E.1. CHILD MORTALITY BY RESIDENCE AND SOCIAL STATUS

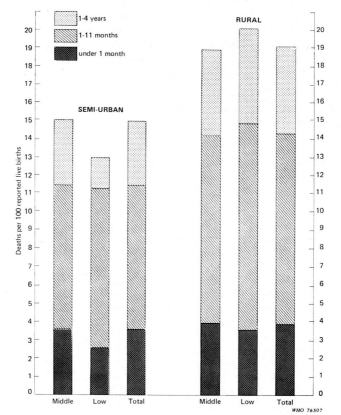

WHO 76507

TABLE 4.E.2. CHILD MORTALITY BY RESIDENCE AND MATERNAL AGE *

Residence	Maternal age	Deaths per 100 reported live births at :					Total reported live births
		<1 month	1–11 months	<1 year	1–4 years	<5 years	
Rural	<20	6.9	6.0	22.9	7.5	30.4	1966
	20–24	4.4	13.7	18.1	6.1	24.2	3394
	25–29	3.0	8.9	11.9	5.9	17.8	2348
	30–34	3.2	6.4	9.6	3.9	13.5	1174
	35–39	4.8	3.0	7.8	4.2	12.0	334
	40–44	6.4	6.4	12.8	0.0	12.8	31
Semi-urban	<20	6.5	13.1	19.6	6.0	25.6	1409
	20–24	4.3	9.6	13.9	4.4	18.3	2336
	25–29	3.5	6.3	9.8	3.5	13.3	1442
	30–34	1.2	6.9	8.1	1.5	10.6	651
	35–39	0.5	5.1	5.6	3.1	8.7	195
	40–44	(0.0)	(0.0)	(0.0)	(0.0)	(0.0)	11

* Figures in parentheses refer to fewer than 25 EW.

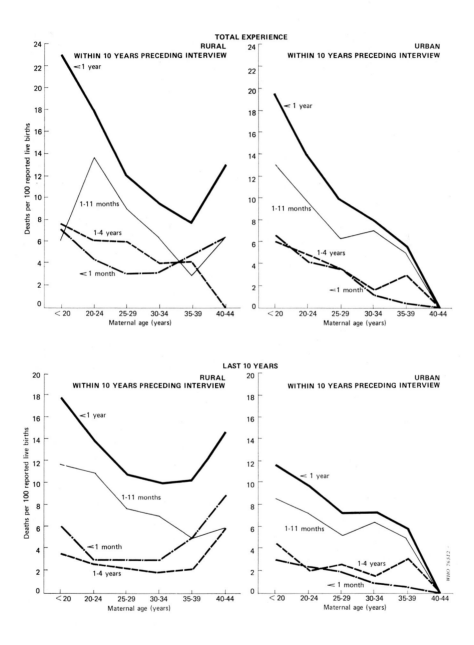

FIG. 4.E.2. CHILD MORTALITY BY RESIDENCE AND MATERNAL AGE:
TOTAL AND DURING PRECEDING 10 YEARS

249

Residence	Age of child at death	Age of mother at interview	Deaths as percentages of live births at maternal age :		
			<25	25–34	35–44
Rural	under 1 month	<25	4.3	—	—
		25–34	5.5	2.7	—
		35–44	5.5	3.3	5.0
		Total	5.3	3.1	5.0
	1–11 months	<25	9.9	—	—
		25–34	15.4	7.9	—
		35–44	15.4	9.5	5.5
		Total	14.5	8.9	5.5
	under 1 year	<25	14.2	—	—
		25–34	21.0	10.6	—
		35–44	20.9	12.8	10.5
		Total	19.8	12.0	10.5
	1–4 years	<25	3.2	—	—
		25–34	5.5	2.0	—
		35–44	10.3	5.8	1.9
		Total	6.9	4.5	1.9
	under 5 years	<25	17.4	—	—
		25–34	26.5	12.6	—
		35–44	31.2	18.6	12.4
		Total	26.8	16.5	12.4
Semi-urban	under 1 month	<25	2.5	—	—
		25–34	4.6	1.7	—
		35–44	7.1	3.4	0.5
		Total	5.1	2.8	0.5
	1–11 months	<25	7.0	—	—
		25–34	11.1	4.8	—
		35–44	12.6	7.6	4.9
		Total	10.9	6.5	4.9
	under 1 year	<25	9.4	—	—
		25–34	15.7	6.5	—
		35–44	19.7	11.0	5.4
		Total	16.1	9.3	5.3
	1–4 years	<25	2.9	—	—
		25–34	4.3	2.2	—
		35–44	7.5	3.1	2.9
		Total	5.2	2.3	2.9
	under 5 years	<25	12.4	—	—
		25–34	20.0	8.7	—
		35–44	27.2	15.1	8.3
		Total	21.3	12.6	8.3

Deaths among recent births (figures above the diagonal lines in Table 4.E.3) show a much less steep decline with maternal age than do those among total live births (those in the rows showing totals).

The mortality experience among children born during the 10 years preceding the interview is shown in Table 4.E.4 and Fig. 4.E.3. Among the rural children, the mortality rates in the first month, the first year, and at 1–4 years showed approximately a reverse J-shaped relationship to maternal age. Death rates at 1–11 months declined consistently with the age of the mother, except for a slight rise in the age group 40–44, while mortality rates under 5 years exhibited a U-shaped relationship to maternal age.

TABLE 4.E.4. CHILD MORTALITY DURING THE 10 YEARS PRECEDING INTERVIEW, BY RESIDENCE AND MATERNAL AGE *

Residence	Maternal age	Deaths per 100 reported live births at :					Total reported live births
		<1 month	1–11 months	<1 year	1–4 years	<5 years	
Rural	<20	6.1	11.7	17.7	3.5	21.2	514
	20–24	2.9	10.9	13.8	2.7	16.5	1071
	25–29	2.9	7.8	10.7	2.2	12.9	1002
	30–34	3.0	7.0	10.0	1.9	11.8	812
	35–39	5.1	5.1	10.2	2.1	12.3	333
	40–44	8.8	5.9	14.7	5.9	20.6	34
Semi-urban	<20	3.1	8.7	11.7	4.5	16.2	358
	20–24	2.4	7.4	9.7	2.1	11.8	762
	25–29	1.9	5.4	7.3	2.5	9.8	684
	30–34	0.9	6.5	7.4	1.6	9.0	445
	35–39	0.5	5.2	5.8	3.1	8.8	194
	40–44	(0.0)	(0.0)	(0.0)	(0.0)	(0.0)	11

* Figures in parentheses refer to fewer than 25 EW.

Among the semi-urban children, on the other hand, deaths steadily decreased as maternal age increased in 3 risk periods : under 1 month, under 1 year, and under 5 years, whereas the decline was somewhat irregular in the 1–11-month and 1–4-year periods.

Child Mortality and Birth Order

Mortality experience among the total births and among births occurring in the 10 years preceding the interview is given in Table 4.E.5 and Fig. 4.E.3. Because of the possible confounding effect of changes in mortality risk factors with time, the 10-year time period is more reliable.

In the rural areas, deaths per 100 live births at under 1 month, at 1–4 years, and at under 5 years gave slightly irregular reverse J-shaped

FIG. 4.E.3. CHILD MORTALITY BY RESIDENCE AND BIRTH ORDER: TOTAL AND DURING PRECEDING 10 YEARS

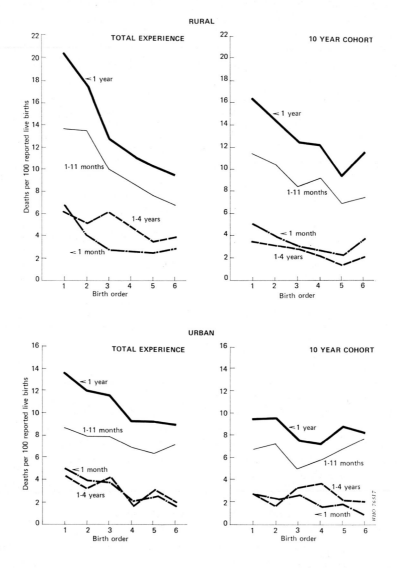

| Residence | Birth order | Deaths per 100 reported live births at: | | | | | Reported live births |
		<1 month	1–11 months	<1 year	1–4 years	<5 years	
Rural Total experience	1	6.8	13.8	20.5	6.2	26.8	2763
	2	4.1	13.6	17.8	5.1	22.8	2345
	3	2.8	10.0	12.8	6.1	18.9	1959
	4	2.6	9.0	11.5	4.7	16.2	1616
	5	2.6	7.7	10.3	3.5	13.8	1278
	6 and over	2.8	6.7	9.5	2.8	12.3	2286
	Total	3.9	10.5	14.3	4.9	19.2	12247
Within 10 years preceding interview	1	5.0	11.4	16.3	3.4	19.7	564
	2	3.9	10.1	14.5	3.1	17.6	517
	3	3.1	8.4	11.5	2.9	14.5	512
	4	2.8	9.3	12.1	2.2	14.3	503
	5	2.3	7.1	9.4	1.4	10.8	490
	6 and over	3.9	7.4	11.3	2.1	13.4	1180
	Total	3.6	8.8	12.4	2.5	14.8	3766
Semi-urban Total experience	1	5.0	8.7	13.7	4.6	18.3	1979
	2	4.1	8.0	12.1	3.7	15.8	1678
	3	3.9	7.9	11.7	4.2	16.0	1327
	4	2.2	7.1	9.3	1.9	11.2	935
	5	2.7	6.5	9.3	2.9	12.2	669
	6 and over	1.9	7.2	9.0	2.0	11.0	1024
	Total	3.6	7.8	11.4	3.5	14.9	7612
Within 10 years preceding interview	1	2.7	6.8	9.5	2.9	12.4	485
	2	2.3	7.2	9.5	1.8	11.3	444
	3	2.6	5.0	7.7	3.2	10.8	379
	4	1.6	5.7	7.3	3.5	10.8	315
	5	1.8	6.9	8.8	2.2	11.0	274
	6 and over	0.7	7.5	8.3	2.0	10.2	557
	Total	1.9	6.6	8.6	2.5	11.1	2454

curves when plotted against birth order, with the highest risks experienced by children of the first birth order. Mortality rates at 1–11 months decreased sharply with the second birth order and then rose sharply until birth order 5, where a decline in rates again occurred. Mortality rates for the whole of the first year decreased with increasing birth order until birth order 3, after which no consistent trend was observed.

No recognizable pattern emerged for the 10-year cohort in the semi-urban area, though mortality rates at 1–11 months tended to rise after birth

Residence	Maternal age	Deaths per 100 reported live births at birth order:					
		1	2	3	4	5	6 and over
Rural	<20	16.6	20.0	22.2	14.3	0.0	—
	20–24	15.5	12.9	11.4	15.2	20.0	19.1
	25–29	17.7	10.0	10.5	10.8	9.6	11.5
	30–34	12.5	20.0	8.0	10.6	4.5	11.2
	35–39	25.0	0.0	—	0.0	8.3	10.4
	40–44	25.0	—	0.0	0.0	—	15.4
	Total	16.3	14.5	11.5	12.1	9.4	11.3
Semi-urban	<20	10.9	14.5	13.3	0.0	—	—
	20–24	8.6	10.5	9.6	6.9	23.3	0.0
	25–29	3.6	2.8	5.7	8.3	7.6	10.6
	30–34	10.0	0.0	2.9	3.7	7.4	9.4
	35–39	0.0	0.0	10.0	13.3	0.0	5.5
	40–44	0.0	—	—	0.0	—	0.0
	Total	9.5	9.5	7.7	7.3	8.8	8.3

order 3, while the rates under 1 month gradually decreased (although not steadily) with increasing birth order.

Child Mortality, Birth Order, and Maternal Age

When child mortality rates are analysed by birth order and maternal age simultaneously, the rates for deaths under 1 month and for 1–11 months become too small for valid conclusions to be drawn. For this reason, only the rate for deaths under 1 year has been given in Table 4.E.6.

Among rural women aged under 20, the relationship between infant mortality and birth order formed an inverted V-shape while, among semi-urban women of the same age, the relationship was V-shaped. The relation between mortality and birth order for the maternal ages between 20 and 24 formed a reversed J-shape in both areas as well as among urban women from 25–29 years old. Among the older age groups, mortality generally exhibited a reversed J-shaped or U-shaped pattern with birth order.

Child Mortality and Preceding Pregnancy Intervals

The relationship between child mortality rates and preceding pregnancy intervals showed a reversed J-shape for all risk periods, in both rural and semi-urban areas (Table 4.E.7 and Fig. 4.E.4).

TABLE 4.E.7. CHILD MORTALITY DURING THE 10 YEARS PRECEDING INTERVIEW,
BY RESIDENCE AND DURATION OF PRECEDING PREGNANCY INTERVAL

Residence	Duration of preceding pregnancy interval (years)	Deaths per 100 live births in 10 years preceding interview, at :					Total live births in past 10 years
		<1 month	1–11 months	<1 year	1–4 years	<5 years	
Rural	<1	6.1	15.6	21.7	3.2	24.9	896
	1	2.6	7.9	10.5	2.6	13.1	1093
	2	1.9	3.6	5.5	1.2	6.7	635
	3	2.1	3.2	5.3	1.1	6.4	281
	4	0.7	1.5	2.2	2.2	4.4	136
	5 and over	0.8	2.4	3.2	0.0	3.2	125
Semi-urban	<1	4.2	12.5	16.7	4.0	20.7	474
	1	1.0	5.5	6.5	2.4	8.9	612
	2	0.7	4.4	5.1	1.5	6.6	408
	3	1.0	5.6	6.6	1.5	8.1	195
	4	0.9	1.8	2.7	0.0	2.7	109
	5 and over	0.6	3.1	3.7	2.5	6.2	158

FIG. 4.E.4. CHILD MORTALITY DURING 10 YEARS PRECEDING INTERVIEW,
BY DURATION OF PRECEDING PREGNANCY INTERVAL

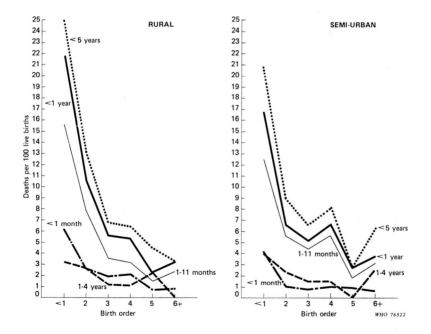

255

Chapter Five

FAMILY FORMATION AND CHILD DEVELOPMENT

I. CHILD GROWTH AND HEALTH

INTRODUCTION

M. R. Bone

The child mortality considered in the previous chapter may be taken as indicative of a much greater morbidity. In developing areas of the world, the combined effects of malnutrition and infections are held to be responsible for the greater part of both morbidity and mortality, besides retarding children's physical development. To the extent that malnutrition and infections are dependent on social and economic circumstances, their prevalence is likely to increase as family growth reduces the resources that can be devoted to each child. It may also be related independently to birth order, if this in turn affects children's susceptibility to the hazards of their environment.

Other studies, reviewed in Part I, have found that young children's health and growth are related to family size : the more siblings a child has, the more slowly he is likely to grow and the more prone he will be to malnutrition and infection. The variation in health and development with birth order, though less frequently investigated, shows a similar relationship : later-born children are at a disadvantage, especially in comparison with the first born.

The specific aspects of growth and health examined in the first part of this chapter are : height and weight, haemoglobin level, intestinal parasitism, nutritional diseases, and infections. The last three and anaemia (indicated by haemoglobin level) interact to varying extents, so that the presence of one increases susceptibility to the others. These conditions were selected because of the relevance of malnutrition and infection.

Most of the data were derived from clinical examination of the eligible women's children under 5 years of age, and from laboratory investigations of blood and stool specimens obtained from them. In addition, the eligible women were asked whether each of their children under 10 years had experienced fever, diarrhoea, or cough lasting for more than one day during the month preceding interview. These 3 symptoms were used as indications of infection.

Despite efforts to do so, clinical and laboratory methods were not standardized across participating areas; and different conditions were included by each area in the disease categories used, since local concern and interest varied. The conditions included and some information on the diagnostic and measurement methods used are outlined in the reports of the individual centres. Because of such differences, it is not permissible to make comparisons of prevalence rates between areas.

Prevalence rates are shown as percentages of examined, or reported, children affected, and mean values are given for height, weight, and haemoglobin level.

For children aged between 6 months and 6 years, and living at sea level, anaemia is considered to exist if the haemoglobin level is below 11 grams per 100 millilitres of venous blood. At greater altitudes, higher limiting values apply.[1]

Information on intestinal parasitism is limited to its presence or absence, and none is provided on the number of parasites present or the egg load.

The reports from the different centres show that the expected relationships between family size and birth order, on the one hand, and morbidity and growth on the other, were found in very few cases. This may be because for most of the areas and cultures covered such relationships did not exist, or were obscured by other more dominant factors. There are, however, technical reasons why real relationships may be hidden.

(a) The samples of children

The intention in every area was to investigate all, or a representative sample, of eligible women's children under 5 years of age. In practice, there were considerable difficulties in persuading women to bring their children for examination and even more so in obtaining blood and stool specimens. Even though the children investigated may have been representative of all the eligible women's children under 5 in terms of age and family size, they may have differed in health. In one area (Teheran), for example, it was early noted that mothers tended to bring for examination only those children who were sick, and special efforts were made to encourage them to bring all their children under 5 years old. A bias of this kind, if it occurred elsewhere, could well mean that any relationships existing were not evident in the group investigated.

---

[1] WHO SCIENTIFIC GROUP ON NUTRITIONAL ANEMIAS (1968) Report, Geneva, World Health Organization (WHO Technical Report Series No. 405).

(b) *The numbers studied*

In most areas, the age and family size subgroups often contained fewer than 25 children and sometimes fewer than 10. With such small numbers, the presence in the group of one or two unusual children, or recording or other errors, would have produced relatively large fluctuations that may have obscured trends.

In the case of weight and height, the comparatively small numbers also meant that children had to be grouped according to years of age. At this stage of life, when growth is rapid, the resulting average value for the year will depend on the way the children's ages were distributed within the year. This, too, may produce fluctuations that conceal trends.

Some evidence that accidental fluctuations were not responsible for obscuring trends comes from the fact that in two areas (Lebanon and Iran) children from the two cultural groups studied differed consistently in height and weight.

(c) *Broadness of categories*

The conditions included in each category varied between areas, but were generally broad. In all areas, for example, " Nutritional Diseases " was interpreted as any evidence of malnutrition, and according to the criteria used the vast majority of children of every age and family size were scored as malnourished. In the circumstances, it may be that relationships between specific diseases and family size were concealed.

In every case, the eligible women's reports of symptoms in their children under 10 years old showed a decline in prevalence as family size increased. This is not only contrary to expectations but is apparently inconsistent with the findings of the clinical investigations on children under 5, which in no case showed an inverse relationship between infection and family size. The difference between the findings of the investigations and the mother's reports might be explicable in terms of the different age ranges and conditions covered, but there is no obvious reason why prevalence should be less in larger than in smaller families, and a more probable explanation is that the more children a woman had, the less she noticed or remembered their minor symptoms.

It was also intended to examine the relationship between family size and the age at menarche of the eligible women's daughters. In the event, it was decided not to use the data for the following reasons :

Firstly, the appropriately aged daughters did not constitute a representative sample or population of all girls living in the area, because daughters of older and dead women were excluded. This shortfall and any resulting bias is, of course, likely to be much greater for teenage and older girls than for children under 5.

Secondly, the information coded and from which the mean age at menarche was calculated was the age of beginning menstruation, if menstruation had begun.

Tanner [1] has pointed out the fallacy of this method : " A procedure that may not give a valid estimate of the mean in cross-sectional data ... is to inquire of all girls ... at which age they first menstruated. Apart from the difficulty of exact recollection by those who had attained menarche several years earlier [2] a more important bias is introduced if there remain any girls who have not yet menstruated. Such girls will exhibit high values for menarcheal age, and if these values are omitted the mean age obtained is spuriously low."

This bias may account for the finding, in all areas, that menarcheal age decreased with increasing birth order, since the age of the girls at interview is likely to vary approximately inversely with birth order—as a rule, the first-born girls will be the oldest and therefore most likely to have passed menarche. Conversely, later born girls will tend to be younger and their mean age at menarche (based on those who have reached it) may be biased in favour of the more precocious.

The effect on the relationship between age at menarche and family size is more obscure, but cannot be assumed to be random. The correct method for cross-sectional studies is to calculate the mean from the proportion of girls of each age, within a specified range (e.g., 9–17 years) who have already menstruated. This method could not be employed, since it was impossible at the tabulation stage to reconstruct their ages.

A. GANDHIGRAM

P. R. Dult, S. Gunasekaran, S. Sethu and P. Padmavethiamma

Sample for Physical and Laboratory Examination

The original intention was to examine all the eligible women's children under 5 years of age. Of such children there were 5705, but only 2700 (47%) accepted examination, and blood and stool specimens were obtained from 25% and 14%, respectively, of all children under 5.

Tables 5.A.1 (a) and (b) compare the children investigated with all children under 5.

The main reason for the children's low attendance rate for medical examination was their mother's reluctance to undergo gynaecological examinations, which were carried out at the same time. Further difficulties beset the collection of stool and blood specimens. Many mothers found obtaining stool specimens difficult and distasteful, and feared their children would be hurt by the extraction of blood samples.

---

[1] TANNER, J. M. (1968) Earlier maturation in man, Scientific American, **218** : 21–27.

[2] This source of error is compounded in the present study because the data are based on the recollections of the girls' mothers.

TABLE 5.A.1. CHILDREN UNDER 5 YEARS INVESTIGATED COMPARED WITH ALL EW'S CHILDREN UNDER 5 YEARS

(a) Distribution by culture

Culture	All EW's children under 5 years No.	Children physically examined	
		No.	%
Muslim	1911	897	47
Scheduled Castes	1026	390	38
Other Hindus	1680	874	52
Vellala	1088	519	48
All cultures	5705	2680	47

(b) Distribution by age

Age (years)	All EW's children under 5 years		Physically examined		Stools examined		Haemoglobin determined	
	No.	%	No.	%	No.	%	No.	%
<1	1169	20	592	22	96	12	151	11
1–2	1122	20	568	21	134	17	256	18
2–3	1125	20	574	21	175	22	321	22
3–4	1190	21	528	20	202	26	355	25
4–5	1099	19	438	16	184	23	338	24
All ages	5705	100	2700	100	791	100	1431	100

Personnel and General Procedure

Six medical officers were appointed to carry out the paediatric examinations. All were new graduates and were given a short period of training in the examination of children and use of the standard form that had been developed for recording results. It soon became clear that, because of the high refusal rate, fewer than 6 medical officers would be required, and after the first few weeks, only 2 were retained.

One graduate and 7 students with matriculation were recruited and given 15 days' training as laboratory technicians by the chief medical officer of the project and a microbiologist.

Results of the physical examination were recorded on a standard form, on which were listed in detail, according to anatomical site, the signs of nutritional diseases (as given by Jelliffe [1]), plus diarrhoea. Specific space was also provided for recording diseases of the respiratory system and "Any other findings".

Results of laboratory investigations were also recorded on a standard form.

A health educator visited each village before the medical examinations began and discussed the study with village leaders. With their help one or more temporary examination centres and laboratories were set up. The medical and laboratory team visited the homes of all those who failed to report for examination.

Height and Weight

(a) *Height*

There was little variation in stature among children of the same age from the 4 cultures. Boys were slightly taller than girls, and children of middle social status were marginally taller than those of low status (Table 5.A.2).

No consistent relationships between height and family size or birth order were evident for children of any culture (Tables 5.A.3 (*a*) and (*b*)).

(b) *Weight*

Children under 1 year of age were weighed using a basket-type spring balance. Older children were weighed fully dressed on bathroom scales of the platform type.

Muslim children weighed rather more than others of the same age. Boys were somewhat heavier than girls (except among Vellalas) and children of low social status tended to be lighter than those of middle status, except among Scheduled Castes, for whom the reverse was true (Table 5.A.4).

There was no consistent relationship between weight and family size for children of any culture, but there was some evidence of a decline in weight with increasing birth order, most clearly amongst Vellala children and, less consistently, among Muslims (Tables 5.A.5 (*a*) and (*b*)).

---

[1] JELLIFFE, D. B. The assessment of the nutritional status of the community, Geneva, World Health Organization, 1966, pp. 43–48 (Monograph Series No. 53).

262

TABLE 5.A.2. MEAN HEIGHTS OF CHILDREN UNDER 5, BY CULTURE, SOCIAL STATUS, AGE, AND SEX *

Culture	Social status	Mean heights (cm) of male (M), female (F), and all (T) children at specified ages (years):														
		<1			1–2			2–3			3–4			4–5		
		M	F	T	M	F	T	M	F	T	M	F	T	M	F	T
Muslim	Middle	70	70	70	77	75	76	86	85	86	92	92	92	96	95	95
	Low	(70)	67	68	77	(74)	76	85	81	83	(87)	88	88	(92)	(93)	93
	Total	70	69	69	77	75	76	85	84	85	91	91	91	95	95	95
Scheduled Castes	Middle	(67)	(64)	65	(81)	(73)	76	(82)	(86)	(84)	(86)	(92)	(89)	(98)	(102)	(99)
	Low	67	67	67	76	76	76	87	83	85	90	92	91	(100)	(96)	98
	Total	67	66	66	78	75	76	85	84	84	89	92	91	99	(97)	98
Other Hindus	Middle	69	69	69	77	77	77	87	84	85	92	89	91	97	97	97
	Low	65	66	66	79	75	77	82	79	81	91	89	90	(95)	94	95
	Total	68	68	68	78	76	77	85	83	84	92	89	91	97	96	96
Vellala	Middle	67	67	67	77	77	77	85	83	84	92	91	91	97	(95)	97
	Low	(68)	(67)	67	(77)	(77)	77	(84)	(83)	83	88	(89)	89	(95)	(93)	94
	Total	67	67	67	75	77	77	85	83	84	91	90	90	97	94	96

* Figures in parentheses refer to fewer than 25 children.

263

TABLE 5.A.3. MEAN HEIGHTS OF CHILDREN UNDER 5, BY CULTURE AND AGE, AND BY FAMILY SIZE OR BIRTH ORDER *

(a) By family size

Culture	Age (years)	Mean heights (cm) in families of size :				Total No. measured
		1 & 2	3 & 4	5 and over	All family sizes	
Muslim	<1	69.6	69.8	68.9	69.5	191
	1–2	75.7	76.2	76.0	76.0	182
	2–3	85.2	84.6	84.8	84.9	195
	3–4	92.4	91.1	90.1	91.0	168
	4–5	96.1	93.4	95.8	94.7	143
Scheduled Castes	<1	64.9	67.2	(68.1)	66.4	90
	1–2	77.0	76.3	(74.5)	76.1	85
	2–3	84.8	83.9	(85.0)	84.4	89
	3–4	(90.6)	92.2	(87.4)	90.7	70
	4–5	(97.5)	96.8	(101.0)	98.2	56
Other Hindus	<1	68.0	70.1	67.5	68.1	188
	1–2	77.6	76.2	76.7	77.0	205
	2–3	82.9	84.0	84.8	83.7	179
	3–4	90.5	90.1	91.3	90.5	162
	4–5	95.6	96.6	97.0	96.5	143
Vellala	<1	67.3	66.7	(67.0)	67.1	113
	1–2	75.9	78.0	(78.0)	76.8	89
	2–3	84.7	82.7	(81.6)	83.6	111
	3–4	90.7	89.1	(91.9)	90.2	125
	4–5	93.2	98.0	(96.2)	95.7	89

(b) By birth order

TABLE 5.A.3 * (continued)

Culture	Age (years)	Mean heights (cm) of children of birth order:				Total No. measured
		1 & 2	3 & 4	5 and over	All birth orders	
Muslim	<1	69.7	70.0	68.9	69.5	191
	1–2	76.1	76.4	75.6	76.0	182
	2–3	85.7	85.2	84.0	84.9	195
	3–4	93.4	91.8	89.0	91.0	168
	4–5	93.3	94.9	96.0	94.7	143
Scheduled Castes	<1	64.5	66.9	68.0	66.4	90
	1–2	77.3	(76.2)	75.2	76.1	85
	2–3	84.6	86.4	32.8	84.4	89
	3–4	(91.4)	(92.9)	87.9	90.7	70
	4–5	(95.7)	(100.4)	(98.5)	98.2	56
Other Hindus	<1	68.5	68.0	67.6	68.1	188
	1–2	77.8	76.5	76.4	77.0	205
	2–3	84.9	82.0	84.0	83.7	179
	3–4	90.1	89.5	92.0	90.5	162
	4–5	95.5	96.4	97.5	96.5	143
Vellala	<1	67.2	67.5	(64.3)	67.1	113
	1–2	76.5	76.2	(78.2)	76.8	89
	2–3	85.8	81.2	(82.8)	83.6	111
	3–4	91.5	89.1	(89.4)	90.2	125
	4–5	95.1	(97.7)	(95.3)	95.7	89

* Figures in parentheses refer to fewer than 25 children.

265

TABLE 5.A.4. MEAN WEIGHTS OF CHILDREN UNDER 5, BY CULTURE, SOCIAL STATUS, AGE, AND SEX *

Mean weights (kg) of male (M), female (F), and all (T) children at specified ages (years):

Culture	Social status	<1			1-2			2-3			3-4			4-5		
		M	F	T	M	F	T	M	F	T	M	F	T	M	F	T
Muslim	Middle	9.3	8.3	8.8	9.1	9.3	9.2	11.0	11.9	11.4	12.9	12.4	12.7	14.3	14.6	14.4
	Low	(8.3)	7.4	7.8	9.8	(8.1)	9.0	10.7	10.5	10.6	(12.2)	11.4	11.7	(12.4)	(12.7)	12.6
	Total	9.1	8.0	8.5	9.3	9.1	9.2	10.9	11.5	11.2	12.7	12.1	12.4	13.8	14.1	14.0
Scheduled Castes	Middle	(7.9)	(6.8)	7.1	(9.5)	(8.3)	8.8	(11.0)	(11.0)	11.0	(10.6)	(13.3)	(11.9)	(13.0)	(13.3)	(13.0)
	Low	7.4	6.8	7.1	9.0	8.8	8.9	11.2	11.1	11.2	12.4	12.7	12.6	(14.3)	(13.1)	13.7
	Total	7.5	6.8	7.1	9.1	8.6	8.9	11.2	11.0	11.1	11.7	12.9	12.4	13.8	13.2	13.6
Other Hindus	Middle	7.9	8.6	8.3	8.9	8.9	8.9	10.7	10.3	10.5	12.2	11.5	11.9	13.3	13.3	13.3
	Low	7.1	6.8	6.9	9.1	8.3	8.7	10.3	9.0	9.7	12.3	11.3	11.0	(12.1)	11.8	12.0
	Total	7.7	8.0	7.9	9.0	8.6	8.8	10.6	9.9	10.2	12.3	11.4	11.9	12.9	12.8	12.0
Vellala	Middle	7.1	7.2	7.2	9.2	8.7	8.9	10.7	12.7	11.6	11.8	12.0	11.9	13.6	(14.3)	13.9
	Low	(7.3)	(6.4)	6.9	(10.4)	(14.6)	12.6	(9.7)	(10.7)	10.3	(11.4)	(11.9)	11.6	(12.8)	(12.7)	12.8
	Total	7.2	7.0	7.1	9.4	10.9	10.2	10.4	11.7	11.1	11.7	12.0	11.8	13.4	13.7	13.5

* Figures in parentheses refer to fewer than 25 children.

Haemoglobin Level

Haemoglobin level, measured as grams per 100 millilitres of venous blood, was determined by the Sahli method.

Blood samples were taken from the heel for infants or from the fingertip for older children ; the specimens were collected by the laboratory technicians during the visit for medical examination and were examined immediately. No consistent differences were evident in mean haemoglobin level among children of different cultures. Those of low status tended to have higher levels than children of middle status, and girls slightly higher levels than boys. The mean level did not appear to be related to age (Table 5.A.6).

There was no indication of any consistent variation in haemoglobin level with either family size or birth order (Tables 5.A.7 (a) and (b)).

Intestinal Parasitic Infestation from Stool Examination

Laboratory technicians took bottles to households in the evening and asked the mothers to provide specimens of the children's stools for the following morning, at which time they were collected by the technicians. The samples were examined before noon of the same day, and the average time between collection of specimens by the technician and investigation was 1–2 hours.

One sample from each child was examined. For the 4 cultures combined 25% of the children provided evidence of infestation. The highest percentage was among Other Hindus—over one-third were infested compared with less than one-quarter of the children of other cultures.

Children under 1 year were least likely to be infested, but otherwise no systematic variation with age was evident.

Because of the comparatively small number of children investigated, tabulation by age, family size, and culture is not useful. Tables 5.A.8 (a) to (c), however, indicate no relationship between infestation and family size.

Infections

All types of infection diagnosed at clinical examination, whether of bacterial, fungal, parasitic, or viral origin, were recorded in this category. In addition, two cases of dental caries, one of eczema, and one of infantile cirrhosis were included.

Fourteen cases of helminthiases (many fewer cases than found from stool investigations) were also found at clinical examination and included in this category.

Of all the children examined, 19% were found to be suffering from infections—22% among the Scheduled Castes and Vellalas and about 18% among Muslims and Other Hindus. Rather more low status than middle status children were affected, but the difference was negligible, except for the Scheduled Castes, among whom 25% of the low status children and 14% of the middle status children had infections.

TABLE 5.A.5. MEAN WEIGHTS OF CHILDREN UNDER 5, BY CULTURE AND AGE, AND BY FAMILY SIZE OR BIRTH ORDER *

(a) By family size

Culture	Age (years)	Mean weights (kg) in families of size :				Total No. weighed
		1 & 2	3 & 4	5 and over	All family sizes	
Muslim	<1	9.8	7.7	7.8	8.5	193
	1–2	9.1	9.4	9.0	9.2	185
	2–3	10.8	10.9	11.9	11.2	193
	3–4	12.7	12.4	12.2	12.4	172
	4–5	15.7	13.4	13.8	14.0	146
Scheduled Castes	<1	7.5	6.9	(7.0)	7.1	93
	1–2	9.2	8.5	(8.8)	8.9	84
	2–3	11.0	11.1	(11.3)	11.1	91
	3–4	(12.0)	12.5	(12.8)	12.4	71
	4–5	(7.8)	13.3	(14.2)	13.6	56
Other Hindus	<1	8.5	7.5	6.8	7.9	190
	1–2	8.8	8.9	8.4	8.8	208
	2–3	10.0	10.2	10.5	10.2	175
	3–4	11.7	11.9	12.1	11.9	162
	4–5	12.6	12.9	13.1	12.9	144
Vellala	<1	7.2	6.9	(7.4)	7.1	114
	1–2	10.2	10.9	(7.0)	10.2	91
	2–3	10.5	12.1	(9.5)	11.1	110
	3–4	11.7	11.8	(12.1)	11.8	121
	4–5	13.8	13.2	(13.2)	13.5	92

TABLE 5.A.5 * (continued)

(b) By birth order

| Culture | Age (years) | Mean weights (kg) of children of birth order: | | | | Total No. weighed |
		1 & 2	3 & 4	5 and over	All birth orders	
Muslim	<1	10.4	7.5	7.7	8.5	193
	1–2	9.2	9.2	9.1	9.2	185
	2–3	11.1	10.4	11.7	11.2	193
	3–4	12.1	12.1	12.3	12.4	172
	4–5	14.7	13.1	14.1	14.0	146
Scheduled Castes	<1	7.5	7.1	6.8	7.1	93
	1–2	9.4	(8.6)	8.7	8.9	84
	2–3	11.5	10.5	11.3	11.1	91
	3–4	(12.1)	(12.8)	12.4	12.4	71
	4–5	(13.5)	(13.7)	(13.5)	13.6	56
Other Hindus	<1	8.6	7.6	7.1	7.9	190
	1–2	8.9	9.0	8.6	8.8	208
	2–3	10.2	10.3	10.2	10.2	175
	3–4	11.8	11.6	12.3	11.9	162
	4–5	12.5	12.9	13.2	12.9	144
Vellala	<1	7.4	6.8	(6.8)	7.1	114
	1–2	10.9	10.3	(8.4)	10.2	91
	2–3	10.6	12.1	(10.3)	11.1	110
	3–4	11.9	11.8	(11.5)	11.8	121
	4–5	13.8	(13.4)	(12.6)	13.5	92

* Figures in parentheses refer to fewer than 25 children.

TABLE 5.A.6. MEAN HAEMOGLOBIN LEVELS OF CHILDREN UNDER 5, BY CULTURE, SOCIAL STATUS, AGE, AND SEX *

Mean haemoglobin levels (g/100 ml) of male (M), female (F), and all (T) children at specified ages (years):

Culture	Social status	<1			1–2			2–3			3–4			4–5		
		M	F	T	M	F	T	M	F	T	M	F	T	M	F	T
Muslim	Middle	(6.5)	(6.6)	6.6	6.7	6.5	6.6	6.6	7.0	6.8	6.7	7.0	6.8	6.6	7.0	6.8
	Low	(7.0)	(7.6)	(7.3)	(7.0)	(7.0)	(7.0)	(7.0)	(6.8)	6.9	(6.7)	(7.5)	7.2	(7.5)	(7.2)	7.4
	Total	(6.7)	6.9	6.8	6.8	6.5	6.6	6.7	6.9	6.8	6.7	7.1	6.9	6.9	7.0	6.9
Scheduled Castes	Middle	(6.6)	(6.9)	(6.8)	(6.9)	(6.5)	(6.7)	(6.4)	(6.4)	(6.4)	(6.2)	(6.8)	(6.5)	(6.6)	(6.4)	(6.6)
	Low	(6.5)	(7.2)	(6.8)	(6.7)	(6.6)	6.7	(7.1)	(6.9)	7.0	(6.5)	(6.4)	6.4	(7.1)	(6.9)	7.0
	Total	(6.6)	(7.0)	6.8	(6.8)	(6.6)	6.7	6.8	6.7	6.8	6.4	6.5	6.4	6.9	(6.8)	6.9
Other Hindus	Middle	(6.6)	(6.8)	6.7	6.7	6.5	6.6	6.4	6.5	6.4	6.8	6.8	6.8	6.9	6.8	6.9
	Low	(7.1)	(6.6)	(6.9)	(7.0)	(6.9)	6.9	6.8	(6.9)	6.9	(6.6)	(6.9)	6.7	(6.8)	(6.8)	6.8
	Total	6.7	(6.8)	6.7	6.8	6.6	6.7	6.6	6.6	6.6	6.7	6.8	6.8	6.9	6.8	6.9
Vellala	Middle	(7.0)	(7.0)	7.0	(6.9)	(6.0)	6.4	(7.1)	(6.3)	6.7	7.3	(6.8)	7.1	6.9	(6.8)	6.7
	Low	(6.3)	(7.0)	(6.6)	(6.2)	(6.9)	(6.7)	(5.3)	(6.8)	6.5	(6.5)	(7.0)	6.8	(6.5)	(6.9)	(6.7)
	Total	(6.8)	(7.0)	6.9	(6.6)	6.4	6.5	(6.6)	6.6	6.6	7.0	6.9	7.0	6.7	6.8	6.7

* Figures in parentheses refer to fewer than 25 children.

270

TABLE 5.A.7. MEAN HAEMOGLOBIN LEVELS OF CHILDREN UNDER 5, BY CULTURE AND AGE, AND BY FAMILY SIZE OR BIRTH ORDER *

(a) By family size

Culture	Age (years)	Mean haemoglobin levels (g/100 ml) in families of size :				Total No. investigated
		1–2	3–4	5 and over	All family sizes	
Muslim	<1	(9.9)	(9.6)	(10.3)	9.9	48
	1–2	9.9	9.7	(9.3)	9.6	75
	2–3	9.9	9.9	(9.9)	9.9	86
	3–4	9.7	10.3	10.0	10.0	111
	4–5	(10.4)	10.2	9.9	10.0	112
Scheduled Castes	<1	(10.0)	(9.9)	(9.1)	9.9	28
	1–2	(9.3)	(9.7)	(10.3)	9.7	44
	2–3	(10.0)	9.7	(9.9)	9.9	55
	3–4	(9.4)	(9.4)	(9.3)	9.3	51
	4–5	(9.1)	10.2	(10.4)	10.0	56
Other Hindus	<1	9.7	(10.0)	(9.7)	9.7	48
	1–2	10.0	9.6	(9.6)	9.7	92
	2–3	9.6	9.6	9.4	9.6	117
	3–4	9.9	9.9	9.7	9.9	111
	4–5	9.9	10.2	9.9	10.0	99
Vellala	<1	(10.0)	(10.2)	(9.9)	10.0	37
	1–2	(9.4)	(9.3)	(9.7)	9.4	45
	2–3	9.6	9.3	(10.9)	9.6	63
	3–4	10.4	9.7	(9.9)	10.2	82
	4–5	10.2	9.3	(10.7)	9.7	71

(b) By birth order

Culture	Age (years)	Mean haemoglobin levels (g/100 ml) of children of birth order :				Total No. investigated
		1–2	3–4	5 and over	All birth orders	
Muslim	<1	(10.4)	(9.6)	(9.7)	9.9	48
	1–2	9.7	(10.0)	9.3	9.6	75
	2–3	9.9	10.0	9.9	9.9	86
	3–4	10.2	9.9	10.0	10.0	111
	4–5	10.6	9.6	10.0	10.0	112
Scheduled Castes	<1	(9.6)	(10.6)	(9.3)	9.9	28
	1–2	(9.0)	(10.0)	(10.0)	9.7	44
	2–3	(9.7)	(9.7)	(10.2)	9.9	55
	3–4	(9.3)	(9.6)	(9.1)	9.3	51
	4–5	(9.7)	(9.9)	(10.3)	10.0	56
Other Hindus	<1	(9.6)	(10.0)	(9.9)	9.7	48
	1–2	10.0	9.4	9.6	9.7	92
	2–3	9.6	9.6	9.4	9.6	117
	3–4	9.9	9.7	9.9	9.9	111
	4–5	10.0	9.9	10.0	10.0	99
Vellala	<1	(9.9)	(10.2)	(9.9)	10.0	37
	1–2	(9.1)	(9.1)	(10.0)	9.4	45
	2–3	(9.6)	9.4	(10.2)	9.6	63
	3–4	10.2	10.0	(10.0)	10.2	82
	4–5	9.7	(9.6)	(10.2)	9.7	71

* Figures in parentheses refer to fewer than 25 children.

TABLE 5.A.8. PREVALENCE OF PARASITIC INFESTATION DETERMINED FROM STOOL EXAMINATION *

(a) By age and family size

Age (years)	Percentage of children infested in families of size :				Total No. investigated
	1 & 2	3 & 4	5 and over	All family sizes	
<1	12	18	(12)	14	96
1–2	33	15	19	25	134
2–3	30	26	32	29	175
3–4	20	19	27	25	202
4–5	22	30	25	27	184
All ages	23	26	25	25	791

(b) By culture and age

Age (years)	Muslim	Scheduled Castes	Other Hindus	Vellala
1	13	15	18	8
1–2	13	26	26	39
2–3	24	20	39	24
3–4	24	24	29	24
4–5	25	16	40	23
All ages	21	21	32	24

(c) By culture and family size

Culture	Percentage of children infested in families of size :				Total No. investigated
	1 & 2	3 & 4	5 and over	All family sizes	
Muslim	18	23	21	21	261
Scheduled Castes	21	20	(20)	21	107
Other Hindus	29	34	33	32	230
Vellala	23	26	(22)	24	193

* Figures in parentheses refer to fewer than 25 children.

272

TABLE 5.A.9. PREVALENCE OF INFECTIONS IN CHILDREN UNDER 5 YEARS OF AGE *

(a) By culture, age, and family size

Culture	Age (years)	Percentage of children with infections in families of size :				Total No. investi- gated
		1 & 2	3 & 4	5 and over	All family sizes	
Muslim	<1	12	23	11	16	199
	1–2	11	15	17	14	188
	2–3	16	18	21	18	198
	3–4	14	29	18	21	171
	4–5	40	11	16	18	141
	All ages	16	19	17	17	898
Scheduled Castes	<1	12	21	(39)	21	91
	1–2	29	29	(29)	29	84
	2–3	22	17	(24)	20	88
	3–4	(26)	17	(24)	21	71
	4–5	(21)	16	(24)	20	56
	All ages	22	20	28	22	390
Other Hindus	<1	21	23	8	19	191
	1–2	19	21	13	19	201
	2–3	14	17	11	15	177
	3–4	25	13	27	20	162
	4–5	13	22	20	19	143
	All ages	19	19	16	18	874
Vellala	<1	16	14	—	14	111
	1–2	32	21	(20)	28	89
	2–3	21	27	(13)	23	105
	3–4	25	17	(29)	23	124
	4–5	21	19	(33)	21	90
	All ages	23	20	22	22	519

(b) By culture and birth order

Culture	Percentage of children with infections for birth order :				Total No. examined
	1 & 2	3 & 4	5 and over	All birth orders	
Muslim	17	19	16	17	898
Scheduled Castes	21	20	25	22	390
Other Hindus	20	17	18	18	874
Vellala	24	21	16	22	519

* Percentages in parentheses refer to fewer than 25 children.

Among Muslims and Scheduled Castes, children who had no siblings were least likely to be infected, but otherwise no relationship was evident between prevalence and either family size or birth order (Tables 5.A.9 (*a*) and (*b*)).

Nutritional Diseases

As mentioned earlier, the form used for recording the results of the clinical examination listed signs of nutritional deficiency in detail. The form, which included space for anthropometric data, was used as a guide by the examining physician, but his final assessment of whether or not the child was suffering from nutritional deficiency was a subjective one. Thus, some children who exhibited none of the specified signs were classified as malnourished because the physician judged them to be below the anthropometric standards for their age.

For the 4 cultures combined, 31% of the children showed signs of these diseases, but the prevalence varied according to the culture. The highest percentage of affected children (47%) was found among the Scheduled Castes and lowest (23%) among the Muslims. Within each culture, more children of low than of middle social status were found to be suffering from nutritional diseases, the differences being most pronounced among the Scheduled Castes and Vellalas (Table 5.A.10). These differences reflect the interaction of socioeconomic conditions and dietary habits. Muslims consume relatively more non-vegetarian food than members of the other cultures and they have the lowest proportion of children with nutritional diseases. Vellalas, being landowning cultivators, could probably afford sufficient milk and milk products for the children. The Scheduled Castes, most of whom live only on a subsistence income (mainly from agricultural labour) are the worst hit with regard to the nutritional level.

TABLE 5.A.10. PERCENTAGES OF CHILDREN WITH NUTRITIONAL DISEASES, BY SOCIAL STATUS AND CULTURE

Social status	Muslim	Scheduled Castes	Other Hindus	Vellala
Middle	22	38	29	23
Low	28	50	39	38
Total	23	47	32	29

Children under 1 year of age were less likely than older children to have nutritional diseases, except among the Scheduled Castes.

Prevalence rose, but erratically, with family size and more systematically with birth order (Tables 5.A.11 (*a*) and (*b*)).

Occurrence of Fever, Diarrhoea, or Cough reported by Eligible Women in Children under 10 during the Month Preceding Interview

Mothers recalled that 12% of their children under 10 had suffered from fevers, 6% from diarrhoea, and 7% from coughs during the preceding

TABLE 5.A.11. PERCENTAGES OF CHILDREN UNDER 5 YEARS FOUND TO HAVE
NUTRITIONAL DISEASES *

(a) By culture, age, and family size

Culture	Age (years)	Percentages of children with nutritional disease in families of size :				Total No. investigated
		1 & 2	3 & 4	5 and over	All family sizes	
Muslim	<1	12	15	25	17	199
	1–2	26	22	22	24	187
	2–3	21	24	22	22	198
	3–4	16	33	29	28	174
	4–5	28	28	29	28	141
	All ages	20	24	26	23	899
Scheduled Castes	<1	32	49	(56)	44	91
	1–2	49	45	(48)	47	85
	2–3	53	43	(30)	44	87
	3–4	(42)	43	(53)	45	71
	4–5	(50)	52	(72)	58	57
	All ages	45	46	51	47	391
Other Hindus	<1	16	20	25	19	191
	1–2	25	38	36	32	293
	2–3	33	46	33	38	177
	3–4	38	39	41	39	162
	4–5	33	39	33	36	143
	All ages	27	37	34	32	876
Vellala	<1	14	24	—	17	111
	1–2	23	32	(40)	27	89
	2–3	30	34	(25)	32	105
	3–4	25	42	(59)	36	124
	4–5	17	40	(67)	31	91
	All ages	22	35	44	29	520

(b) By culture and birth order

Culture	Percentage of children with nutritional disease for birth order :				Total No. investigated
	1 & 2	3 & 4	5 and over	All birth orders	
Muslim	20	22	27	23	899
Scheduled Castes	41	45	53	47	391
Other Hindus	26	33	38	32	876
Vellala	24	32	37	29	520

* Figures in parentheses refer to fewer than 25 children.

TABLE 5.A.12. REPORTED OCCURRENCE OF FEVER, DIARRHOEA, AND COUGH
AMONG CHILDREN UNDER 10, DURING THE MONTH PRECEDING
MOTHER'S INTERVIEW

(a) By culture and family size

Culture	Condition	Percentage of infections reported by EW with families of :				Total No. of children in age group
		1 & 2	3 & 4	5 and over	All family sizes	
Muslim	Fever	22	15	15	17	3550
	Diarrhoea	11	8	5	8	3550
	Cough	14	9	7	10	3550
Scheduled Castes	Fever	16	7	5	9	1854
	Diarrhoea	8	4	2	4	1854
	Cough	10	5	2	5	1854
Other Hindus	Fever	16	11	8	11	3105
	Diarrhoea	9	5	3	6	3105
	Cough	10	5	3	6	3105
Vellala	Fever	11	7	7	8	2088
	Diarrhoea	6	2	3	3	2088
	Cough	8	3	2	5	2088

(b) By culture and birth order

Culture	Condition	Percentage of infections reported by EW for birth order :				Total No. of children in age group
		1 & 2	3 & 4	5 and over	All birth orders	
Muslim	Fever	18	16	16	17	3550
	Diarrhoea	8	7	7	8	3550
	Cough	11	8	9	10	3550
Scheduled Castes	Fever	10	7	10	9	1854
	Diarrhoea	5	3	5	4	1854
	Cough	7	4	5	5	1854
Other Hindus	Fever	13	10	5	11	3105
	Diarrhoea	6	6	5	6	3105
	Cough	7	6	5	6	3105
Vellala	Fever	10	7	7	8	2088
	Diarrhoea	5	3	3	4	2088
	Cough	6	4	3	5	2088

month. Reported prevalence was rather higher among Muslim children than others.

The percentages said to have exhibited each of these symptoms declined with increasing family size, and, except in the case of diarrhoea, with rising birth order (Tables 5.A.12 (a) and (b)).

276

B. TEHERAN

A. Majd and B. D. Navidi-Kasmaii

Sample for Physical and Laboratory Examination

It was decided to examine all the children under 5 years old of the eligible women selected for gynaecological examination. 50% of the eligible women were included by taking all those living in every second street block used at the interview sampling stage. This system yielded 1579 children under 5 years belonging to all the eligible women.

During the first few days of the medical examination it became apparent that some women were bringing only their sick children to the clinic. The healthy children of these women were therefore fetched by the project's social worker, and it was made clear to all the women that all their children under 5 years, whether healthy or sick, should be brought for examination. They were told that unless all their children under 5 were brought, none would be examined.

Comparisons of the age and birth order distributions of the paediatric sample with those of all the eligible women's children under 5 revealed no statistically significant differences, nor were any such differences found in cultural and social status (Table 5.B.1).

There is therefore no reason to suppose that the paediatric sample differed in any way from the eligible women's other children under 5 years of age.

Personnel and General Procedure

The paediatric examinations were conducted in the local clinics by one paediatrician and recorded on a standard form. She was aided by a nurse, who measured heights and weights. Two laboratory technicians took blood samples and investigated the blood and stool specimens in the laboratories of the School of Public Health.

Height and Weight
(a) Height

Armenian children were on the whole taller for their age than Muslim children. Boys were slightly taller than girls of the same age, and children of middle status women were a little taller than those of lower status women (Table 5.B.2).

No relationship was evident between stature and family size or birth order (Tables 5.B.3 (a) and (b)).

TABLE 5.B.1. CHILDREN UNDER 5 YEARS INVESTIGATED COMPARED WITH ALL EW'S CHILDREN UNDER 5 YEARS

(a) By culture and social status

Culture	Middle social status				Low social status				Total			
	All children under 5		Medically examined		All children under 5		Medically examined		All children under 5		Medically examined	
	No.	%	No.	%	No.	%	No.	%	No.	%	No.	%
Muslim	685	100	265	43.6	1325	100	607	45.8	2010	100	872	43.4
Armenian	742	100	357	48.1	1752	100	350	46.5	1494	100	707	47.3
Total	1427	100	622	43.6	2077	100	957	46.1	3504	100	1579	45.1

(b) By age (all children under 5)

Age (years)	All children under 5		Medically examined		Haemoglobin determined	
	No.	%	No.	%	No.	%
<1	697	19.9	286	18.1	268	17.6
1–2	502	14.3	228	14.4	224	14.7
2–3	731	20.9	309	19.6	303	19.8
3–4	778	22.2	370	23.4	357	23.4
4–5	797	22.7	386	24.5	374	24.5
All ages	3504	100.0	1579	100.0	1526	100.0

TABLE 5.B.1 *(continued)*

(c) By age (under 1 year)

Age (months)	All children under 1 year		Medically examined	
	No.	%	No.	%
<1	58	8.3	15	5.2
1–6	377	54.1	164	57.3
6–12	262	37.6	107	37.4
All ages under 1 year	697	100.0	286	100.0

(d) By birth order

Birth order	All children under 5		Medically examined	
	No.	%	No.	%
1	790	22.5	324	20.5
2	751	21.4	352	22.3
3	628	17.9	279	17.7
4	414	13.2	324	14.2
5	328	9.5	154	9.7
6 and over	543	15.5	246	15.6
All birth orders	3504	100.0	1579	100.0

279

TABLE 5.B.4. MEAN WEIGHTS OF CHILDREN UNDER 5, BY CULTURE, SOCIAL STATUS, AGE, AND SEX *

Mean weights (kg) of male (M), female (F), and all (T) children at specified ages (years) :

Culture	Social status	<1			1-2			2-3			3-4			4-5		
		M	F	T	M	F	T	M	F	T	M	F	T	M	F	T
Muslim	Middle	(7.5)	(6.5)	7.0	(9.1)	8.8	8.9	11.4	(10.4)	11.0	13.0	12.4	12.7	14.7	14.4	14.5
	Low	6.6	6.0	6.2	8.8	8.3	8.5	10.6	10.2	10.4	12.4	12.0	12.2	14.3	13.8	14.0
	Total	6.9	6.1	6.5	8.9	8.5	8.7	10.9	10.3	10.6	12.6	12.1	12.4	14.4	14.0	14.2
Armenian	Middle	6.7	6.9	6.8	10.6	(9.8)	10.3	11.7	11.3	11.5	13.8	13.6	13.7	15.5	15.1	15.3
	Low	6.9	6.4	6.7	(10.0)	9.1	9.5	11.7	10.6	11.3	13.7	12.7	13.3	15.4	14.5	14.9
	Total	6.8	6.6	6.7	10.3	9.4	9.9	11.7	11.0	11.4	13.8	13.1	13.5	15.4	14.8	15.1

* Figures in parentheses refer to fewer than 25 children.

TABLE 5.B.5.   MEAN WEIGHTS OF CHILDREN UNDER 5, BY CULTURE AND AGE, AND BY FAMILY SIZE OR BIRTH ORDER *

(a) By family size

Culture	Age (years)	Mean weights (kg) in families of size:				Total No. weighed
		1 & 2	3 & 4	5 and over	All family sizes	
Muslim	<1	6.1	6.7	7.1	6.5	154
	1–2	8.6	8.6	8.9	8.7	141
	2–3	10.7	10.5	10.6	10.6	154
	3–4	12.2	12.3	12.6	12.4	199
	4–5	14.1	14.2	14.3	14.2	204
Armenian	<1	6.8	6.8	(6.6)	6.7	136
	1–2	10.0	10.0	(9.1)	9.9	101
	2–3	11.2	11.5	11.7	11.4	143
	3–4	13.3	13.6	13.8	13.5	181
	4–5	15.1	15.2	14.9	15.1	196

(b) By birth order

Culture	Age (years)	Mean weights (kg) of children of birth order:				Total No. weighed
		1 & 2	3 & 4	5 and over	All birth orders	
Muslim	<1	6.2	6.1	7.1	6.5	154
	1–2	8.7	8.9	8.5	8.7	141
	2–3	10.8	10.5	10.6	10.6	180
	3–4	12.4	12.2	12.5	12.4	199
	4–5	14.1	14.2	14.2	14.2	204
Armenian	<1	6.7	6.8	6.6	6.7	136
	1–2	10.0	9.8	(10.0)	9.9	101
	2–3	11.2	11.6	11.4	11.4	143
	3–4	13.5	13.2	14.0	13.5	181
	4–5	15.2	15.1	14.9	15.1	196

* Figures in parentheses refer to fewer than 25 children.

283

(b) Weight

All children were weighed by the same nurse using a lever balance. Children under 1 year were weighed without clothing and those over 1 year were weighed with minimum clothing. The average weight of such minimum clothing for the age of the child and the season was then deducted from the recorded weight.

Armenian children were heavier, as well as taller, than Muslim children of the same age. Boys weighed on average more than girls, and children of middle status women more than those of low status women (Table 5.B.4).

Weight was evidently related neither to family size nor to birth order (Tables 5.B.5 (a) and (b)).

Haemoglobin Level

Haemoglobin level, measured in grams of haemoglobin per millilitre of venous blood, was determined by the cyanmethaemoglobin method. Blood samples were extracted by fingerprick and were investigated immediately after extraction.

The mean haemoglobin levels rose with age, but there were no consistent differences between the cultures, nor between the social classes within each culture (Table 5.B.6).

No relationship was found between mean haemoglobin level and either family size or birth order (Tables 5.B.7 (a) and (b)).

Intestinal Parasitic Infestation

Only 69 stool samples were obtained and none of these provided evidence of infestation. No conclusions can be drawn in view of the poor response rate.

Prevalence of Infections

Any infection, including dental caries, that was detectable at clinical examination was included in the category " Infections ", whether of viral, fungal, parasitic, or bacterial origin.

Infections were more prevalent among Muslim than among Armenian children (46% compared with 33%), and within each culture slightly more of the low status than the middle status children were found to have infections (Muslim: middle 43%, low 48%; Armenian: middle 31%, low 35%). However, more of the middle status Muslim children than of the low status Armenian children had infections. In both cultures, children who had no siblings were least likely to show evidence of infection, whilst children in families of 6 or more were most likely to do so. There was therefore an overall rise in prevalence with family size (Table 5.B.8 (a)).

TABLE 5.B.6. MEAN HAEMOGLOBIN LEVELS OF CHILDREN UNDER 5, BY CULTURE, SOCIAL STATUS, AGE, AND SEX *

Culture	Social status	Mean haemoglobin levels (g/100 ml) of male (M), female (F), and all (T) children at specified ages (years) :														
		<1			1-2			2-3			3-4			4-5		
		M	F	T	M	F	T	M	F	T	M	F	T	M	F	T
Muslim	Middle	(10.9)	(10.6)	10.7	(10.2)	10.1	10.2	10.1	(10.8)	10.4	10.4	11.0	10.7	(12.0)	11.2	11.5
	Low	10.1	10.3	10.2	9.9	10.3	10.1	10.6	10.4	10.5	11.1	10.9	11.0	11.4	11.2	11.3
	Total	10.3	10.4	10.4	10.0	10.2	10.1	10.4	10.5	10.5	10.9	11.0	10.9	11.6	11.2	11.4
Armenian	Middle	10.2	(9.0)	10.1	9.8	(10.6)	10.1	10.6	10.6	10.6	11.3	11.0	11.2	11.3	11.8	11.5
	Low	9.6	10.1	9.8	(10.1)	(9.9)	10.0	10.4	10.7	10.5	11.1	10.7	10.9	11.3	11.5	11.4
	Total	9.9	10.0	9.9	10.2	10.2	10.1	10.5	10.7	10.6	11.2	10.9	11.1	11.3	11.6	11.5

* Figures in parentheses refer to fewer than 25 children.

TABLE 5.B.7. MEAN HAEMOGLOBIN LEVELS OF CHILDREN UNDER 5, BY CULTURE AND AGE, AND BY FAMILY SIZE OR BIRTH ORDER *

(a) By family size

Culture	Age (years)	Mean haemoblobin levels (g/100 ml) in families of size :				Total No. investigated
		1 & 2	3 & 4	5 and over	All family sizes	
Muslim	<1	10.6	10.2	10.3	10.4	139
	1–2	9.7	10.5	10.4	10.1	128
	2–3	10.4	10.6	10.4	10.5	165
	3–4	10.9	10.9	10.9	10.9	185
	4–5	11.4	11.3	11.4	11.4	181
Armenian	<1	10.1	9.8	(10.0)	10.0	129
	1–2	9.9	10.3	(10.2)	10.1	96
	2–3	10.6	10.3	11.0	10.6	143
	3–4	11.0	11.1	11.3	11.1	172
	4–5	11.6	11.5	11.3	11.4	193

(b) By birth order

Culture	Age (years)	Mean haemoglobin levels (g/100 ml) of children of birth order :				Total No. investigated
		1 & 2	3 & 4	5 and over	All family sizes	
Muslim	<1	10.5	10.2	10.3	10.4	139
	1–2	9.7	10.6	10.4	10.1	128
	2–3	10.9	10.6	10.4	10.5	165
	3–4	10.9	11.0	10.9	10.9	185
	4–5	11.4	11.3	11.4	11.4	181
Armenian	<1	10.1	9.7	(10.1)	10.0	129
	1–2	9.9	10.2	(10.2)	10.1	96
	2–3	10.6	10.4	10.8	10.6	143
	3–4	11.1	11.0	11.2	11.1	172
	4–5	11.4	11.6	11.3	11.5	193

* Figures in parentheses refer to fewer than 25 children.

The prevalence of infection was lowest in first-born children and highest in those of fifth and higher birth orders (Table 5.B.8 (b)).

TABLE 5.B.8. PREVALENCE OF INFECTIONS IN CHILDREN UNDER 5 YEARS OF AGE

(a) By culture and family size

Culture	Percentage of children with infections in families of size :				Total No. investigated
	1 & 2	3 & 4	5 and over	All family sizes	
Muslim	43	48	49	47	872
Armenian	31	35	38	33	702

(b) By culture and birth order

Culture	Percentage of children with infections for birth order :				Total No. investigated
	1 & 2	3 & 4	5 and over	All birth orders	
Muslim	43	47	51	47	879
Armenian	31	35	36	33	707

TABLE 5.B.9. REPORTED OCCURRENCE OF FEVER, DIARRHOEA, AND COUGH AMONG CHILDREN UNDER 10, DURING THE MONTH PRECEDING MOTHER'S INTERVIEW

(a) By culture and family size

Culture	Condition	Percentage of infections reported by EW with families of :				Total No. of children in age group
		1 & 2	3 & 4	5 and over	All family sizes	
Muslim	Fever	42	32	27	33	3879
	Diarrhoea	22	11	9	14	3879
	Cough	38	28	22	29	3879
Armenian	Fever	31	22	20	25	3227
	Diarrhoea	14	7	5	9	3227
	Cough	26	18	15	20	3227

(b) By culture and birth order

Culture	Condition	Percentage of infections reported by EW for birth order :				Total No. of children in age group
		1 & 2	3 & 4	5 and over	All birth orders	
Muslim	Fever	35	33	30	33	3879
	Diarrhoea	16	11	13	14	3879
	Cough	32	27	25	29	3879
Armenian	Fever	27	22	23	25	3227
	Diarrhoea	11	8	6	9	3227
	Cough	22	18	17	20	3227

287

Occurrence of Fever, Diarrhoea, or Cough reported by Eligible Women in Children under 10 during the Month Preceding Interview

Mothers reported that 29% of their children under 10 had suffered from fever, 12% from diarrhoea, and 25% from coughs during the month preceding the interview.

More Muslim than Armenian children were said to have had each symptom, but within each culture there were no differences between social status groups.

For both cultures there was a decline in the percentages reported affected as family size and birth order rose, the only exception being for Armenian children of sixth and higher order births (Table 5.B.9). This differs from the paediatric evidence on a wider range of infections among children aged under 5 years, according to which the infections were least prevalent among only children and first-born children.

C. BEIRUT *

I. Lorfing, C. Churchill, J. Azar and H. Zurayk

Sample for Physical and Laboratory Examination

It was originally decided to examine all the children under 5 years old of random samples of 1000 of the women interviewed (500 from each cultural group). The initial refusal rate, however, was high and the investigators finally accepted for examination all children under 5 whose mothers were prepared to bring them to the examination centre. The total number examined was 1209.

In these circumstances, it is possible that the children examined differed in some ways from those of all the women interviewed. In fact, it was found that they did not differ significantly in family size, birth order, or age. There remains the possibility, however, that they differed in other respects, for example, in their health, which would have been crucial.

Personnel and General Procedure

The paediatric examinations were conducted by 2 paediatricians, and the laboratory tests by a qualified technician at the American University Hospital laboratories under the supervision of the Department of Clinical Pathology.

---

* Owing to the disturbed political situation prevailing in the Lebanon during the last months of the study, it was not possible to revise the various tables to make them comparable with those of the other centres.

4. Environmental Theatre

RICHARD SCHECHNER
THE PERFORMANCE GROUP

Schechner, Richard, *Environmental Theatre* (New York: Hawthorn Books, Inc., 1973) 339 pages.

——, *Essays on Performance Theory. 1970–1976* (New York: Drama Books Specialists, 1977) 212 pages.

——, *Makbeth: After Shakespeare* (Schulenburg, Texas 78956: I.E. Clark, 1978) 53 pages.

—— and The Performance Group, *Dionysus in 69* (New York: Farrar, Straus and Giroux, 1970).

THE BREAD AND PUPPET THEATRE

Falk, Florence, 'Bread and Puppet: *Domestic Resurrection Circus*' *Performing Arts Journal*, II, 1 (Spring 1977), 19–30.

Schumann, Peter, 'With the Bread & Puppet Theatre; An Interview', by Helen Brown and Jane Seitz, *The Drama Review* (T38), XII, 2 (Winter 1968), 62–73.

—— and others, Several articles in *The Drama Review* (T47), XIV, 3 (September 1970), 35–96.

Shank, Theodore. 'The Bread and Puppet's Anti-Bicentennial: *A Monument for Ishi', Theatre Quarterly* (London), V, 19 (September–November 1975) 73–88. With 28 photos by the author.

Towsen, John, 'The Bread and Puppet Theatre: *The Stations of the Cross*' *The Drama Review* (T55), XVI, 3 (September 1972) 57–70.

SNAKE THEATER

Weiner, Bernard, 'Theater in Sausalito: Snake's Masks and Puppets', *Theater* (Yale School of Drama), X, 1 (Fall 1978), 84–9.

Wren, Scott Christopher, 'Snake Theater Here and Now', *New Performance* (San Francisco), I, 4 (1979).

5. New Formalism

ROBERT WILSON

Wilson, Robert, '*A Letter for Queen Victoria*' in *The Theatre of Images,* edited by Bonnie Marranca (New York: Drama Books Specialists, 1977) pp. 46–109.

——'. . . I Thought I Was Hallucinating', *The Drama Review* (T76), XXI, 4 (December 1977), 75–8.

——, '*The $ Value of Man*' in *Theater* (Yale School of Drama), IX, 2 Spring 1978), 90–109.

—— '*I Was Sitting on My Patio This Guy Appeared I Thought I Was Hallucinating*' in *Performing Arts Journal* (11/12), IV, 1 and 2 (1979) 201–18.

SUZANNE HELLMUTH AND JOCK REYNOLDS

Shank, Theodore, 'California Cool: Soon 3, Hellmuth–Reynolds, Snake Theater', *Performing Arts Journal* (12), IV, 3 (1980) 72–85.

ALAN FINNERAN
SOON 3

Finneran, Alan, 'An Interview' by Michael O'Connor, *New Performance* (San

Bibliography

2. Primary Explorations

THE LIVING THEATRE

Beck, Julian, *The Life of the Theatre* (San Francisco: City Lights Books, 1972).

Biner, Pierre, *The Living Theatre,* translated from the French by Robert Meister (New York: Avon Books, 1972) 256 pages.

Brown, Kenneth H., *The Brig,* With an Essay on The Living Theatre by Julian Beck and Director's Notes by Judith Malina (New York: Hill and Wang, 1965) 107 pages.

Malina, Judith, *The Enormous Despair.* Her diary August 1968–April 1969 (New York: Random House, 1972) 249 pages.

—— and Julian Beck, *Paradise Now:* Collective Creation of The Living Theatre (New York: Vintage Books, 1971) 154 pages.

Rostagno, Aldo, with Julian Beck and Judith Malina, *We, The Living Theatre,* A Pictorial Documentation by Gianfranco Mantegna . . . of *Mysteries and Smaller Pieces, Antigone, Frankenstein, Paradise Now* (New York: Ballantine Books, Inc., 1970) 240 pages.

THE OPEN THEATRE

Chaikin, Joseph, *The Presence of the Actor; Notes on the Open Theater, Disguises, Acting, and Repression* (New York: Atheneum, 1972) 161 pages.

——, 'Closing the Open Theatre', interview by Richard Toscan, *Theatre Quarterly,* IV, 16 (November–January 1975) 36–42.

Open Theater, The, *Three Works (Terminal, The Mutation Show, Nightwalk),* edited by Karen Malpede (New York: Drama Book Specialists, 1974) 191 pages.

Pasolli, Robert, *A Book on the Open Theatre* (New York: Bobbs–Merrill Company, Inc., 1970) 127 pages.

3. Theatre of Social Change

THE SAN FRANCISCO MIME TROUPE

Davis, R.G., *The San Francisco Mime Troupe: The First Ten Years* (Palo Alto, California 94303: Ramparts Press, 1975) 220 pages.

San Francisco Mime Troupe, *By Popular Demand: Plays and Other Works* (San Francisco: San Francisco Mime Troupe, 1980).

Shank, Theodore, 'Political Theatre as Popular Entertainment', *The Drama Review* (T61), XVIII 1 (March 1974) 110–17.

——, 'The San Francisco Mime Troupe's Production of "False Promises"', *Theatre Quarterly* (London, TQ27), VII, 27 (Autumn 1977) 41–52.

EL TEATRO CAMPESINO

Morton, Carlos, 'Teatro Campesino', *The Drama Review* (T64) XVIII, 4 (December 1974) 71–6.

Shank, Theodore, and Adele Edling Shank, 'Chicano and Latin American Alternative Theatre', in *Popular Theater for Social Change in Latin America,* edited by Gerardo Luzuriago (Los Angeles: U.C.L.A. Latin American Center, University of California, Los Angeles, 1978) pp. 213–33.

Valdez, Luis., 'El Teatro Campesino; Interviews' by Beth Bagby, *The Drama Review* (T36), XI 4 (Summer 1967) 70–80.

——, *Actos* (San Juan Bautista, California: El Centro Campesino Cultural, 1971) 145 pages.

Bibliography

1. The Alternative Theatre

The best sources are the following periodicals:

The Drama Review (1955–67 called *Tulane Drama Review)*
   721 Broadway, Room 600, New York, N.Y. 10003, U.S.A.
Performing Arts Journal
   P.O. Box 858, Peter Stuyvesant Station, New York, N.Y. 10009, U.S.A.
Theater (formerly *Yale/Theater)*
   Box 2046 Yale Station, New Haven, Connecticut 06520, U.S.A.

Banes, Sally, *Terpsichore in Sneakers: Post-Modern Dance* (Boston: Houghton Mifflin Co., 1980) 292 pages.

Goldberg, RoseLee, *Performance: Live Art 1909 to the Present* (New York: Harry N. Abrams, Inc., 1979) 128 pages.

Kaprow, Allan, *Assemblage, Environments, and Happenings* (New York: Harry Abrams, 1966) 342 pages.

Kirby, Michael, *Happenings; an Illustrated Anthology* (New York: E.P. Dutton, 1965) 288 pages.

——, *The Art of Time; Essays on the Avant-Garde* (New York: E.P. Dutton, 1969) 255 pages.

Kostelanetz, Richard, *The Theatre of Mixed Means; An Introduction to Happenings, Kinetic Environments, and Other Mixed-Means Performances* (New York: The Dial Press, 1968) 311 pages.

—— (ed.), *Esthetics Contemporary* (New York: Prometheus Books, 1978) 444 pages.

Loeffler, Carl E. (ed.), *Performance Anthology: Source Book for a Decade of California Performance Art* (San Francisco: Contemporary Arts Press, 1980) 500 pages.

Marranca, Bonnie (ed.), *The Theatre of Images* (New York: Drama Books Specialists, 1977) 256 pages.

194

References

and Elizabeth LeCompte interview on 'Acting/Non-Acting' by Scott Burton, *Performance Art Magazine* 2 (New York) 14–16.

    3. Historical information about Squat Theatre is from the company.